WILDLIFE
LAW ENFORCEMENT

WILDLIFE
LAW ENFORCEMENT

by

William F. Sigler

Head and Professor
Department of Wildlife Management
Utah State Agricultural College

WM. C. BROWN COMPANY PUBLISHERS
Dubuque, Iowa

Printed in the United States of America

Preface

The compilation of a text on wildlife law enforcement is long over-due. The author of this volume is to be complimented for pioneering this much-needed work.

All too often the law enforcement officer is variously referred to as a "flat-foot," "copper," "bull," or by some other term which reflects the dignity of work which society requires be done. The public, being sovereign, calls a man to perform a public service, underpays him, and then permits him to be castigated and belittled by the very element of our society which all of us seek to be protected against--the violator of the laws which we insist must be cast upon our statute books.

In a sense, we Americans are a perverse people--that is, in the sense that we want and must have government, but want to be governed as little as possible. This is not a criticism, but a compliment to the nature and temperament of all Americans.

The man on the "beat" is usually the first contact we have with "the law." The enforcement officer, who issues the "tickets," is the person upon whose head is heaped the scorn and abuse of casual and persistent violators of law and order. The officer of high moral standards and thorough, scientific training is able to combat public apathy and condemnation much more efficiently than the appointee who is chosen because of political influence, or because he is "available" for want of other means of earning a livelihood. This first contact with a representative of the law is usually the most impressionable one. From it, opinions are formed. These opinions are the formative basis of public policy.

In ordinary talk we refer to the professions. We like to think of our sons as engaged in an educational pursuit which will lead them into a profession--likely a doctor, lawyer, engineer, or certified public accountant. Webster confines the definition of a professional man to "one of the three learned professions, especially theology, law, and medicine." Time, progress, and the intricacies of social life with expanding populations make a broader definition of the professions more to the point. We often hear the expression that so and so is a professional soldier, meaning, of course, that he has been trained in the art of making war. Why not, therefore, create a corps of professionally-trained wildlife law enforcement officers?

It is with this thought in mind that this work is presented for those who would so mold their lives that they will be not merely the "flat-foot on the beat," but one who utilizes all of the tools at his command to make himself efficient, scholarly, and worthy of public confidence.

Enforcement is a harsh word. It implies compulsion. The connotation of the word "compliance" tends more to sooth the nerves and heart of the outdoor man and woman. You will find much in this volume devoted to public education which seeks to avoid violation of law, rather than to capture and convict the violator after the act.

This first work of its kind is a step in the right direction and should create the urge in subsequent authors to build upon this foundation. It should instill in the minds of instructors and students a desire to attain a more perfect understanding of the role played by those who will engage in the pursuit of wildlife law enforcement.

Geo. D. Preston

Foreword

It has long seemed apparent that schools training wild-life management men were overlooking an opportunity in not including enforcement training in their courses. A growing number of states are raising both the qualification standards and entrance salaries of their law enforcement personnel, but many schools have been reluctant, despite repeated suggestions, to train men for this type of work.

I was therefore much interested when Dr. Sigler started to develop a course in this field some years ago. From this beginning, he has developed a carefully worked-out training program and this well-prepared text.

This text has been prepared as the result of this teaching experience and should provide much help and guidance as similar courses are initiated. It is well documented and should stimulate interest in a field that offers a growing employment opportunity for trained men. Human nature being what it is, there will be a need for good enforcement men as far in the future as anyone can foresee.

This book includes an outline of the basic legal knowledge that officers must have, but more important it provides valuable information on enforcement methods, preparation and presentation of evidence, and the relation of the enforcement staff to the other work of the department.

This book should help materially in providing well-trained men for this phase of management, and I for one am delighted to see it.

Ira N. Gabrielson

Acknowledgments

These people have reviewed the manuscript and made helpful suggestions. Several of them have also contributed material by talks before law enforcement classes at Utah State Agricultural College.

Clarence Cottam, Director, Welder Wildlife Foundation and former Assistant Director, U. S. Fish and Wildlife Service.

Federal Bureau of Investigation.

Paul R. Felt, English Instructor, Logan, Utah.

Ira N. Gabrielson, President, Wildlife Management Institute.

George O. Hendrickson, Professor of Zoology, Iowa State College.

Hawley Hill, District Conservation Officer, Idaho Fish and Game Department.

William J. Hilty, Personnel Officer, Idaho Fish and Game Department.

George H. Kelker, Professor of Wildlife Management, Utah State Agricultural College.

Spencer Kimball, Former Dean, University of Utah School of Law.

Lee W. Kuhn, Associate Professor, Fish and Game Management, Oregon State College.

Leslie E. Lahr, Assistant Chief of Patrol Conservation Education, California Fish and Game Department.

J. P. Linduska, Chief, Branch Game Management, U. S. Fish and Wildlife Service.

William B. Morse, Wildlife Management Institute.

George D. Preston, Former County Prosecutor and Attorney at Law, Logan, Utah.

Henry Milton Reeves, Game Management Agent, U. S. Fish
    and Wildlife Service.

Earl Sparks, Game Warden, Utah Fish and Game Depart-
    ment.

John Stewart, Assistant Professor of Journalism, Utah
    State Agricultural College.

Joseph N. Symons, Professor of Sociology, Brigham Young
    University.

Wendell Twitchell, District Conservation Officer, Idaho
    Fish and Game Department.

In addition, three sources of material were drawn on
frequently. They are:

Callaghan, F. P._____Instructions for the guidance of
    U. S. game management agents (restricted). Wash-
    ington, D. C.: U. S. Fish and Wildlife Service.
    p. 68.

United States Army. 1951. Criminal Investigations.
    Washington, D. C.: U. S. Government Printing Office,
    Dept. of the Army Field Manual F.M. 19-20. p. 258.

United States Government. 1951. Manual for courts-
    martial. Washington, D. C.: U. S. Government
    Printing Office. p. 665.

These people have contributed material by talks before
classes in wildlife law enforcement at Utah State Agricultural College:

Wendell B. Anderson, Professor of Political Science, Utah
    State Agricultural College.

William J. Cayais, Salt Lake County Prosecutor, Salt Lake
    City, Utah.

Jess Dally, former Warden, Utah Fish and Game Depart-
    ment.

J. Perry Egan, Director, Utah Fish and Game Department.

C. N. Feast, former Director, Colorado Fish and Game
    Department.

Newell Gardner, Warden Supervisor, Wyoming Fish and
    Game Department.

Frank Groves, Director, Nevada Fish and Game Department.

Merrill Hand, former Chief Law Enforcement Officer, Utah Fish and Game Department.

Lewis M. Jones, Judge, First Judicial District of Utah.

Russ Knowles, Police Captain, Logan, Utah.

Ross Leonard, Director, Idaho Fish and Game Department.

J. B. Low, leader, Utah Cooperative Wildlife Research Unit.

Harry Lyman, Game Management Agent, U. S. Fish and Wildlife Service.

L. J. Merovka, Regional Supervisor Game Management Division, U. S. Fish and Wildlife Service.

Hack Miller, Sports Editor, Deseret News-Telegram.

Carl Mueller, Game Management Agent, U. S. Fish and Wildlife Service.

T. B. Murray, former Director, Idaho Fish and Game Department.

Ray Nelson, Editor, Herald-Journal, Logan, Utah.

Golden Peay, Chief Law Enforcement Officer, Utah Fish and Game Department.

D. I. Rassmussen, In Charge of Wildlife Management, Region Four, U. S. Forest Service.

Herb F. Smart, Attorney at Law, Salt Lake City, Utah.

Floyd Thompson, Game Management Agent, U. S. Fish and Wildlife Service.

Clinton D. Vernon, former Attorney General, State of Utah.

Introduction

<u>Purpose and scope</u>

The purpose of this text is to present wildlife law enforcement as an integral part of the total program of wildlife management. Since each of the forty-eight sovereign states has a separate and distinct set of laws and regulations governing the managing and taking of fish and game, it is evident that such a discussion must deal only with fundamentals and general principles.

The text is addressed (1) to professional wildlife personnel who, it is hoped, will find in it not only new cause for self-dedication to an honorable and important calling but also a useful guide for office and field use; (2) to students of wildlife courses in colleges and universities who see in the wildlife service an interesting and promising career; and (3) to sportsmen, often the most ardent lay supporters of a wildlife law enforcement program, who will gain a better understanding of the enforcement officer's viewpoints and duties.

The necessity for an adequate knowledge of general and technical aspects of law enforcement is obvious to wildlife officers. A small bit of additional information may result in greater efficiency and higher achievement, and it car conceivably save an officer from a costly or even fatal mistake. Although it is impossible to predict every situation that may confront an officer, many of the important ones are discussed in varying degrees. Beginning officers should find much value herein, and experienced men will undoubtedly uncover new ideas.

All wildlife employees must have a working knowledge of basic law, since they are occasionally called upon to act as enforcement agents. In fact, in some states, all employees are deputy agents. The administrator himself must be interested in and cognizant of all phases of law enforcement if he is to understand and appreciate the problems of that division of the program.

This is not a legal document and should not be accepted as one in the United States or elsewhere. When legal information is needed, the individual should consult code books and proclamations of the respective states and the United States, as well as treaties between the United States and foreign governments.

Extreme technical treatment of the material has been avoided in order to help the reader not schooled in law to obtain a rapid and lucid view of the whole picture of wildlife law enforcement. For those who would like to plumb deeper into the subject, however, there has been added an extensive bibliography covering most phases of the subject. Other aids to an understanding of this important field consist of a glossary of legal terms; official forms, charges, and specifications employed in a hypothetical case; and sample examination questions used in connection with the course of wildlife law enforcement taught by the author.

Wherever it was felt that the points made throughout the text would be clarified thereby, the author has used illustrative materials. These include actual and hypothetical incidents and situations involving law violations, and also brief accounts of court cases and rulings. These materials, together with the sample examination questions and the glossary, should serve to sharpen the "legal sense" of the student or beginning officer and permit him to evaluate with increased discrimination the legal aspects of the enforcement officer's responsibilities.

Plan of organization

Chapter one shows the need for adequate wildlife laws and for effective enforcement through an historical review of wildlife management and present-day practices. The legal basis for the various state and federal laws comprise the material for chapters two, three, and four, wherein are treated (a) the problems of state versus federal ownership of and jurisdiction over the nation's wildlife resources, and (b) the rights of private citizens.

Chapter five deals with the problem of wildlife law violation by minors, adults, and members of certain American Indian groups and offers possible solutions. Chapters six, seven, and eight are devoted to a discussion of the officer's qualifications and professional preparation; departmental procedures; use of code books and indexes; legal and tech-nical problems involved in making the arrest; and the reserve-warden system.

The material in chapter nine deals with the officer in court and explains the preparation and use of the brief, the officer's role as a witness for the prosecution, and estab-lished courtroom practices and procedures. The complex subject of evidence--its nature, identification, collection, and preservation--comprises the theme of chapter ten. In chapter eleven the author provides a view of the possible future status of the wildlife law enforcement program.

In appendices A, B, and C appear, respectively, defi-nitions and legal terms; forms, charts, and specifications used in wildlife law violations; and sample examination questions. Finally, there is a bibliography of sources cited in the body of the text and a bibliography of sources reach-ing beyond the scope of the text.

In the selection of the photographs of officers perform-ing their various duties, the author has attempted to make the text material more concrete and vivid and to humanize the often little-understood and little-appreciated work of the wildlife law enforcement officer in America.

Table of Contents

    Program for the Individual Poacher   74
    Program for the Community   75

  Summary.   76

VI. The Wildlife Law Enforcement Officer. . . . 77

  Responsibility and Calling   77
  Historical Sketch of Policing Agencies 77

    Police Systems in England   77
    Police Systems in North America.   79
    Game Wardens   79

  Personal Qualifications   80
  Professional Qualifications   82

    Point of View.   82
    Education   82
    Code of Ethics   84

  Employment   87
  Professional Duties   87

    Wildlife Management   87
    Educational Programs.   87
    Law Enforcement.   89

  Knowledge of State Wildlife Laws and Court
    Rulings   89

    Code Books   89
    Indexes   91

  The Uniform   94
  Side-Arms   94
  The Official Automobile   96
  Reserve Wardens   97

    The California System   97
    The New Mexico System.   98

VII. Tactics of the Arrest   100

  Definition of Arrest   100
  Types of Arrest.   100

    Non-Warrant Arrest   100
    Warrant Arrest   102
    Misdemeanor on Complaint   102
    Citizen's Arrest   103

Chapter   Page

List of Illustrations

WILDLIFE
LAW ENFORCEMENT

Photograph by Don Wooldridge
Courtesy Missouri Conservation Commission.

Protector of all he sees.

CHAPTER I

The Problem of Wildlife Law Enforcement

LAW ENFORCEMENT IN THE OVER-ALL PROGRAM

Wildlife law enforcement has occupied man's attention in varying degrees throughout a large part of history. Its position in the over-all wildlife program is shown below:

1. Establishment of protected areas which are generally known as preserves, sanctuaries, reserves, or refuges;
2. Environmental manipulation (habitat improvement);
3. Control of enemies, sometimes listed as predator control;
4. Artificial replenishment or stocking;
5. Restriction of the harvest, now known as wildlife law enforcement.

Each phase is dependent on one or more of the others for its success. Without this tie-in the entire wildlife management program falters or fails.

HISTORICAL PERSPECTIVE OF WILDLIFE MANAGEMENT

In order to develop a better understanding of this enforcement phase of the program, wildlife management is presented in historical perspective.

Early Landuser-Hunter Behavior Patterns

It is interesting to speculate as to what happened, even before recorded history, to mankind and his social organization. The early nomadic family groups lived from the uncultivated lands. Their interests were in hunting, fishing, and grazing, but there was no proprietary interest in the land itself. Agricultural settlements soon encroached on this wilderness but left the uncultivated part for anyone who was interested in supporting himself. It appears probable that even in prehistoric times farmers were encroaching upon the established state of nature.[1]

Later, as the land itself became a source of wealth, its control was about the only way of acquiring more wealth than a man could carry in his pockets. It therefore became natural for a person to acquire title to as much land as he could in order to transmit his wealth to his descendants. In those very early days material possession was probably a matter of force rather than of legal title. It was not until much later that the law recognized and protected personal property.

At first there was little proprietary interest in any land other than that which was tillable. However, it soon became apparent that control of surrounding land was necessary to cultivate and manage arable land. Depredation by nomadic wilderness dwellers probably brought this about. Consequently, large and powerful families developed land holdings around tilled land. These landlords became the rulers and nobility of their time.

Early English Backgrounds

The following quotation from Nelson[2] reveals how the idea of privilege became associated in the public mind with the hunting of game:

> To begin with the time of the Britons, when their Princes and great Lords had no Occasion to set apart Places for the Preservation of Game and Beasts of Venary, (their Bruery, i.e. Thickets and uncultivated Lands, being such Nurseries and Shelter for them), it was the Interest of both Princes and Lords rather to destroy than preserve them.
>
> During the Wars between the Britons and Saxons, so many of the Britons were killed, and so many fled from the conquering Saxons, that the cultivated Lands were more than sufficient to maintain the Conquerors and the miserable Britons who staid amongst them; for at that Time there were no foreign Markets where the Saxons traded with the Produce

---

1. S. Dale Furst, Jr. 1946. Outlook in wildlife law enforcement. Delivered before the International Assn. of the Game, Fish, and Forestry Commissioners, Denver, Colorado. p. 1.
2. William Nelson. 1762. The laws concerning game. Of hunting, hawking, fishing and fowling, etc., and of forest, chases, parks, warrens, deer, doves, dove - cotes, conies. 6th edition. London: Printed by E. Richardsen and C. Lintot for T. Waller. 255 pp.

of their Lands. When the Saxons found themselves Masters
of the British Lands and People, the Saxon Captains, as Con-
querors, in Common Council agreed to divide the Lands they
had taken amongst themselves, their Friends and Companions
in Conquest.

The Woods, Wastes, and Bruery Lands, that were not appropriated to any particular Persons, remained to the Chief
Captain, who in Process of Time assumed the Title of King,
who, as Occasion offered, granted Parcels of such Woods to
whom he thought fit. . . .More and more useless Woods were
appropriated and improved; and as Improvements were made,
the Game and Beasts of Venary retired from thence for Shel-
ter into the unfrequented Woods, thither the Saxon Kings, that
took Delight in Hunting, went for their Diversion, where was
such Plenty of Game, that there was no Occasion for restraining Laws to preserve them. . . .

. . .but in Edgar's Time. . .he having an elegant Taste prohibited Hunting his Deer, and appointed Officers to preserve
all Game of the Table, in his Woods, who so rigorously put in
Execution their Orders, that the Nobility and Gentry were
prevented of taking their diversions and their Tenants of
their respective Rights; At length this arbitrary Procedure of
the Officers grew to so great a Grievance, that Noblemen,
Gentlemen, and Farmers, made great Complaints for Want
of a Law to ascertain the King's Prerogative and the People's
Privilege in this Case; on which King Canute, through his
innate Goodness and Justice, in a Parliament holden at Win-
chester in 1016, brought the Proceedings to a Certainty, that
all men might know what they should, and should not do, by
publishing Forest Laws, therein setting out the Rounds of his
Forests, and limiting the Power of the Forest Officers. . . .

William the Conqueror laid waste thirty-six Towns in
Hampshire to make a Forest. . .and his Forest Officers. . .
exercised such arbitrary Rule, as to abridge even the great
Barons of the Privileges they enjoyed under the Saxon and
Danish Kings; not at all regarding the liberties given to the
Subject by Canute's Forest Laws.

His Son William Rufus is recorded in History for the
Severity of his Proceedings against all that hunted in his
Forests; inflicting the Punishment of Death upon such as
killed a Stag or Buck in his Forests, without any other law
than that of his own Will. . . .

In the Reign of King John these and other Oppressions,
having exasperated the Barons, they took up Arms. . .and
marched to Northampton. . .from whence they sent Letters
to the Earls, Barons and Knights that adhered to the King,
and if they would not desert the perjured King, and join them
in asserting their Liberties, they would proceed against them
as public Enemies.

These Threats drew from the King most of the Barons that
had adhered to him, which Defection left the King hopeless and
induced him. . .to let the confederated Barons know he would

grant them the Laws and Liberties they desired: Upon which a Meeting of King and Barons was agreed to be on the fifteenth of June, 1215, at Runnymede between Stains and Windsor, where a conference began between the Barons that adhered to the King and the confederated Barons, who were so superior in Number to the King's Barons, that he seemed to make no difficulty of granting the Laws and Liberties demanded; which were drawn up as the confederated Lords thought fit, in two Charters, vis. The Great Charter, and the Charter of the Liberties and customs of the Forest.

Wildlife Control During the Middle Ages

At the time European land-holding families were acquiring lands, European culture was just emerging from the greatest moral, financial, and spiritual depression in recorded history. In this period of the Dark Ages, men were extremely desperate, superstitious, and confused. The result was many changes in the habits of the people, including a loss of interest in hunting and fishing.

When the interest in hunting and fishing was lost, the urge to control it subsided. Probably this was tied up with a scarcity of wild game and an inability to harvest it safely away from controlled land holdings. Once the right to hunt and fish was relinquished to the landowner, he must have quickly seen the advantage of reserving it for himself, even though this right was not known as such at that time. Consequently, the landowner used all possible methods of declaring the game and fish his own and made it a crime for anyone else to hunt or kill. Landowners then hunted and fished for either sport or food and controlled the land, prohibiting all others from even trespassing. Those among the peasantry who had lived by fishing and hunting were then forced to become poachers and outlaws. Consequently, the situation developed in Europe to the point where the game laws were written and enforced for the benefit of ruling classes, and the full weight of the law and social stigma fell upon those who harvested this game without permission of the landowner. Thus, there grew up in the mind of the general public the idea that fish and game laws were for the benefit of the favored few.

European Traditions in North America

Much later, large areas of North America were settled by agricultural people from Europe. These people brought with them a tradition of resentment against fish and game

Figure 1. Checking licenses initiates one of many officer-sportsman meetings.

7

laws. Furthermore, since there appeared to be an inexhaustible supply of wildlife in early North America, conservation measures were not considered necessary.

Wildlife management in America

According to Gabrielson, [3] the first game laws in America were probably the hunting privileges granted in 1629 by the West Indies Company to persons planning colonies in New Netherlands, the provisions regarding the right of hunting in the Massachusetts Bay Colonial Ordinance of 1647, and the New Jersey Concessions of Agreement of 1678.

At the time of the American Revolution, 12 colonies had enacted limited closed seasons. In this regard the history of many states is typified by that of Pennsylvania where a handful of conservationists, led by John M. Phillips, pushed through early wildlife laws and convinced the general populace that it should live up to these laws. [4]

As wildlife populations began to dwindle, it became apparent that law enforcement alone was not the entire answer to wildlife preservation. Even severe restrictions or closed seasons were not bringing back harvestable numbers. [5]

Control of enemies came next. This dealt more with big-game predators than with enemies of small game or fish. Efforts and results have been confused by the fact

---

3.   Ira N. Gabrielson. 1951. Wildlife management. New York: The Macmillan Co. p. 56.
4.   William F. Schultz, Jr. 1953. Conservation law and administration. New York: Ronald Press. pp. 23-25.
5.   For an interesting and authoritative account of the problems of wildlife management in this country, the reader's attention is directed to two papers by Clarence Cottam, former Assistant Director, U. S. Fish and Wildlife Service:

    The Why of Migratory Waterfowl Regulations, read before the annual meeting of the International Association of Game, Fish, and Conservation Commissioners, Memphis, Tennessee, September 15, 1950;

    Fifty Years of Progress and Handicaps in Wildlife Management in the United States, read before the International Association of Game, Fish, and Conservation Commissioners, Rochester, New York, September 10-11, 1951.

that predator control designed primarily to benefit domestic livestock, and predator control for the benefit of wildlife, have not been clearly differentiated.

Soon after predator control began, some areas were set aside as wildlife sanctuaries. The first was Yellowstone National Park, which was established in 1894. In theory, the game would become abundant in these areas and move outside to produce hunting. How miserably this can fail on occasion was being demonstrated in 1954 by the north (Gardner) Yellowstone National Park elk herd, which is literally eating itself out of food and still refuses to emigrate, except in very severe winters, out of the refuge to where it may be hunted.

Today, wildlife managers rarely recommend refuges except in the case of waterfowl or rare species. There are examples, however, of where the continued existence of a remnant species depends almost entirely on effective law enforcement and an adequate refuge. Some of these include the trumpeter swan, key deer, California condor, whooping crane, and the ivory-billed woodpecker. The passenger pigeon is extinct, presumably as a result of uncontrolled, wholesale slaughter.

One of the early artificial stocking ventures was on a game farm in Illinois in 1905. This experiment has since been repeated in varying degrees to replenish game and fish in every state. Originally, stocking was used to put more game before the gun; that is, the animal stocked was the one harvested. This practice is still being used. It soon became apparent in these early ventures that even when a high percent of the game was recovered, the cost was prohibitive. Furthermore, research shortly demonstrated that, in many areas, relatively little of the original stock was ever recovered. The emphasis was then shifted to replenishment of breeding stock and a search for exotic species to fill unoccupied ecological niches. Stocking on a "put and take" basis is now used primarily to fulfill special requirements (example, trout), and within economic limitations.

Perhaps because the first four methods have succeeded only in part, the turn to habitat improvement has been forced. This technique, now in its infancy both as an art and a science, is the hope of the future. [6]

FACTORS INFLUENCING SOUND MANAGEMENT

Several factors influence sound management of wildlife resources. Among these are (1) more and better information on the resources; (2) fluctuations in the number of wild animals available to the sportsman; (3) a changing philosophy in regard to how much and how game should be harvested by an individual within and outside lawful regulations; (4) the ever-increasing number of posted areas which either restrict or prohibit hunting and fishing; (5) changes in the number of sportsmen going afield; and (6) the development of more efficient methods of harvest.

One of the most sensational happenings has been the violent fluctuations in the number of wild animals, particularly waterfowl. Ducks and geese have ranged all the way from the countless millions in the "good old days" of market-hunting to the terrifying few of the early 30's. The typical market-hunting days as described by Day[7] in the following quotation were a far cry from 1930, when the most frequent prediction was to the effect that waterfowl hunting was gone forever.

> Greedy game markets. . . readily accepted game of all sorts as shipments came from the great slaughtering grounds. No section of the country that had a good supply of wildlife escaped. Expert hunters, working six and sometimes seven days a week, from daybreak to dark, killed every game bird within reach.

An increase in the number of technically-trained men has resulted in more adequate information for use in setting seasons and bag limits. In regard to the changing philosophy of management, such trends as "fishing for fun" (releasing all but two or three fish) and debunking the claims of the meat hunter are going to affect drastically the laws of the future.

There has been an increase of all types of posted areas. These limited or complete closures have many variations: no hunting; hunting by the landowner and a few friends;

---

6. William F. Sigler. 1954. What is wildlife management? Utah Fish and Game Bulletin 10.12:1-2.
7. Albert M. Day. 1949. North American waterfowl. New York: Stackpole and Heck, Inc. pp. 44-45.

theoretically open-sale-permit units which, in practice, operate as private clubs; and truly private clubs. All of these areas tend to restrict the take, or the number of participants, and create new problems for fish and game departments, since management is in part placed in the hands of private individuals.

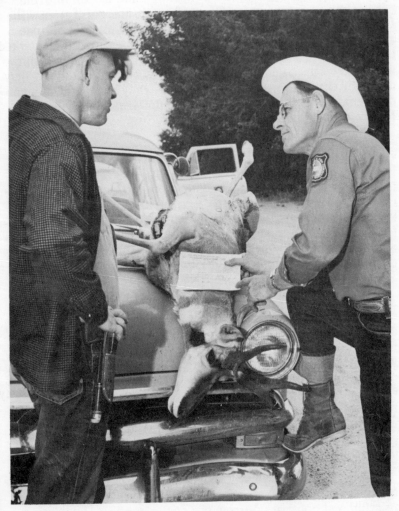

Photograph by Paul Lake
Courtesy Wyoming Game and Fish Department

Figure 2. Management information on a once nearly extinct species.

Perhaps the greatest single influence on wildlife laws has been the ever-increasing human population, with its corresponding hunter and fisherman increase. This becomes readily apparent when one considers the numbers of red-clad and hip-booted sportsmen who, with improved weapons and other gear and modern methods of transportation, are increasingly taking to field and stream.

A few of them, unfamiliar with or disregardful of wildlife law and lacking the background and training of sportsmen and woodsmen of earlier generations, move like Attila's Huns over the wildlife habitats, slaughtering and depleting without regard to need or to the rights of others. What they do not strip bare with their weapons, they threaten to burn out with their carelessly-tended camp fires and thoughtlessly-discarded matches and cigarettes.

A WILDLIFE LAW ENFORCEMENT PROGRAM

As was pointed out, law enforcement alone is not the entire answer to wildlife preservation. Indeed, it is obvious that the best wildlife law enforcement agency, operating under ideal conditions, cannot produce fish and game in a desert. On the other hand, the best habitat cannot produce good hunting, fishing, or trapping without adequate regulation and enforcement.

The need for adequate law enforcement should not be confused with the desirability of sometimes relaxing restrictions. For example, it is frequently necessary to modify laws in order to permit the sportsman to take more warm-water fish and to kill more deer. However, it is desirable to enforce all existing laws, and certain limitations on harvesting methods will always be necessary. This suggests the need for laws and regulations that are wisely conceived, for an adequately-trained body of professional people to administer these laws, and for strengthened support from the courts.

The heart of such an enforcement program would seem to be an enlightened public opinion, for unless wildlife legislation and control do grow out of the demands of an aroused populace, a large proportion of our wildlife resources may be sacrificed to the interests of special groups or of misguided individuals.

Basically, wildlife legislation is passed either as the result of pressure from special interests or because of professional recommendations. In the first instance, an individual or a group may wish to alter the time of season or the bag limit to better suit his or its needs. It should be emphasized, however, that many individuals and organizations that lobby for conservation measures are motivated by sound thinking and the desire for good, long-range management; and some advocates of what may be labeled undesirable or controversial legislation are honest in their views.

Because of the divergent points of view concerning wildlife resources, some over-all custodial power is

Courtesy Iowa Conservation Commission

Figure 3. Good dogs mean more bagged birds.

Figure 4. Planting multiflora rose to help pheasants.

needed to set up and give direction to an optimum wildlife law enforcement program that will insure the conservation of the resources for the enjoyment and profit of all the people. Such custodial power lies within the province of the state and can be controlled largely through the agency of the state fish and game department. The subject of state jurisdiction over wildlife resources is discussed in the following chapter.

CHAPTER II
State Jurisdiction Over Wildlife

INHERENT JURISDICTION

We have seen[1] that before the signing of the Magna Charta at Running Mead, ownership of wildlife vested exclusively in the person of the king, and that after the signing, ownership vested in the office of the king, to be held in sacred trust for the people.

Colonists who settled America carried the common law of England with them. After the Revolution the question arose as to whether or not the newly independent colonies had a common law. It was decided that the common law of England plus English statutes, prior to the Revolution, were applicable where conditions permitted. It was believed that the State had in effect acquired the title of the King, and the State in its sovereign capacity held the game in trust for the people; therefore, no statute was necessary to invest it with the ownership of wildlife. For this reason it has been deemed unnecessary to examine the statutes of the various states as regards the ownership of wildlife.

Referring to this transfer of power from king to colony, the court has stated, in part:

> Undoubtedly, this attribute of government to control the taking of animals <u>ferae naturae</u>, which was thus recognized and enforced by the common law of England, was vested in the colonial governments, where not denied by their charters, or in conflict with grants of the royal prerogative. . . .[2]

At the Constitutional Convention of 1787 the state delegates invested the Federal Government with certain powers, but they did not mention the control of wildlife; therefore, except in the case of wildlife on federal lands and migratory birds, control resides in the state.

The right of states to govern the taking of fish and game was established in the famous case of Geer v.

---

1. <u>Infra.</u>, p. 3.
2. Geer v. Connecticut, 161 U. S. 519, 527-528.

Photograph by Jim Sherman
Courtesy Iowa Conservation Commission

Figure 5. A quick check, then back to fishing.

Connecticut. [3] In this case the right of the state to regulate and control the manner in which wild game may be taken is sustained on two grounds: (1) the sovereign ownership of wild animals by the state, and (2) the police power of the state, which flows from its duty to preserve for its people

---

3. Ibid.

a valuable food supply. The court recognized the authority of the state to control the taking of wildlife in the following rulings:

> . . . It is. . . certain that the power which the colonies thus possessed passed to the State with the separation from the mother country, and remains in them at the present day, insofar as its exercise may be not incompatible with, or restrained by, the right conveyed to the Federal Government by the Constitution. [4]

> It is not to be doubted that the power to preserve fish and game within its borders is inherent in the sovereignty of the State. . . . [5]

> It is admitted that, in the absence of Federal legislation on the subject, a State has exclusive power to control wild game within its borders and that the South Dakota law was valid when enacted, although it incidentally affected interstate commerce. [6]

In State v. Lessard, [7] a case involving ownership, action was brought against Edward O. Lessard and others by the state for killing, taking into possession, and holding a whale. This whale was killed in an inland Oregon slough in Multnomah County. The state contended that the whale was a royal sovereign fish. The defendant was acquitted and the state appealed on the following grounds: (1) the whale was owned by the state and the defendants had wrongfully seized it; (2) whales within coastal or inland waters of the state are royal fish which belong to the state, and hence the killing of a whale in an inland slough and keeping possession of its body without consent of the state is actionable. The Supreme Court ruled in part: (1) the complaint is sufficient; (2) it is clearly stated in several cases that the whale in inland waters is the property of the state, and killing and holding without state permission is wrong. There is a different rule for fish (as opposed to the whale, a mammal), and the defendant improperly applied the other rule. The Supreme

---

4. Ibid.
5. Geer v. Connecticut, 161 U. S. 519, 527-528; Ward v. Racehorse, 163, U. S. 504, 507.
6. Geer v. Connecticut, 161 U. S. 519; Silz v. Herterber, 211 U. S. 31. Carey v. South Dakota, 250 U. S. 118, 120.
7. State v. Lessard (Ore.) 29 Pac. 2nd 509.

Court reversed the decision in favor of the plaintiff (state) and instructed the lower courts to rectify their mistakes.

The state's trusteeship as regards wildlife is clearly pointed out in the case of State of Arkansas v. Mallory, wherein the Supreme Court of Arkansas held:

> Since then (Magna Charta), the ownership of wild animals, so far as vested in the sovereign, has been uniformly regarded as a trust for the benefit of the people; and we think that clearly, in effect, the title and ownership of the sovereign has been held to be only for the purposes of protection, control, and regulation. . . but nowhere do we find that in modern times has the absolute and unqualified ownership of such animals by government been asserted and exercised further than for the purposes of controlling and regulating the taking of the same. On the other hand, we find frequent denials of the right of government to do more. [8]

POLICE POWER

Grounds are frequently advanced to support the right of the state legislature to impose regulations governing the taking of wildlife. A common one is the police power, which entitles the state to regulate the public health, safety, morals, and welfare of the people. Indeed, the cases which hold that as between a state and the citizen the state has the right to regulate the taking of game do not base that right upon absolute ownership of that game by the state, but upon the police power. They say that the game belongs to all the people and that the state, sovereign by virtue of its police power, regulates the taking of the game for the benefit of all, so that the few who are favorably situated may not reap the benefit of the game to the exclusion of those handicapped by distance and other considerations. In Geer v. Connecticut[9] the court reviews the matter fully and shows that the various nations have always regarded the game as belonging to all the people in common, and that the state has regulated the killing of game, not on the ground of ownership, but as sovereign, acting for the benefit of all.

In Missouri v. Holland[10] the court said, "To put the claim of the State upon title is to lean upon a slender reed." Also, in McKee v. Gratz,[11] the court maintained:

---

8.   Arkansas v. Mallory, 73 Ark. 236, 83 S. W. 955, 67 L. R. A. 773.
9.   Geer v. Connecticut, 161 U. S. 519, 527-528.
10.   Missouri v. Holland, 252 U. S. 416, 434.
11.   McKee v. Gratz, 260 U. S. 127.

> It (the Circuit Court of Appeals) rightly, as we think, held that the statutes declaring the title to game and fish to be in the State spoke only in aid of the State's power of regulations and left the plaintiff's interest what it was before.

In some states private ownership of game, such as bison or waterfowl, is recognized. However, unless the laws make definite exceptions, it should be assumed that wild game is in the custody of the state.

LIMITATION OF STATE JURISDICTION

This custodial power of the state may be exercised in any way that does not contravene the provisions of the federal constitution. Whenever conflict does arise in this regard, the authority of the state must yield to a valid exercise of power by the Federal Government. A court ruling to this effect reads:

> . . . it is clear. . . that the right to regulate the taking and use of game and fish is, generally speaking, in the State as an attribute of its sovereignty, subject only to valid exercise of authority under the provisions of the Federal Constitution.[12]

12.　United States v. 2271.29 acres of land, etc. (31 F (2d0) 617).

CHAPTER III

Federal Jurisdiction Over Wildlife

Wherever the paramount interests of the people are concerned, the authority of the Federal Government takes precedence over that of the states. This principle applies to all areas of interest, including the area of wildlife control.

SOURCE OF FEDERAL AUTHORITY

In 1787, sixty-five delegates from the several states met to draft the Constitution of the United States. Out of the work of the convention came the principle of the division of power between the states and the Federal Government. Many powers were delegated by the states, but those not specifically delegated reside inherently in the states.

Although among these residual powers is the one giving control of wildlife to the states, the Federal Government exercises jurisdiction over migratory wildlife. This jurisdiction stems from the authority vested in the Government to (1) create and regulate a federal government, (2) make treaties, (3) regulate foreign and interstate commerce, and (4) levy and collect taxes.

Jurisdiction Over Wildlife Habitats

Item one above refers to the power of Congress "to dispose of and make all needful Rules and Regulations respecting the Territory or other Property belonging to the United States. . . ."[1] Under this authority Congress has the power to set aside lands or territory for the creation of national monuments, national parks, national refuges, and national forests. This gives the Government control over the habitats of all wildlife in these areas as well as in such territories as Alaska, Puerto Rico, the Philippine Islands before their independence on July 4, 1946, extensive military holdings, and, since 1932, the District of Columbia.

---

1.   Constitution of the United States, Article IV, Section 3, clause 2.

Jurisdiction Over Migratory Wildlife

Control over migratory wildlife may be exercised by reason of item two, the treaty-making power vested in the president. "He shall have Power, by and with the Advice and Consent of the Senate, to make Treaties, provided two-thirds of the Senators present concur. . . ."[2]

Ducks, geese, and swans are examples of wildlife that are migratory in habit and cross state and international lines. Control, supervision, and management, therefore, become an international problem and are subject to treaty power.

Jurisdiction Over Deer

Although the Federal Government does not and may not control the right to kill deer (outside federally-owned lands), it may and therefore does exercise the right, under the provisions of item three, "to regulate Commerce with foreign Nations, and among the several States, and with the Indian tribes,"[3] to control shipments of carcasses in interstate commerce.

Authority to Enforce Wildlife Laws

"The Congress shall have Power to lay and collect Taxes, Duties, Imposts and Excises. . . ."[4] This power gives the agents of the Branch of Game Management of the U. S. Fish and Wildlife Service in the Department of Interior the right to enforce federal game laws.

Authority to Manipulate Wildlife Populations

The Constitution has been interpreted to also allow the Federal Government to manipulate wildlife populations through the general welfare clause.[5] Under this, Congress has established, as part of the U. S. Fish and Wildlife Service, branches of Predator and Rodent Control, Fish Hatcheries, Wildlife Research, Fishery Research, River Basin Studies and Federal Aid.

---

2. Ibid., Article II, Section 2, clause 2.
3. Ibid., Article I, Section 8, clause 2.
4. Ibid., Article I, Section 8, clause 1.
5. Ibid.

Authority to Implement Controls

Finally, the Federal Government has the power to implement its control over wildlife by reason of the right of Congress "to make all laws which shall be necessary and proper for carrying into Execution the foregoing Powers, and all other Powers vested by this Constitution in the

Photograph by Don Wooldridge
Courtesy Missouri Conservation Commission

Figure 6. Hunter success from the man who knows.

Government of the United States, or in any Department or Officer thereof. "6

FEDERAL WILDLIFE LAWS

Although each state has its own set of wildlife laws, there are federal laws that are common to all states. Inasmuch as all conservation officers will be called upon to enforce them at one time or another, it seems desirable to present the highlights. The laws are given in their chronological order.

The Lacey Act

The first federal law pertaining to game, the Lacey Act of 1900, 7 regulates the interstate commerce of game. Any person transporting illegally-taken wild animals or birds across a state line is in violation of the Lacey Act. Briefly, action can be taken against anyone who delivers for shipment or knowingly receives for shipment wild animals or birds imported contrary to the laws of a foreign country or state, or who makes false records or accounts or ships or transports any package not properly labeled or tagged.

There is another section that prohibits the importation of certain birds and animals into the United States or district thereof, regardless of state law. These include the mongoose, the so-called "flying foxes" or fruit bat, the English sparrow, the starling, and such other birds and mammals as the Secretary of the Interior may prohibit.

The Lacey Act is not applicable to domesticated animals, such as fox, mink, marten, fisher and other furbearers or karakul and chinchilla when they are in captivity, but applies to them when they are in the wild. Such furbearers in captivity must be reared according to the laws of the state wherein they are confined. The Lacey Act applies to wild animals (mammals) and the birds, but excludes all cold-blooded animals, such as fish, reptiles, and amphibians. It applies to the animal, or any part thereof, including eggs, plumage, nest, hide, or trophy. All wild animals or birds transported, carried, or conveyed in interstate or foreign

---

6. Ibid., Article I, Section 8, clause 18.
7. Amended June 25, 1948, 62 STAT. 687, 18 U. S. C. SS 43-44 3054 and 3112.

commerce shall be plainly labeled with the names and addresses of the shipper and the consignee, and with an accurate statement of the contents as regards species and number.

Any person convicted of violating the Act shall be fined not more than $500, or imprisoned not more than six months, or both. All wild animals or birds involved in the violation shall be forfeited. They must be held for disposition by federal court and, unless so ordered, may not be returned to the state from which they were shipped.

The Migratory Bird Treaty Act

In 1916, the United States concluded a treaty with Canada (with the permission of Great Britain) for the protection of migratory birds;[8] and in 1936, a treaty for the protection of migratory birds and game mammals was concluded between the United States and the United Mexican States. This law provides that, except as permitted by regulations, it is unlawful to pursue, hunt, take, capture, kill, possess, offer for sale, barter, purchase, exchange, deliver for shipment, cause to be shipped or exported, any migratory birds, any part thereof, or any egg, or nest of such a bird.

The Secretary of Interior[9] is authorized and directed to establish seasons and the method of hunting, shipping, transporting, and carrying birds, their eggs, or nests, or any part thereof, as warranted by such conditions as are compatible with the biological aspects of migratory bird management.

It is unlawful to ship, transport, or carry by any means whatsoever, migratory birds, or parts, or nests, from one state, territory, or district to another in violation of the laws of either state, territory, or district.

---

8. Act of July 3, 1918, 40 STAT. 755, as amended by June 20, 1936, 49 STAT. 1555--16 U. S. C. 703-711.
9. The Bureau of Biological Survey, Department of Agriculture, and the Bureau of Fisheries, Department of Commerce, were transferred to the Department of Interior, effective July 1, 1939, 53 STAT. 813. This transferred to the Secretary of Interior the functions of the Secretary of Agriculture relating to wildlife, and the Secretary of Commerce relating to fisheries.

Courtesy Washington Department of Game

Figure 7.   Checking a limit of Mallard.

Any employee of the Department of Interior, authorized by the Secretary of Interior, may enforce the provisions of the Migratory Bird Treaty Act without a warrant, and has the authority, with a search warrant, to search any place pursuant to his duties as an enforcement officer under this Act. Any person, association, partnership, or corporation who is convicted of violating the Migratory Bird Treaty Act shall be deemed guilty of misdemeanor and shall be fined not more than $500, or imprisoned not more than six months, or both. Nothing in the Act prevents states or territories from making or enforcing any regulations regarding migratory birds which are not inconsistent with the provisions of the Migratory Bird Treaty Act. The states may, if they so desire, give further protection to migratory birds, nests, and eggs, but they may not extend or change the laws in any way to be less restrictive than the Federal Act. The Act prohibits the breeding of migratory game birds on farms and reserves, or the sale of birds so bred except under proper regulations and permit.

Migratory Bird Hunting Stamp Act

The Migratory Bird Hunting Stamp Act [10] was created to supplement and support the Migratory Bird Treaty Act, and it does this by providing funds for the acquisition of areas as sanctuaries and breeding grounds for development and administration, and for the protection of certain birds.

The term "migratory waterfowl" as used in this Act means wild ducks, geese, and brant. No person over 16 years of age shall take any migratory fowl unless at the time of the taking he carries on his person an unexpired federal migratory-bird hunting stamp which has been validated by his signature written in ink across the face of the stamp. Any person taking or attempting to take migratory waterfowl shall upon request exhibit the stamp to an officer of the state or of the Federal Government. However, no stamp is required of federal or state institutions or official agencies collecting birds for propagation; or by the resident, owner, tender, or sharecropper on his premise or by officially designated agents of the Department of Interior.

These stamps are sold by the Post Office Department and expire the 30th of June. No expired stamp is valid under the Migratory Bird Hunting Stamp Act. This Act does not authorize a person to take waterfowl otherwise than in accordance with regulations adopted by the Federal Government and the state involved, and it does not, in any case, take the place of a required state license. No person other than the

---

10. Act of March 16, 1934, 48 STAT. 451, as amended June 15, 1935, 49 STAT. 379, June 28, 1941, 55 STAT. 356, and August 12, 1949, 63 STAT. 599--600, 16, U. S. C. 718-718i.

one validating the Migratory Bird Hunting Stamp may use it for any purpose during the period of validity. No person shall alter, mutilate, imitate, or counterfeit any stamp authorized by the Act. Any person violating the provisions of the Act shall be deemed guilty of a misdemeanor, and when convicted in court shall be fined not more than $500, or imprisoned not more than six months, or both. The Secretary of Interior is authorized to cooperate with states and territories in the enforcement of this act. The Migratory Bird Hunting Stamp is not required of persons who merely possess waterfowl.

Black Bass Act

Originally the Black Bass Act[11] covered black bass only; at present all fish are covered. A fish in a particular state is any animal so defined by that state, territory, or the District of Columbia. The Act provides that fish when taken illegally within one state and transported over the state line are in violation of the Black Bass Act when the state line is crossed.

The word "person" includes company, partnership, corporation, association, and common carrier. It is unlawful for any person to deliver or knowingly receive for transportation, or knowingly to transport, any fish from one state, territory, or district to another, if the fish were taken illegally; or if the state, territory, or district in which they were taken specifically forbids transportation outside of that area. No person shall knowingly purchase or receive any fish which have been transported or taken in violation of the Act.

Any package containing fish which is to be transported or delivered in interstate commerce shall be clearly marked on the outside of the package with a statement of the number of each species. Any species of fish transported into any particular state are subject to the laws of that state. Designated employees of the Department of the Interior may

---

11.   Act of May 20, 1926.
      Amended July 30, 1947, 61 STAT. 517--16 U. S. C. 851-856.
      Amended July 16, 1952, to include all fishes, including salt water fish and shell fish. Exception, Section 10 not changed. Does not apply to steelhead trout legally taken in Columbia River between Washington and Oregon.

enforce this Act and arrest without warrant any person
violating the law in the presence of the officer. Persons
when arrested must be taken immediately before a court
of competent jurisdiction. Officers finding fish being transported in violation of the Act shall seize the fish and place
the person in custody. Any person violating the Act shall
upon conviction be punished by a fine not exceeding $200, or
be imprisoned for a term of not more than three months,
or both. This Act does not apply to steel-head trout (Salmo
gairdneri) legally taken in the Columbia River between the
states of Washington and Oregon.

Bald Eagle Act

This Act protects the bald eagle[12] within the United
States and any state subject to its jurisdiction, except
Alaska. It expressly prohibits anyone from taking, possessing, selling, purchasing, bartering, offering for sale,
transporting in any manner the bald eagle or a part thereof,
including the nest or egg. The exception to this is when the
bird is taken for scientific or exhibition purposes under
proper permit. However, no permit can be issued to an
individual to continue in possession of the bald eagle. This
Act does not interfere with the possession or transportation
of such birds dead or alive, or any part, nest, or egg which
were lawfully taken prior to June 8, 1940. A bald eagle
taken dead or alive in Alaska cannot be sold in the United
States or any other place which is under the jurisdiction
of the United States, except Alaska. Any person violating
this Act, if convicted, shall be fined not more than $500,
or imprisoned not more than six months, or both.

FEDERAL VERSUS STATE
RESPONSIBILITIES

Even though, by reason of the constitutional provisions,
the major areas of federal and state authority over wildlife
control seem to be well defined, there are several areas
wherein exist differences of opinion as to the proper division of responsibility for wildlife control. A study of the
views expressed by Connery[13] respective to the issues

---

12. Act of June 8, 1940, 54 STAT. 250--16 U. S. C. 688.
13. Robert H. Connery. 1935. Governmental problems in wildlife conservation. Columbia University Press. pp. 53-80.

involved leads one to summarize his ideas in the following statements:

1. It is easy to say let either the states or the federal government handle all game matters, but this cannot be done;

2. States have no international rights by which to protect birds, mammals, or fishes outside their respective boundaries;

3. States cannot dictate rules and regulations on federal properties, and game has no priority over timber, oil, minerals, and recreations for being singled out for special consideration;

4. Federal influence should be primarily promotional, with regulations secondary;

5. The states should be chiefly regulatory, but have strong promotional and educational programs to supplement the federal developments.

These statements are indicative of the trends that are actually taking place in the area of wildlife management. There are, however, notable exceptions with respect to division of responsibility.

Wildlife on National Forests [14]

Considerable difference of opinion exists, for example, as to the proper division of authority over wildlife on national forests. The material under this section presents the case for federal control.

The legislation providing for the National Forest Administration Act of June 4, 1897, is based on the power of Congress "to dispose of and make all needful Rules and Regulations respecting the Territory or other Property belonging to the United States. . . ."[15]

Legal rulings based on this constitutional provision have been rendered by the various federal courts. With regard to the power held by Congress, Judge Sibley stated:

. . . but the Congress still has the power, under the supreme law of the land, to make such regulations as are needful, Congress being the judge of what is needful. It is probable that it

---

14. This material is, in part, from a file prepared by the senior attorney solicitor's office, U. S. Forest Service, Ogden, Utah. Permission to reproduce it is contained in a letter to the author from S. R. Standing, Assistant Regional Forester, dated December 27, 1954.
15. Constitution of the United States, Article IV, Section 3, clause 2.

is the exclusive judge of what is needful. Certainly any regulation looking to the use or disposal or the safety of the property is needful if Congress so conceives it. It is well settled that Congress, in making regulations, may not only deal with them itself, but may, after providing a general scheme, delegate the details to some officer or commission. [16]

In Shannon v. United States [17] the Circuit Court of Appeals for the Ninth Circuit said:

> The Federal Constitution delegates to Congress the general power absolutely and without limitation to dispose of and make all needful rules and regulations concerning the public domain, and this independent of the locality of the public land, whether it be situated in a State or in a territory. . . the exercise of which power cannot be restricted or embarrassed in any degree by said legislation. . . . The rights given by the State statutes to the subjects of the State extend only to the lands of the State. They end at the borders of the Government lands. At that border the laws of the United States intervene, and it is within their province to forbid trespass. Such laws being within the power of Congress, it is not necessary to discuss the question whether it is sovereign power or police power, or what be its nature, for there is no power vested in the State which can embarrass or interfere with its exercise.

The Supreme Court of the United States, in referring to this constitutional provision in Kansas v. Colorado, [18] held:

> The full scope of this paragraph has never been definitely settled. Primarily, at least, it is a grant of power to the United States of control over its property. That is implied by the words "Territory or other property."

This control over its property gives the Government the rights of a private ownership. In United States v. Light [19] the court maintained:

> The United States can prohibit absolutely or fix the terms on which its property may be used. As it can withhold or reserve the land, it can do so indefinitely.

In Utah Power and Light Co. v. United States [20] the Supreme Court held:

---

16. United States v. Gurley, 279 Fed. 874.
17. Shannon v. United States, 160 Fed. 870.
18. Kansas v. Colorado, 206 U. S. 46, 89.
19. United States v. Light, 220 U. S. 523.
20. Utah Power and Light Co. v. United States, 389.

And so we are of the opinion that the inclusion within a
State of lands of the United States does not take from Congress
the power to control their occupancy and use, to protect them
from trespass and injury and to prescribe the conditions upon
which others may obtain rights in them, even though this may
involve the exercise in some measure of what commonly is
known as the police power. "A different rule," as was said in
Camfield v. United States, [21] "would place the public domain of
the United States completely at the mercy of the State legislation."

Wildlife on the national forests is a resource of the
land and waters as are forage and timber. Federal control
should therefore extend to all phases of wildlife regulation.
This control is provided for by the National Forest Administration Act, in defining the duties and powers of the Secretary of Agriculture. [22] The Act provides that he may
make such rulings and regulations and establish such service as will insure the objects of such reservations, namely,
to regulate their occupancy and use and to preserve the
forest thereon from destruction.

It is believed that the regulation by the Secretary of
Agriculture of hunting upon the national forests is permissible as a means of fire prevention and for the protection of
forest growth against damage. While the Secretary has the
authority in periods of extreme fire danger to entirely close
national forest areas to all use, nevertheless it is recognized by the U. S. Forest Service that such action is rather
drastic and should be avoided, if practicable. It sometimes
happens that as a result of protective measures the game
increases to a point where, for the protection of the forest
growth and forage and to prevent soil erosion, it is necessary to drastically reduce the game.

In Hunt v. United States [23] the Supreme Court upheld
the right of the Secretary of Agriculture to kill large numbers of deer on the Kaibab National Forest and Grand Canyon National Game Preserve, since it was shown that such
action was necessary to protect the national forest and the
game preserve, and also the animals themselves. The
deer had increased to such large numbers that the forage
was insufficient for their sustenance, with the result that

---

21.   Camfield v. United States, 167 U. S. 518.
22.   Act of February 1, 1905, 33 STAT. 628.
23.   Hunt v. United States, 278 U. S. 96.

they had greatly injured the lands by overbrowsing upon and killing the young trees, shrubs, bushes, and forage plants. Thousands of the deer had died because of insufficient forage.

The court said that the power of the United States thus to protect its property did not admit of doubt. The lower court states in its decree that it should not be construed to permit the licensing of hunters to kill deer within the reserves in violation of the state game laws (19 F. 2d, 634). The Supreme Court said that while the Solicitor General of the United States did not concede the authority of the court to impose this limitation upon the Secretary's authority, he was content to let the decree stand. The Court therefore accepted the opinion and decree of the lower court, with the modification that all carcasses of deer and parts thereof shipped outside the boundaries of the reserve should be plainly marked with tags or otherwise, in such manner as the Secretary of Agriculture might provide, to show that they were killed under his authority within the limits of the reserves.

Following the Kaibab decision, the Circuit Court of Appeals for the Fourth Circuit[24] held that the Secretary of Agriculture could cause surplus deer on the Pisgah National Forest and Game Preserve in North Carolina to be killed for the protection of the lands of the United States without regard to state law. The lands involved in this case were purchased by the Government under the Weeks Law.[25] The state, by legislative act of 1915,[26] gave its consent for the Federal Government to make all such rules and regulations as it should deem necessary with respect to game animals.

Congress, in 1916,[27] authorized the President to establish preserves for the protection of game animals, birds, or fish; and prohibited, under penalty, the hunting, catching, trapping, or killing or the willful disturbance of any kind of game animal, bird, or fish, except under such rules and regulations as the Secretary of Agriculture may, from time to time, prescribe.

---

24. Chalk v. United States, 114 F (2d) 207.
25. Act of March 1, 1911 (36 STAT. 961; 16 U. S. C. 513).
26. N. C. Code Ann., 1939, Sec. 2099.
27. Act of August 11, 1916 (39 STAT. 446, 476; 16 U. S. C. 683).

The court ruled that this constituted an acceptance by Congress of the state cession of jurisdiction. It also held, however, that without regard to this cession and acceptance of jurisdiction, the Secretary had authority to take the action which he did.

Judge Luse of the U. S. District Court for Wisconsin said that it was within the power of Congress to regulate fishing and the hunting of wildlife, other than migratory birds, as an incident to the acquisition and control of the land for the purpose of the Migratory Bird Treaty. So here the Secretary of Agriculture, having the broad power to regulate the occupancy and use of the national forests for all purposes, certainly can regulate hunting. [28]

The Knox Opinion [29]

One of the reasons the U. S. Forest Service did not assert full control over the fish and game within the national forests is that some of its former law officers felt that it did not have such authority in view of an old opinion rendered by Attorney General Knox. But in that opinion, Mr. Knox said the authority given the Secretary to regulate the occupancy and use of the national forests was sufficient to enable him to regulate hunting, were it not for other legislative considerations affecting the question. He states:

> I have little doubt that, if unaffected by other legislative provisions and other considerations, the general and specific powers conferred upon the Secretary would be sufficient for this purpose. But these must be read in the light of other legislative action and non-action, and of other considerations to which I shall refer. The various statutory provisions which may have a bearing upon the question are too numerous to permit here more than a very general reference to them. [30]

A careful reading of the Knox opinion will show that it is based mainly upon the premise that there was an implied license to hunt upon the public lands of the United States and that he did not believe that Congress intended to cut off that license by the creation of the national forests.

There was also an implied license to graze on the public lands, which license was the basis of many private

---

28.   United States v. 2271.29 acres of land, etc. (31 F (2d0) 617).
29.   November 29, 1901 (23 Atty. Gen. 589).
30.   Ibid., pp. 591-592.

fortunes.[31] But the Supreme Court did not allow this to interfere with civil and criminal prosecutions for grazing on the national forests contrary to the regulations. In United States v. Light[32] the court said:

> There thus grew up a sort of implied license that these lands, thus left open, might be used so long as the government did not cancel its tacit consent (Buford v. Houtz, 133 U. S. 326). Its failure to object, however, did not confer any vested right on the complainant, nor did it deprive the United States of the power of recalling any implied license under which the land had been used for private purposes (Steele v. United States, 113 U. S. 130; Wilcox v. Jackson, 13 Pet. 513).

And in the Grimaud case,[33] which was a criminal action for grazing sheep on a forest contrary to the regulations, the court held:

> Thus the implied license under which the United States had suffered its public domain to be used as a pasture for sheep and cattle, mentioned in Buford v. Houtz, 133 U. S. 326, was curtailed and qualified by Congress, to the extent that such privilege should not be exercised in contravention of the rules and regulations (Wilcox v. Jackson, 13 Pet. 498, 513).

> If, after the passage of the Act and the promulgation of the rule, the defendants drove and grazed their sheep upon the reserve, in violation of the regulations, they were making an unlawful use of the government's property. In doing so, they thereby made themselves liable to the penalty imposed by Congress.[34]

Obviously, these decisions apply to hunting as well as to grazing; and the Knox opinion has thus lost its main premise. Its reference to the fact that Congress has enacted special game legislation in some instances is no real argument against the full exercise of the authority to regulate the occupancy and use of the national forest, which the Knox opinion said is without doubt in itself broad enough to include regulation of hunting and fishing.

A special act means nothing more than that a particular situation has been called specifically to the attention of Congress, and that Congress has therefore acted on that situation. There are special acts relating to some other phases

---

31.   Buford v. Houtz, 133 U. S. 320; United States v. Light, 220 U. S. 523; United States v. Mid-West Oil Co., 236 U. S. 459, 475.
32.   United States v. Light, 220 U. S. 523.
33.   United States v. Grimaud, 220 U. S. 506.
34.   Ibid., p. 521.

of national forest regulation, but this does not mean that the Secretary of Agriculture cannot exert as to other similar situations the full extent of the regulatory power conferred. For example, section 55 of the penal code makes it a criminal offense to trespass on what was formerly known as the Bull Run National Forest but is now a part of the Oregon National Forest and the watershed of the city of Portland. That does not prevent the Secretary from taking similar action for the protection of watersheds of other states, as he has done in many instances.

In the light of this discussion it would seem that the Federal Government is within its rights when, in the paramount interests of the people of the United States, it attempts to control wildlife on national forests. The present policy of the Federal Government appears to be that of allowing the states to control harvests on public lands where there is an open season. For example, on national forests and lands under supervision of the U. S. Bureau of Land Management, state agencies set the seasons and patrol the area throughout the year.

Federal Regulation of Migratory Birds

Another area of friction between the Federal Government and the states concerns the jurisdiction over wildlife that is migratory. A waterfowl management treaty, signed by Canada and the United States (with the approval of Great Britain) in 1916, and by Mexico and the United States in 1937, forms the legal basis for federal control over these birds.

After the Canada treaty was signed by the President, it was contested on the grounds that it invaded states' rights. The Supreme Court decision, written by Justice Holmes, sustained the Enabling Act of Congress. Under this Act waterfowl and certain other migratory birds were declared to be under the jurisdiction of the Federal Government. The law appointed the U. S. Biological Survey (part of the U. S. Fish and Wildlife Service since 1939) as the government agency which should administer the law. Justice Holmes, who gave the decision, emphasized the following legal features:

1. The National Government has been delegated powers to make treaties; so this did not contradict the 10th amendment;

2. That acts of Congress are the supreme law of the land when made in pursuance of the constitution;
3. That treaties are likewise when made under authority of the U. S.;
4. That the treaty did not contravene any prohibitory clause in the constitution;
5. That it dealt with the subject recognized by international custom as the proper one for treaties;

Photograph by Paul Lake
Courtesy Wyoming Game and Fish Department

Figure 8. A sportsman is advised where to hunt.

6. That therefore it was valid and the law carrying it into effect was constitutional;
7. That it was recognized that the state in its sovereign capacity owned animals ferae naturae;
8. That also the states' title exceeded an individual's;
9. A State could never prevent the National Government from exercising a right to make treaties regulating this subject.

In Cochrane v. United States [35] the Circuit Court of Appeals for the Seventh Circuit said:

> It is impossible to deal with migratory birds on the basis of their being the property of the State or of the State's having an exclusive property interest in them. Ordinarily, an attribute of property and of property rights is possession. Moreover, it is equally impossible even to identify the birds after they have passed from one State to another and returned to the State where they were hatched. It is unbelievable that the framers of the Constitution intended to leave this form of valuable property, which did not vest in the individual and which could not be controlled by the State, unprotected and fated to total destruction. It is not a matter of sentiment, but of common sense.

Exemplification of the power of Congress is found in the recent case of Missouri v. Holland, [36] in which the court sustained the act of Congress for the provisions of the Migratory Bird Treaty against an attack upon its constitutionality on the ground that it was an invasion of the sovereignty of the State. There the court said:

> The State, as we have intimated, founded its claim of exclusive authority upon an assertion of title to migratory birds, an assertion that is embodied in statute. No doubt it is true that as between a state and its inhabitants the state may regulate the killing and sale of such birds, but it does not follow that its authority is exclusively of paramount powers.
>
> As most of the laws of the United States are carried out within the states and as many of them deal with matters which in the silence of such laws the state might regulate, such general grounds are not enough to support Missouri's claims. Valid treaties, of course, "are as binding within the territorial limits of the states as they are elsewhere throughout the dominion of the United States." [37] No doubt the great body of private relations usually falls within the control of the state, but a treaty may override its power (p. 434).

---

35.   Cochrane v. United States, 92 f. (2d) 623 cert. denied, 303 U. S. 636
36.   Missouri v. Holland, 252 U. S. 416, 435.
37.   Baldwin v. Franks, 120 U. S. 678, 683.

Here a national interest of very nearly the first magnitude is involved. It can be protected only by national action in concert with that of another power. The subject matter is only transitorily within the state and has no permanent habitat therein. But for the treaty and the statute, there soon might be no birds for any powers to deal with. We see nothing in the Constitution that compels the Government to sit by while a food supply is cut off and the protectors of our forest and our crops are destroyed. It is not sufficient to rely upon the states. The reliance is vain, and were it otherwise, the question is whether the United States is forbidden to act. We are of the opinion that the treaty and statute must be upheld.

CHAPTER IV

Rights of Private Citizens Under Wildlife Law

OWNERSHIP OF WILDLIFE A PRIVILEGE

Since the state owns the game in its wild state and in its sovereign capacity, it follows that an individual cannot obtain absolute property right to game except upon such conditions, restrictions, and limitations as the state permits. Further, the individual acquires absolute property right to wildlife only as a matter of privilege and not as a right. The state can and does impose conditions under which an individual may acquire property rights to wildlife. Either the legislature alone or the legislature and the state fish and game department may impose conditions deemed necessary and expedient, so long as these do not contravene any principle of the Constitution.

It was held in Indiana that when a citizen accepts the state's grant, he also accepts it impressioned with all the restrictions and limitations. And when he acquires property under a game license, he does so with the full notice of his qualified rights, and that if he loses that which he has taken or held possession of upon forbidden terms, he has lost nothing in its forfeiture that belonged to him. [1]

In the case of Magner v. People[2] it was held that to hunt and kill game is a boon or privilege granted expressly or impliedly by sovereign authority, but not a right inherited by each individual. Consequently, nothing is taken away from the individual when he is denied a privilege, such as limited hunting seasons. The individual may no longer acquire ownership of game by capturing, killing, or reclaiming, except as permitted by law.

---

1. Smith v. State, 155 Ind. 611, 612, 613.
2. Magner v. People, 97 Ill. 320, 333, 334.

ACQUIRING OWNERSHIP OF WILDLIFE

There are two ways that an individual can gain legal title to wildlife. He may provide his own brood stock and have his property set up as a game farm or fish hatchery under proper permit, or he may take wildlife under legal regulations and reduce it to his possession. The following discussion deals with the latter provision.

The pros and cons of reducing game to possession are discussed in the case of Dapson v. Daly. [3]   In this case the plaintiff sued for the carcass of a deer killed by the defendant. The plaintiff wounded the deer and was in the act of pursuing it when the defendant fired at the deer. The deer immediately dropped and was dead when the defendant reached it. The defendant carried the carcass away, after which he was sued by the plaintiff for its recovery. The court refused to order the carcass returned to the plaintiff for the following reasons:

1. The plaintiff failed to show that he had taken possession of the deer even though it had been wounded by him.
2. Evidence presented in court indicated that the fatal shot had been fired by the defendant, and thus the animal was taken into possession by him from a.wild state.
3. The plaintiff failed to show that he was entitled to the rights of a huntsman, and subsequently to the possession of a deer, since he failed to produce a hunting license (being the plaintiff the burden of proof rested with him). In order to gain possession of the carcass the plaintiff, in addition to showing that the deer was taken into possession, had to show that he was authorized to take the game into possession.

On these grounds the case was dismissed.

Other cases that clarify the rights, title, and remedies of hunters in respect to game which is being pursued, or which has been killed or wounded, follow in annotated form.

---

3.   Dapson v. Daly, Massachusetts Supreme Judicial Court, 1926, American Law Reports, Vol. 49. pp. 1496-1530.

Game

1. The pursuit of a wild animal gives no title thereto; and an action will not lie against a man for killing and taking an animal _ferae naturae_, though the killing was done in view of another who started it and was on the point of taking it. But, on the other hand, title may accrue to one though he has not actually seized the body of the animal, as where he has ensnared the animal or has actual dominion over it by such means as will prevent its escape. [4]

2. The instant a wild animal is brought under the control of a person, so that actual possession is practically inevitable, a vested property interest in it accrues, which cannot be divested by another intervening and killing it. [5]

3. A partridge shot by one hunter and picked up by a second hunter was alive but in a dying condition. The court ruled that the partridge was in possession of the first hunter since it had been sufficiently reduced to possession. [6]

Fish

1. Where fish have been caught in a net which has not been drawn in and from which it is not absolutely impossible, but practically so, for them to escape, the owners of the net have acquired. . . a property in them. . . . [7]

2. But in State v. Thomas[8] it was held that the owner of fish traps containing an opening about 3 1/2 feet square through which the fish entered did not have a property in the fish while in such traps, since the court ruled that the avenue of escape must be closed, or the chance of escape at least reduced to a minimum.

RIGHTS OF THE PROPERTY OWNER

The mere fact that a landowner posts his property against hunting, fishing, or trespassing in no way gives him title to the game. The state holds ownership of game within its boundaries, but the individual owner of real estate has an interest in the game on his premise. This is not an absolute interest, but rather a qualified one. That is, no one has the right to go on his premises, without permission, to hunt or fish. [9]

---

4. 12 R. C. L. 3, p. 686.
5. Liesner v. Wanie, 1914 (156 Wis. 16; 50 L. R. A., N. S. 703, 145 N. W. 374).
6. Reg. v. Roe, 1870 (22 L. T. N. S. England, 414).
7. State v. Shaw, 1902 (67 Ohio St. 157, 60 L. R. A. 481, 65 N. E. 875, 14 Am. Crim. Rep. 405).
8. State v. Thomas, 1901 (11 Ohio S. & C. P. Dec. 753).
9. DuPont Company, The. 1930. Wild game--its legal status. The DuPont Co., p. 39.

Courtesy Washington Department of Game

Figure 9. Promoting good farmer-sportsman relations is part of an officer's job.

In Minnesota the Court held that the individual has the right to exercise exclusive and absolute domain over his property, and the unqualified right to further restrict taking game. [10]   In other words, the restriction does not modify the act but prohibits it.

A private owner has the exclusive right to hunt on his land and may prohibit others. [11]   In the case of L. Realty Co. v. Johnson, [12] the Supreme Court of Minnesota said:

> While true that the title to all wild game is in the State and the owner of premises whereon it is located has only a qualified property interest therein, yet he has the right to exercise exclusive and absolute dominion over his property, and incidentally the unqualified right to control and protect the wild game thereon.

A state license does not authorize hunting on the lands of a private owner.   A Wisconsin court maintained:

> No person has a right to go upon the land of another against the latter's will, or to so intrude upon the right of such other to the exclusive use of lands for any purpose merely because he possesses a State license to hunt. Such a license does not affect the relations of the licensee with such other in the slightest degree. A violation of the latter's rights by such person, which would be an actionable wrong if he were not armed with such a license to hunt, would be such a wrong if he were so armed. It is a mistaken notion that such a license gives the holder thereof any right whatever to trespass upon the property rights of others. [13]

The Wisconsin court also ruled:

> The exclusive use of one's own property is a right protected by the Constitution. The Legislature cannot authorize another to enter the premises for the purpose of taking game. [14]

In fact, the owner's rights include the right to prohibit a hunter from shooting over the premises of an adjoining owner, or from going on the premises to retrieve game which has fallen there. [15]

RIGHT TO PROTECT PROPERTY FROM DAMAGE BY WILDLIFE

The right of property owners to protect their property even at the expense of wildlife that are responsible for

---

10.   L. Realty Co. v. Johnson, 92 Minn. 363, 364, 365.
11.   Ohio Oil Co. v. Indiana, 177 U. S. 190; Kellogg v. King, 114 Cal. 378, 46 Pac. 166; Sterling v. Jackson, 69 Mich. 488, 37 NW, 845; L. Realty Co. v. Johnson, 92 Minn. 363, 100 NW 94.
12.   L. Realty Co. v. Johnson, 92 Minn. 363, 364, 365.
13.   Diana Shooting Club v. Lamoreux, 114 Wis. 44.
14.   Ibid.
15.   Whitaker v. Stangvick, 100 Minn. 3, 386.

damage to it has been recognized by the courts. In Kentucky the Court of Appeals ruled that a landowner can kill game when it is doing damage to his lands. [16]

Masden sued the Kentucky State Fish and Game Department for damages resulting to his lands by deer from a nearby refuge, claiming the laws made it impossible to protect his land. He obtained a judgment in the amount of $2,079 against the state. The state appealed, claiming he could have protected his property.

The Kentucky Court of Appeals ruled that the state's contention was correct, that most states give the private citizen the right to protect his property from wild game even to the extent of killing game that is in the act of doing damage. Furthermore, they said the state is not liable for damage, but nothing prohibits the state from payment of fair damage claims. They ruled the estimate of damages was unclear and evasive, whereupon they reversed the judgment with directions to grant appellants a new trial.

In the case of willful destruction of game, as a result of alleged property damage, the true intent of the law may be difficult to ferret out. For example, in State v. Burk[17] the defendant was charged with illegal possession of an elk on two counts, contrary to the statutes of the State of Washington.

The defense held that the killing was justified because elk had in the past, and were then, causing damage to the defendant's property. District Court had found that the defendant did not show sufficient damage or cause for justification of killing an elk, and therefore restricted that information from the jury. The verdict of "guilty" was upheld in Superior Court.

The case was appealed to the Supreme Court on the following grounds: (1) one who kills elk to defend self or property is not guilty; (2) testimony was withheld which would help the jury to decide the justification of killing elk; (3) the defendant might show recent past injury by the band of elk,

---

16. Commonwealth of Kentucky, et al., v. Masden, Vol. 169, American Law Reports: 101, Kan.
17. State v. Burk, 15938 Supreme Court of Washington, 1921; Pacific Reporter, 195:16-20.

some of which he killed; (4) the defendant, prosecuted for killing elk, was entitled to show damage done by the band of elk. The state contended that he was not justified in killing elk because the statute meant that the elk were more precious than the amount of damage done. However, the Constitution gives a man the right to protect his property. So the questions were: Were the proceedings correct, and did the damage justify the illegal act?

(1) The court held that the act of killing an elk to protect oneself or property was justifiable if the damage was sufficient to warrant the killing, and the defendant had a right to show the necessity for his act.

(2) The court ruled that the defendant's testimony was sufficient to attempt to show justification. Also testimony on past damage was admissible not to show justification for killing the elk but to show the capacity of the elk to do damage.

(3) The court contended that at no time did the court have the right to judge whether testimony on damage was sufficient or not, that this was the responsibility of the jury.

(4) The court ruled that the defendant could show damage by the elk band so as to justify the killing of the two elk if these elk were part of the band. The Supreme Court reversed the judgment and the case was remanded for a new trial.

FINAL AUTHORITY

A point that should be kept in mind is that fish and game laws are passed by state legislators and administered by state and federal enforcement agencies, but they are interpreted by judges and juries. It has been said that a law is nothing more than a prediction of what a judge or a jury will do under a particular circumstance. In borderline cases one may find that it is often impossible to predict what a verdict will be. In such cases great stress is placed on the interpretation of the law. It is entirely possible that two courts may interpret a ruling in such diverse ways that one court might convict an individual for certain offenses and another court might acquit him.

CHAPTER V

Violation of Wildlife Law

TYPES OF LAW VIOLATION
IN GENERAL

Basically, there are two types of law violation. Classical writers speak of crimes and of misdemeanors. The first comprise acts that are mala in se, or wrong in and of themselves. Violations of morals, such as homicide and theft, serve as examples. Misdemeanors comprise acts said to be mala prohibita, or acts which are wrong merely because they are prohibited by law. In this category come such acts as traffic or wildlife violations.

In other words, fish and game offenses are wrongful acts because society has seen fit to make them so by acts of legislation, or their equivalent, and not because these offenses outrage our morals. It must be admitted, however, that some law enforcement personnel believe that in certain flagrant cases our morals are outraged and that the offenses should be punishable as crimes.

MAJOR CLASSES OF WILDLIFE LAW
VIOLATIONS AND COURT RULINGS

Regardless of how efficient a law enforcement agency may be, it is a foregone conclusion that violations will occur. Wildlife violations may be classified under five headings. [1] They are: (1) taking or attempting to take wildlife out of season; (2) taking or attempting to take wildlife in an illegal place; (3) improper or no license; (4) illegal gear; and (5) illegal possession. An example of each class is given below. In addition, a number of court rulings are cited in order to help the officer develop judgment in what

---

[1] Many administrators believe that an analysis of any complete set of fish and game regulations will show that the majority of them are of a nature designed to equalize opportunity of taking game by sportsmen, rather than an effort to reduce the kill. In other words, conservation is primarily managing the people taking the game, rather than managing the game.

have been considered, for one or more reasons, border-line cases. Presumably, these rulings are at present final in the states involved and may influence judgment in other states.

Out-of-Season[2]

This violation may result from either fishing or hunting after hours or on days when the season is closed.

Case.[3] The defendant was convicted in county court of violating the state game law by illegally killing a deer. He appealed on the grounds that the evidence was insufficient to sustain the judgment. The evidence is as follows: Two men working on the forest reserve heard a shot. They investigated and found the defendant and another man armed with rifles; and one man had hair and blood on his clothing, apparently from a deer. When the arresting officers followed the tracks of the two defendants, they found a dead deer, still warm, about 175 steps from where they had met the defendants. The deer had been killed with a rifle. The defendant did not take the stand and offered no testimony.

The Supreme Court ruled that the evidence, though circumstantial, was sufficient to sustain the judgment. The verdict was affirmed.

Case.[4] This case of killing elk out of season to protect private property is almost identical to that of the State v. Burk.[5]

Illegal Place

It is a violation to seek fish and game in closed areas, refuges, on closed streams, and generally on posted private property.

Case.[6] Defendant Aragon, the plaintiff in this case, was a justice of the peace for Alamosa County. He convicted several persons of illegally hunting on private land without first obtaining permission from the owner and assessed a $25 fine on each person. The case was appealed to the district court,

---

2. There is a definite relationship between out-of-season and illegal possession. Many persons involved in out-of-season violations are actually charged with illegal possession, since it is difficult to apprehend the violator in the act. Laws which put a definite limit on how long game may be held therefore destroy alibis for post-season hunting.
3. Robinson et al. v. State, Vol. 258 Pacific Reporter; 1073 Oklahoma.
4. State v. Rathbone, Vol. 100 Pacific Reporter, 2nd series; 86 Montana.
5. State v. Burk, Vol. 195 Pacific Reporter, 16 Washington.
6. Aragon v. People, ex. rel. Medina et al., Vol. 218 Pacific Reporter, 2nd series; 744 Colorado.

and writ of prohibition against further action or steps to collect fines was asked for on the grounds that the statute did not
provide a penalty for the offense; thus no prosecution was possible. The District Court reversed the decision and upheld
the writ.

The justice of the peace appealed to the Supreme Court.
This court ruled that even though no penalty was provided in
the specific section setting forth the violation, the penalty was
provided in a later section of the statute specially put in to
cover the violations of the preceding sections. The penalty,
as set forth for the preceding violation, was a fine of not less
than $25 or more than $250, or by imprisonment in the county
jail for not less than ten days or more than three months, or
by such fine and imprisonment.

This section adequately covered the section stating the violation; thus the justice of the peace did not exceed his jurisdiction, and the judgment of the district court was reversed and
cause remanded with directions for further proceedings in accordance with the views expressed by the Supreme Court.

Case.[7] The defendant was convicted in District Court of hunting game on purportedly posted land. The case was appealed
to the Supreme Court of New Mexico.

The law states clearly that a person must both post and
publish his intentions of closing his land, both in English and
in Spanish, before the law against trespass will apply. The
plaintiff only posted and published his intentions in English,
and even though the plaintiffs could read English, the law
against trespass was not in effect on the land because the requirements were not met. The law is very clear and strictly
construed; thus the decision was reversed, and orders to District Court were issued to reverse its decision and release the
defendants from its custody.

Improper License

The law is violated by a person who uses a license
improperly made out, who uses a residence license when he
is entitled only to a nonresidence license, who uses a license
issued to other than himself, or who fails to display a visible
license as required.

Case.[8] The defendant in this case was a game warden who had
violated the rights of an alien by arresting him for improper
license and illegal possession of deer meat. The alien had
lived in Colorado for five years prior to buying a resident
hunting license on which no false statements were made. The
case hinged on the right of an alien to lawfully purchase a

---

7. State v. Barnett et al., Pacific Reporter, 2nd series, Vol. 245; 833,
   N. Mex.
8. Herzig v. Feast et al., Pacific Reporter, 2nd series, Vol. 259; 288,
   Colorado.

hunting license. The first case had not been prosecuted in justice court; so no disposition was given it. The law made a distinct specification between residents and non-residents but made
no distinction against resident aliens.

The District Court had ruled against the alien and for the
warden, but the Supreme Court reversed the ruling and remanded the case with directions, on the grounds that an alien
can lawfully buy a big-game license, kill, and possess game
on the license; and the warden's action in this case was wanton
and reckless disregard for the alien's rights. The warden
should have made sure the law applied to aliens in regard to
licenses before subjecting the person to arrest.

Case.[9] The defendant was convicted of fishing without a
license, and he appealed. The circumstances of the case were
odd. Two game rangers saw five men seining a slough. They
did not arrest them then but blocked the road and found six
men, two of whom did not have a license, leaving the pond.
The defendant's clothing was dry and no evidence was given
that he participated in the seining. Furthermore, the pond
was land-locked (no inlet or outlet to other waters) and was
completely within privately owned land. However, a license
is required for seining in waters over which the state has
jurisdiction.

The Appellate Court ruled that the evidence purporting to
show the defendant was seining was insufficient and circumstantial at best. They also ruled that the state has no authority to regulate fishing in private, land-locked lakes where
fish do not have free access to waters outside the lake and
are not free to pass in waters to and from the same. The
judgment and sentence of the county court were reversed and
the defendant released.

Illegal Gear

It is against the law in most states to use a 22-caliber
gun to hunt deer, to use a shotgun that will hold more than
three shells when attempting to take migratory waterfowl,
or to use too many hooks on fishing gear, or worms on a
stream open only to artificial fly fishing.

Case.[10] Defendant Tyler was tried for illegally taking fish.
He was using a pole with a line run through eyes on the pole
and with a large hook at the end of the line. The hook could
be pulled up and made stationary at the end of the pole and
used as a gig. He had snagged one channel catfish. By law,
the catfish is a game fish, and the use of a gig is unlawful.

---

9.   Washburn v. State, Pacific Reporter, 2nd series, Vol. 213; 870,
     Oklahoma.
10. State v. Tyler, Pacific Reporter, 2nd series, Vol. 166; 1015,
     Oklahoma.

Courtesy Washington Department of Game

Figure 10. Special permits as well as licenses are required in some areas.

Tyler argued that he was not using the pole as a gig, but witnesses testified differently. He also said everyone else was fishing in this manner and that the fish would have died anyway because of low water. The court ruled that even if others were violating the law, that did not excuse the offense, and that the dying fish were a problem of the state fish and game department, to be handled by them and not by Tyler.

Tyler had been discharged by the county court and in this way escaped further prosecution. However, the case was decided in favor of the state.

Case.[11] Defendant Baxter was convicted of catching salmon with a net and fined $300. The jury trial was appealed on grounds that the evidence was not sufficient to secure a conviction, that court erred in giving instructions to the jury on circumstantial evidence, that the nets used in court were not the same ones as those taken from him, and that the defense was not permitted to cross-examine a witness.

The charges were stated by prosecution as follows: two game wardens saw a man setting nets but did not arrest him at the time. Later, they arrested a man whom they identified as the man seen earlier. The man had three nets in his boat, one containing fish.

The court ruled that the evidence was sufficient for a jury to deliver a verdict of guilty and for a court to sustain it. In cases of this kind, the Supreme Court reviews the case and decides if the evidence is sufficient for a jury to bring in a verdict. Very seldom will the Supreme Court overrule a jury's decision if the evidence is sufficient, even when the Supreme Court does not agree with the verdict.

The Court further ruled that the instructions to the jury about circumstantial evidence were correct because circumstantial evidence is competent evidence, is often as good as actual evidence, and may often be the only type that exists. As for the nets, the three in question were kept separate and were not proven to be the wrong ones. The court said they would have no great bearing on the case anyhow. The witness that was not cross-examined was later called by the defense and examined completely; so the defendant had no complaint. The verdict of the jury and trial court was affirmed.[12]

---

11.   State v. Baxter, Pacific Reporter, 2nd series, Vol. 132; 1022, Washington.

12.   The officers could have saved time and money by placing the man under arrest when they saw him committing the crime. If this were not possible, he could have and should have been kept under constant surveillance until the arrest could be effected. Also, the need for absolute identification of evidence by the officer is shown. The nets should have been, if they were not, very plainly marked and stored in such a manner as to leave no doubt, at a later time, as to their role as competent evidence in this case. For a more complete discussion of evidence, see Chapter 10.

Photograph by Don Wooldridge
Courtesy Missouri Conservation Commission

Figure 11. Confiscation of illegal gear is occasionally necessary.

Case.[13] The defendant was convicted in the Custer County
Court of unlawfully catching channel catfish out of the Washita
River by means of a wire trap. He appealed the decision to the
Oklahoma Criminal Court of Appeals.

Two statutes could have been used in this case. One prohibits catching game fish by any means other than hook and line,
and classifies channel catfish as game fish. The other law
prohibits catching certain game fish by means of nets, net
seines, gun, wire trap, pot, snare, or gig, but does not name
channel catfish as a game fish. This last statute was the basis
of the defense. However, the court ruled that the information
in the complaint, to wit "unlawfully catch about 25 channel
catfish out of the Washita River by means and use of wire trap"
was sufficient to institute proceedings under the statute declaring hook and line as the only legal way to catch game fish.

The defendant claimed he only happened upon the trap and
took fish from it but disclaimed ownership of the trap. However, by taking the fish from the stream by the wire trap,
with or without ownership, he violated the first statute given
above. The judgment and sentence of the county court were
affirmed.

Case.[14] The defendants were convicted in probate court of
attempt to kill deer with the aid of a spotlight, and they appealed to the District Court. Here the judgment was reversed
and the proceedings dismissed. The state appealed to the
Supreme Court.

The complaint sets forth the acts committed by these men
who were using a spotlight on their car after dark to locate
deer, which they intended to kill or attempt to kill. They had
loaded rifles which they intended to use in an attempt to kill
the deer. However, no evidence is presented of any actual
attempt to kill deer, and it must be assumed the actual attempt if not witnessed did not occur. The statute which applies reads, in part: "Provided, also, that it shall be a misdemeanor to take, kill, or attempt to kill any game with the
aid of a spotlight, flashlight, or artificial light of any kind."

The court ruled the statute, as worded, does not make it
unlawful to hunt deer with a spotlight. The complaint cites the
statutes and also sets forth the acts committed, but only goes
so far as to show hunting the animals and not an attempt to kill
them. The facts show only planning or preparation, which is
not stated in the statute as a crime.

---

13.   Kephart v. State, Pacific Reporter, 2nd series, Vol. 299; 244,
      Oklahoma.
14.   State v. Schirmer et al., Pacific Reporter, 2nd series, Vol. 211;
      762, Idaho.

The defendant cited a number of cases to show precedence. [15] The appelant also cited cases, [16] but these did not apply because they were all from Texas, and the Texas statute involved makes it an offense to hunt game with the aid of a light. The judgment of the District Court was affirmed.

Case. [17] The defendants were charged with illegally taking fish. The information charged that the defendants ". . .did then and there. . .catch and take fish with their hands. . . ." and referred to the statute that reads, in part, "It shall be unlawful for any person to take, catch, or kill any game fish. . . ." Nothing is said of non-game fish. The fish caught by the defendants were "mudcats" and not game fish as specified by the statute.

The defendants were tried, and a demurrer to the information was sustained by the county court. The state appealed. The Supreme Court ruled that the statute does not prohibit taking non-game fish by hand, and the statutes cannot be expanded or extended to cover cases that are not clearly within their scope. The judgment and demurrer were affirmed.

Illegal Possession.

A person violates the law when he possesses game beyond the legal possession limit of time, or possesses animals on which there is no open season (unless he can otherwise show legal ownership).

Case. [18] Defendant Miller caught five kelp bass in waters off the Mexican Coast. The fish were taken legally in all respects; however, upon landing at San Diego, a game warden asked the defendant to fill out a form declaring his catch, and a permit to bring the fish into California would have been issued. The defendant refused to comply and was arrested, tried, and convicted. The conviction was upheld through all the courts to the appelate department of the Superior Court of San Diego County.

The defendant appealed the case on the grounds that the fish and game code did not state that it was a crime, and the state has no right to restrict commerce, since this is the job of the Federal Government.

15. State v. Adder, A. L. R. 22 A. L. R. 219; Dooley v. State, 170 So. 96; West v. Commonwealth, 157 S. E. 538; State v. Wood, 103 N. W. 25; State v. Hurley, 64 A 78; Gustine v. State, 97 So. 207; State v. Rooney, 236 P 826.
16. Galloway v. State, 69 S. W. 2nd 89; Protect v. State, 133 S. W. 2nd 581; West v. State, 210 S. W. 2nd 585.
17. State v. Weindel et al., Pacific Reporter, 2nd series, Vol. 2, 599 Oklahoma.
18. People v. Miller, Pacific Reporter, 2nd series, Vol. 22; p. 496, California.

Court ruled that the code was very clear on the crime of transporting fish, because an officer was present and the defendant's signature on an application for a permit to import fish was all that was required. The states may pass laws necessary to conserve fish and game or laws pertaining to the bringing in of food, which includes fish and game. The judgment was affirmed.

Case. [19] Defendant Worth was convicted in Superior Court of illegal possession of the carcass of a deer. He had killed the deer, while driving, by hitting it with his car. He then took the deer home and did not notify the game warden. The state contended, rightly, that the defendant had no right to possess the deer. Worth appealed to the Massachusetts Supreme Judicial Court, contending that the possession of the carcass was lawful, that the possession was not prohibited by statute, and that the wording of the statute ". . . except as provided in this chapter" was equivalent to the wording ". . . in violation of this chapter."

The Court ruled that the possession was not lawful, inasmuch as the property right in game is with the state and no person has a right of possession. Also, the deer was not taken during the lawful season nor while it was destroying property or as a result of property protection. These are the only ways one can legally possess a deer. The fact that the deer was not illegally killed is immaterial to the possession. Also the word "provided" is not similar to "violation" in this instance. The exceptions asked by the appellant were overruled.

Case. [20] Officer Rogers was informed by a forest-service officer that Evans and Acuff, the defendants, had received a fire permit on forest reserve land. When the warden went to check the campers, he found them in the woods wearing bloody clothing. They directed him away from, rather than to, their camp. However, he located the camp and asked the men for permission to search. This permission was denied and enforced by covering the officer with rifles. Later, permission was granted, but the men followed the officer around with their rifles pointed at him. He found a rack, 204 feet from the camp, containing sacks of elk meat and elk meat being smoked. There was a well-worn path between the camp and the rack. A stew pot of elk meat was found still steaming along the trail. Parts of elk, including antlers, were near by. The officer attempted to arrest the men, but they resisted by pointing their rifles at him. Finally Acuff surrendered, but Evans left the camp and was apprehended later in town. The men were convicted by a jury in circuit court and sentenced to $500 fine and three months in jail, each. They appealed.

19.   Commonwealth of Massachusetts v. Worth, American Law Reports, Vol. 125, 1196 Massachusetts.

20.   State v. Evans et al., Pacific Reporter, 2nd Series, Vol. 22, 496 Oregon.

The defendants claimed the Court should not have allowed the district attorney to say the defendants put the officer "through an ordeal." The Court ruled that in view of the circumstances, this was permissible, and on the light side of what could be said. The Court ruled that, though circumstantial, the evidence was sufficient to show possession if believed by the jury. The defendants claimed the officer had no search warrant and no reason to believe a crime was committed. The Court pointed out that no warrant was necessary to search on forest or public land, and reason was justified by the blood on the men's clothing. The very act of resisting the search and arrest is, by statute, prima-facie evidence of the violation of the law by the persons resisting. This resistance was also taken into consideration when sentencing the defendants, and the Supreme Court ruled the sentence to be within legal bounds. The Supreme Court could find no error in the proceedings and affirmed the judgment.

Case. [21] Mr. Pulos was tried and convicted of illegal possession of a duck under the statute which reads, in part, "It shall be unlawful. . .at any time between January 15 and September 1 of any year, to take, kill, injure, destroy, or have in possession any wild duck."

The defendant argued that the duck was killed during the lawful season and was stored as food. He was obviously relying on the case of State v. Fisher. [22] Also, he contended that it was unfair to allow killing on one day and prohibit as unlawful the possession of the kill on the day after. He claimed the duck was lawfully reduced to his possession, being then his property with the state having no right to take it from him. He appealed to the Supreme Court.

The Supreme Court ruled that the Fisher case did not apply because the working of the statute, passed after the Fisher case, was very clear on possession at any time other than open season. Court agreed that the law might not be absolutely fair; however, it pointed out that the law does not make a person hunt on the last day of the season nor does it make a person kill more ducks than he or his friends can consume before the season ends. Furthermore, the title to wild game is with the state, and no person has an absolute property right to wild game; that hunting and taking game is a privilege subject to the regulations and restrictions of the law-making powers. The Court cited cases supporting this position[23] and affirmed the judgment.

21.   State v. Pulos, Pacific Reporter, Vol. 129; p. 128, Oregon.
22.   State v. Fisher, Pacific Reporter, Vol. 98; p. 713, Oregon.
23.   State v. Ashman, 135 S. W. 325; Ex. Parte Maier 37 Pac. 402; Sherwood v. Stephans, 90 Pac. 345.

Figure 12. Inspecting an excellent bag of Canadian Geese.

Case.[24] Mr. Fisher was tried and convicted in county court of illegally possessing deer meat after the season closed. The verdict was upheld in District Court, and the case was appealed to the Supreme Court. The violation was based on a statute that reads, in part, ". . . any person. . . having in possession any deer, or carcass, or part of a deer during the season when it is unlawful to take or kill such deer shall be guilty of a misdemeanor."

Fisher tried to explain the deer was killed legally during the season and was not unlawfully possessed. The District Court ruled he was in possession during off season and instructed the jury in that manner, thus obtaining a judgment of guilty.

The Supreme Court ruled that, whether intended or not, the words "such deer" in the statute referred to deer that were taken or killed during the time when it was unlawful to kill deer. Thus, deer that were killed legally did not fall under the category of this statute. The defendant had a right to show legal possession and the judgment was ruled erroneous and reversed. A new trial was ordered.

Case.[25] The defendant was convicted on two counts, one for killing a deer and one for illegal possession of parts of the deer killed. He appealed on the grounds that he did not kill the deer and he did not have the head of the deer in his possession. Also, an acquittal on an earlier count made him immune to these charges. He contended, in addition, that there was an error in instructions to the jury.

The undisputed evidence in condensed form is as follows: Defendant and two friends planned a deer hunt out of season. One man killed a small deer; another, a large buck; and the defendant, nothing. They carried the deer to a car, the defendant carrying the head of the large deer, which was hidden in a shack and later found by a deputy game warden. Defendant was acquitted on the killing of the small deer.

The Supreme Court ruled that the planning and carrying out of the hunt itself made the defendant equally guilty, even though he did not actually kill the deer. Also, he hid the deer head and could be said to be in possession of it, even though it was not on his person. The two acts of killing two deer were absolutely separate acts, unrelated in their commission; thus acquittal on one gave no immunity to the other. The instructions to the jury on accessory to the fact was in error; however, not all errors make judgment reversals necessary. The conviction and sentence of the lower court were affirmed.

Case.[26] A complaint was issued, charging defendant Miles with offering a reward for display of a game animal. Miles

---

24. State v. Fisher, Pacific Reporter, Vol. 98; p. 713, Oregon.
25. Stewart v. People, Pacific Reporter, Vol. 264; p. 720, Colorado.
26. State v. Miles, Pacific Reporter, 2nd series, Vol. 105; p. 51, Washington.

operated a sporting goods store and offered $10 for the largest deer displayed at his store during the deer season. The Fish and Game Commission had made it illegal to display game by virtue of powers granted to it for the taking of game. However, the regulation concerning the Commission's powers to pass rules regulating the taking of game does not mention displaying of game. The court ruled that the displaying of game could not have a logical connection affecting the taking of game, and the Commission had overstepped its authority by ruling against the display of game. The Superior Court had ruled for the defendant, and the Supreme Court affirmed the judgment.

Case. [27] The defendants, the Vissers, were convicted of illegal possession of deer, namely two fawns, during closed season and were fined $250 and costs. They appealed, claiming that the officers had not seen them in possession of the deer or been closer than 20 feet to the deer. The story was that these three men, the Visser brothers, were seen in the woods on state land after a series of shots had been heard. The officer found a car parked and a man, John Visser, approaching the car. Visser carried a rifle that had apparently been recently fired. However, this charge was not pressed. The two other men were seen in the woods hiding, but when told to come forward, they ran into the brush and escaped. The officer found two dead and still warm fawns 20 feet from where the men had been hiding. These two men were later arrested, one wearing clothing that was covered with blood and deer hair. No testimony was offered by the defendant.

The Supreme Court ruled that the evidence was sufficient, if believed by a jury, which it was, to reasonably show possession. Even though no one saw the men with the deer, it was illegal to possess these deer, whether observed or not. The circumstantial evidence supported a conviction, and the lower court had given correct instructions to the jury. The verdict and judgment were affirmed.

Case. [28] This case is discussed under the heading of improper license.

VIOLATIONS AND WILDLIFE MANAGEMENT

Violations of wildlife laws may be considered in another way: from the standpoint of management. Certain violations result in the taking of extra fish or game, and others do not.

Hunting out of season usually takes game which otherwise would not be taken. Hunting and fishing in improper

27. State v. Visser et al., Pacific Reporter, 2nd series, Vol. 61; 1284, Washington.
28. Herzig v. Feast et al., Pacific Reporter, 2nd series, Vol. 259; 288, Colorado.

places, such as refuges, probably take extra game (although much of it would never become available for legal take), but hunting on property that is posted frequently does not, although it may be in violation of both the fish-and-game and the civil law.

The use of an improper license, such as buying a residence license when a person is eligible only for a non-residence license, probably does not take additional game, but such practice may cost the state the additional amount of revenue. Licenses which are made out improperly, but for which the correct fee has been paid, do not take extra game. Improperly tagged animals, such as the use of a deer tag, does not take additional game (unless the tag is reused). The failure to wear a properly purchased, visible license when the law so requires does not take additional game.

The use of illegal gear may or may not take extra game, depending on the efficiency and use of the gear. Illegal possession, such as holding game overtime, does not take extra game, although it may permit game to be held so long that it is no longer suitable for table use.

VIOLATIONS INVOLVING MINORS

It appears that the problem of handling juveniles is becoming increasingly difficult. This is perhaps true to a greater degree in fish and game cases than in many other types of violations. Possibly this is partly because of the increased number of violations and partly because of the lack of specialized training of the officers handling these cases.

In dealing with juveniles, the officer must recognize that the rights of both the parent and the child are involved. The rights of parents to care for their children and exercise discretion in meeting the children's needs to the best of their ability must be maintained, as must the equally basic rights of the child to his personal liberty, to freedom from other than parental or normal community restraint.

For this reason, when a juvenile is apprehended in connection with a wildlife law violation, the officer should first ascertain the names of the child and his parents, their address, and telephone number. Then, instead of making an

arrest he may issue a citation. [29] He may or may not take
up the gear involved. Of course, if the minor becomes
obstreperous, the officer may consider it desirable to
make the arrest and take him to the nearest police station,
to be held until the parents are notified and come for him.
The disposition of the case then rests with the juvenile
court.

The philosophy regarding the handling of juvenile of-
fenders has changed drastically over the past 50 years.
Happily, that old-time judge is on his way out who, looking
at a defendant, snaps, "It says here you are guilty of shooting pheasants out of season. That will be $50!" Today, not
only has "snap justice" been replaced by what is known as
individualized justice, but also a new type of court, for
juveniles, has steadily been establishing itself as an essential part of the judicial system. Although juvenile courts
are perhaps not as well known or as widely distributed as
they should be, their underlying philosophy--that a child involved in delinquency is in need of treatment rather than
punishment--is now rather generally accepted.

VIOLATIONS INVOLVING AMERICAN INDIANS

Before visiting Indian reservations, an officer should
report to the superintendent of the reservation and advise
him of the purpose of his visit. Whenever possible, officers
should keep the superintendent acquainted with all state and
federal laws that may concern Indians. As a general rule,
Indians not complying with wildlife regulations on reservations are not arrested but taken to the superintendent, and
the case is turned over to him. An Indian who violates outside the refuge is treated as any other citizen. They should
not, however, be arrested if they claim legal exemption
from federal laws or if they question the validity of the regulations or if there appears to be an unsettled, legal question involved. For example, in State v. Arthur[30] it was
held that because of a treaty made many years before between the United States and a representative chief of the
Indians that the Indians could hunt and fish on certain lands
of the white man without restriction. This treaty was

---

29.   See Chapter VII, p. 103, for a discussion of the use of the citation.
30.   State v. Arthur, Pacific Reporter, 2nd series, Vol. 261; p. 135,
      Idaho.

upheld because the hunting, while outside the Indian reservation, was within the bounds originally set up by the treaty.
It states in part:

> Prosecution of a member of Nez Perce Tribe of Indians for
> having killed deer out of season on national forest lands, which
> were outside the boundaries of the reservation but within the
> exterior boundaries of lands ceded to the federal government
> by Nez Perce Tribe, in violation of state law and regulations
> of state fish and game commission. The District Court,
> Tenth Judicial District, Idaho County, Harry J. Hanley, J.,
> entered an order sustaining defendant's demurrer and entered
> judgment dismissing the action and discharging defendant, and
> the state appealed. The Supreme Court, Thomas, J., held
> that under treaty between United States and Nez Perce Indians,
> reserving right to such Indians to hunt upon open and un-
> claimed land, such Indians are entitled to hunt at any time of
> the year in any of the lands ceded to the federal government.
> The judgment was affirmed.

In view of the importance of this ruling, especially in
the Great Basin states, a presentation of the key points
underlying the judgment seems to be in order. These points
deal with the status of treaties of the Federal Government
versus states' rights and with the rights of Indians under
treaty.

Treaties

1. A treaty entered into in accordance with constitutional
requirements has force and effect of legislative enactment
and is, for all purposes, equivalent to Act of Congress, and
becomes law of the United States and states, and is binding
upon each sovereignty, not withstanding contrary provisions
in constitutions or laws of states. [31]

2. In case of conflict between treaty of the United States
and provisions of state constitution or statutory enactment,
whether enacted prior or subsequent to making of treaty,
treaty will control. [32]

3. The repeal of treaty provisions by implication is not
favored.

Indians

1. Admission of Idaho into the union did not operate to repeal the right reserved by treaty to Nez Perce Indians to hunt

---

31.   United States Constitution of America, article 6, clause 2.
32.   Idem.

upon open and unclaimed lands within the state. The Organic
Act and Idaho Constitution both recognize this treaty right.[33]

2. In determining meaning of provision of treaty between
United States and Nez Perce Indians reserving right or privilege of hunting to Indian tribes, recourse would be had to
negotiations between the tribes and the United States Government relative to subject matter and the practical construction
and intent.[34]

3. Within treaty between the United States and the Nez
Perce Indians reserving right to Indians to hunt upon "open
and unclaimed lands, " the quoted phrase was intended to include and embrace such lands as were not settled and occupied
by whites under possessory rights or patent or otherwise appropriated to private ownership, and was not intended to and
did not exclude lands, title to which rested in Federal Government, and, therefore, a member of such tribe has the right
under the treaty to hunt deer in National Forest Reserve established on land ceded by Indians to the United States.[35]

4. Under treaty between the United States and the Nez
Perce Indians reserving the right to such Indians to hunt upon
open and unclaimed land, such Indians are entitled to hunt at
any time of the year in any of the lands ceded to the Federal
Government, though such lands are outside boundaries of their
reservation and, therefore, such an Indian could not be prosecuted for having killed deer on National Forest lands, which
were outside boundaries of reservation but within exterior
boundaries of lands ceded to Federal Government, in violation
of state law and regulations of fish and game commission.[36]

PHYSICAL HAZARDS INVOLVING
WILDLIFE OFFICERS

The duties of the wildlife law enforcement officer are
exacting and not a little hazardous. Because of the nature
of his contacts with sportsmen and violators, he is sometimes regarded as <u>persona non grata</u>. When, in the discharge of his duties, he arouses the emotions of those surprised in the violation of wildlife law, he is in physical
danger from frustrated, angry, and confused men, men who
are sometimes acting also under the influence of alcohol.

33.　　Act of July 3, 1890, 26 STAT. 215; <u>Treaty between United States
and Nez Perce Indians</u>, June 11, 1855, 12 STAT. 1957; <u>Constitution</u>,
article 21, section 19; <u>Nez Perce Treaty</u>, June 9, 1863, 14 STAT.
647; <u>Nez Perce Treaty</u>, May 1, 1893, 28 STAT. 327; <u>Act of March
3, 1863</u>, 12 STAT. 808.

34.　　<u>Treaty between United States and Nez Perce Indians</u>, June 11, 1855,
12 STAT. 1957.

35.　　<u>Idem</u>. Also: <u>United States Constitution of America</u>, article 1, section 10; article 6, clause 2.

36.　　Treaty, <u>op. cit</u>. Also: <u>Idaho Constitution</u>, sections 36 to 104.

This danger may materialize in the form of threats to or acts of violence upon his person. In either case, those responsible are guilty of assault and, perhaps, battery, and are liable to court action. On the other hand, the wildlife enforcement officer may lay himself open to charges of assault and battery if he uses more force than is called for in effecting an arrest. These terms are defined below.

Assault

An attempt or offer with unlawful force or violence to do bodily harm to another is assault. It is not necessary that the attempt or offer be consumated. Pointing an unloaded pistol at a person who knows the weapon to be unloaded is not an attempt to do bodily harm, if the assailant realizes his inability to shoot the victim, and if the potential victim is not frightened. However, such an act may be an assault if the victim is put in reasonable fear of bodily injury by the act. Contrariwise, aiming a loaded weapon at someone who is not aware of the act is nevertheless committing assault, since the intent is to do bodily harm. Raising a fist or club over a person's head is an assault.

On the other hand, picking up a.club is not in itself an assault if there is no attempt to use it. Threatening words in themselves do not constitute assault. For example, a hunter who waves a shotgun about but proclaims at the same time that while he is sorely tempted he, nevertheless, has no intention of using it, is not committing assault. However, if the gun is at any time pointed at another person, the hunter may be charged with careless handling of firearms. It is not assault if one person fires a weapon at another who is obviously beyond the range of the weapon.

Aggravated Assault

This is an assault committed with a dangerous weapon or by other means or force likely to produce death or grievous bodily harm. Grievous bodily harm means serious bodily injury. That is, the natural and probable consequences of a particular act might result in death. Dangerous weapons are not necessarily firearms. It has been held that bottles, broken glass, rocks, pieces of pipe, boiling water. drugs, rifle butts, and so forth, can inflict death or grievous bodily harm. On the other hand, an unloaded pistol, when used as a firearm rather than a bludgeon, is not a dangerous weapon.

Battery

An assault in which the attempt to do or offer to do bodily harm is consummated by inflicting such harm is called a battery. This may be defined as an unlawful and intentional or culpably negligent application of force to the person of another by a material agent used directly or indirectly.

It may be a battery to push, spit on, or even cut the clothes of another person, or to cause him to take poison or to run into him with an automotive vehicle. Throwing a stone into a crowd of people may be a battery on anyone whom the stone hits. It may be a battery if a person is injured as a result of indirect motion. For example, a person may push a second one who falls against the third and injures him. The first person has committed a battery, if the act was intentional.

If an injury inflicted is unintentional and without culpable negligence, the offense is not committed. It is not a battery to lay hands on another to attract his attention or to seize someone to prevent a fall.

Proof of a battery will support a conviction of assault, since an assault is necessarily included in a battery. In order to constitute an assault the act of violence must be unlawful and it must be done without legal justification or excuse and without the lawful consent of the person affected.

THEORIES FOR CRIME

The reasons given for having committed intentional violations are diverse and sometimes ingenious. Some of the more valid reasons given by violators of wildlife law are that wildlife has damaged personal property or the honest belief that the game belongs to the land owner. In some places, violators express the all-too-recent view that game laws should not be enforced. However, attitudes toward game laws frequently represent the outlook of an individual or of a family, rather than that of an entire group.

Down through the ages many theories have been advanced concerning the reasons for crime in general. These theories form part of the history of crime, as seen through the eyes of some leading criminologists.

Courtesy Federal Bureau of Investigation

Figure 13. A firearms examiner comparing a specimen cartridge with the Standard Ammunition File.

During medieval and even early modern times one of the most accepted of the many explanations for crime was that it was due to depravity and the instigation of the devil. During this period such subjects as chairs, insects, and hogs were tried for various crimes. This age, known for its executions by brutal methods, had largely passed by the middle of the nineteenth century.

In 1775 the philosophy of Hedonism, also known as the philosophy of eat, drink, and be merry for tomorrow we die, was applied to penalogy by Beccaria. This held that if the subject acted of his own free will and accord, that the pleasure of one act was balanced against the pains of another. Beccaria worked to make punishment less arbitrary and severe, but contended that the pleasure gained from an illegal act is balanced against the pain of punishment, if and when the criminal is apprehended and convicted.

Lombroso and his followers, in 1876, stated that it was necessary to study the criminal rather than the crime in order to deal effectively with crime. However, his principal contention was that criminals constitute a born type and that they can be recognized by physical characteristics. This theory was later modified somewhat, but Lombroso still insisted that some were born criminals and that all other criminals approached that type. A further refinement of this was that criminal types, such as thieves, could be recognized by certain physical characteristics.

All of this has been amply demonstrated to be false. However, some people still believe it today, due in part to observing such things as facial expressions, haircuts, dress, and mannerisms. Undoubtedly, the general appearance of people in police lineups and prisons contributes much to this philosophy. The Lombrosian theory has been debunked for criminal acts in general, and there is no reason to believe that it has any validity in fish and game violations.

In 1905 the so-called "mental testers" advanced the theory that crime was the result of feeble-mindedness. This contention stated in part that a feeble-minded person was not able to appreciate the meaning of the law or to foresee the consequences of his act. The present viewpoint is that the relationship between crime and feeble-mindedness is generally slight. The theory of psychopathy or neo-Lombrosianism is today regarded as no more justified than the Lombrosian theory that criminals constitute a distinct type.

Emotional instability and drug addiction may and do account for scattered crimes, but for very few of the fish and game violations. Alcoholism may be connected with a lawless attitude. Sutherland[37] states:

---

37.   Edwin H. Sutherland. 1947. Principles of criminology. 4th ed. Philadelphia: J. B. Lippincott Co. pp. 114-115.

Moreover, there has been for a long time a distinct relationship between alcohol and respect for law. . .but in both systems respect for law was distinctly decreased by the practices connected with alcohol.

However, in regard to sportsmen it is more likely that the game is in less danger from someone using excessive amounts of alcohol than from a sober person. Where firearms are involved, the primary danger from such a person is to himself and to his immediate companions rather than to game in the area.

The last and most acceptable theory in regard to the cause of crime is the sociological, or group and social processes theory. In this broad area centers the most reliable of the explanations of crime. It is probable that the cause of most fish and game violations can be successfully explained by this theory.

CRIME AS LEARNED BEHAVIOR

According to this theory, criminal behavior is learned from criminals, through association with people who are proficient or versed in various phases of criminal behavior. It is not inherited, nor is it commonly resorted to by one not already trained in crime.

Thus, the principal part of the learning occurs from within an intimate personal group. Sutherland refers to this as the "Differential Association Theory." Close friends and relatives usually influence a particular person much more than do such outside influences as movies, newspapers, and books. Sutherland makes the following statement:[38]

The chance that a person will participate in systematic criminal behavior is determined roughly by the frequency and consistency of his contacts with the patterns of criminal behavior. If a person could come in contact only with lawful behavior he would inevitably be completely law-abiding. If he could come in contact only with criminal behavior (which is impossible, since no group could exist if all of its behavior were criminal), he would inevitably be completely criminal. The actual condition is between these extremes. The ratio of criminal acts to lawful acts by a person is roughly the same as the ratio of the contacts with the criminal and with the lawful behavior of others. It is true, of course, that a single

---

38. Ibid. Edwin H. Sutherland, 1939. Principles of Criminology. 3rd Edition, Philadelphia: J. B. Lippincott Co. page 6. Permission to quote granted by publisher in letter to author dated August 10, 1955.

critical experience may be the turning point in a career. But these critical experiences are generally based on a long series of former experiences and they produce their effects generally because they change the person's associations. One of these critical experiences that is most important in determining criminal careers is the first public appearance as a criminal. A boy who is arrested and convicted is thereby publicly defined as a criminal. Thereafter his associations with lawful people are restricted and he is thrown into the association with other delinquents. On the other hand, a person who is consistently criminal is not defined as law-abiding by a single lawful act. Every person is expected to be law-abiding, and lawful behavior is taken for granted because the lawful culture is dominant, more extensive, and more pervasive than the criminal culture.

FACTORS INFLUENCING VIOLATIONS

The cause of crime suggests the remedy. If criminal behavior is learned behavior, then the educative process involved can be controlled. Effective control should result in a reduction of crime, including wildlife law violations.

It should be emphasized that no amount of education alone will prevent all unlawful acts. The extensive education and public relations program in narcotics and traffic has not decreased the necessity for law enforcement. However, where effective law enforcement exists, the violation rate is substantially lower than in areas where it is lacking. The relative value of an educational program is sometimes a highly debated and perhaps somewhat academic question. The educational program's effectiveness is dependent upon so many factors that results are often hard to predict; however, it is a tool that must be maintained and developed to the utmost.

Some of the factors involved may be called inhibiting factors, for while they do not strike at the roots of the problem, they do tend to lessen the incidents of crime.

Fear of Punishment

Certainly the factor of fear enters into the problem. Some administrators of educational programs firmly believe that potential violators are or can be deterred by fear--fear of fines, of jail sentences, of adverse publicity, or of social stigma. However, sociologists point to the fact that pickpockets in England were caught plying their trade in a crowd which was watching a convicted pickpocket being hanged by his thumbs. They believe that willing cooperation is more healthy and longer lasting than is compliance because of fear.

It has been said, in the case of traffic violations, that 15 per cent are habitual violators, 15 per cent do not violate, and 70 per cent may be influenced by a number of items. If this is true of wildlife law violators, then certainly the 70 per cent should receive a treatment designed primarily to educate rather than punish.

Desire for Gain

Although violations constantly occur because otherwise well-meaning and law-abiding citizens misunderstand or are ignorant of the laws they violate, this is not the case with the individual who decides to take his chances in full knowledge of his wrong-doing. Such a violator is generally motivated by a desire for gain, and unless his fear of punishment is stronger than this desire, a violation occurs. If desire is overcome by fear, then to all intents and purposes the potential violator remains a law-abiding citizen.

Fear is not the answer. Emphasis must be specifically directed toward nullifying the desire of the individual to commit the act. This perhaps over-simplifies the obvious and very urgent necessity for an excellent public education-information program.

Opportunity to Violate the Law

Another factor commonly present in the willful violation of wildlife law is the opportunity to do so. Wild animals are so widespread that the opportunities of committing violations against them are numerous, and at times it is difficult if not impossible for enforcement personnel to eliminate or neutralize these opportunities. Nevertheless, there are times when opportunity can be lessened. For example, if officers can patrol the area or disperse the animals, it is possible to counter the invitation to easy game-law violation offered by migrations of salmon or other spawning fish and by movements of big-game animals through narrow passes.

EDUCATIONAL PROGRAMS

Inhibiting factors by themselves cannot solve the problem. At best they can but constrict the flood until more adequate but long-range measures become operative. Such measures include programs of education wisely conceived and conducted to teach the reason for wildlife laws and to promote a better understanding of the broad meaning of the term "sportsmanship."

These programs of education can be developed each with a different group in mind, because each group will require a slightly different angle of attack. One group includes children and their parents; another, the chronic poachers; and a third, the community at large.

Program for Juveniles

One method of preventing law violations on the part of minors is to work with parents. This includes stressing to adults the unfairness of teaching children illegal techniques and attitudes such as, "It is not too bad to violate a fish and game law." It should be emphasized to parents that it is very important for children to have proper hunting and fishing companions who set a good example for them in the field. Even house guests who may discuss hunting and fishing experiences, sometimes with very imaginative and elaborate examples, should be chosen with care. Every emphasis should be made to show how important it is to display a high type of sportsmanship, which is one requirement of good citizenship.

Parents normally impress their young offspring more than does anyone else. If the sportsmanship of the father and mother is above reproach at all times, only rarely does the child go astray. It has been said that the younger generation wants a faith. It may well be that out-of-doors activities can aid in kindling and building this faith.

Additional emphasis should be given to promoting sportsmanship in cartoons, comic books, movies, television, and conservation magazines in general. Perhaps one of the widest fields involves the comic strips, the comic books, and the radio programs, since these reach a great number of young people each day.

According to Wertham,[39] an increasing number of judges and educators have come to the conclusion that certain of

39.   Frederick Wertham. 1954. Let's look at the comics. Scouting 42.7:2-3, 19-20.

the present-day comic books contribute directly to crime by
teaching youngsters how to commit various crimes. The
average parent has no idea that every conceivable type of
crime is described in detail in some comic books. These
comic books, under the guise of showing how to catch criminals and demonstrating that crime does not pay, are actually teaching children how to steal, rob, lie, cheat, assault,

Photograph by Paul Lake
Courtesy Wyoming Game and Fish Department

Figure 14. A bit young, but interested.

break and enter, and to commit almost every conceivable type of present-day crime. They even go so far as to show how to conceal evidence and how to evade detection once the criminal is approached. If juvenile delinquency can actually be traced to crime-comic books, as many prominent people think it can, then it is high time that conservationists look to this source of miseducation to further understand the causes of wildlife violations.

The defense against bad comic books would appear to be to induce the young readers to turn to good reading. Perhaps this could be accomplished in part by persuading at least some of the writers of comic strips to produce technically correct and morally acceptable types of comic books, which could be used as a positive rather than as a negative force.

It should be emphasized that there are some notable exceptions to this type of comic book, and there are some newspaper comic strips, such as "Mark Trail," which not only emphasize good sportsmanship, but go to great trouble and detail to be technically correct. However, comic strips that appear in the 1,500 odd newspapers across the country are strictly censored, whereas the so-called comic magazines are not censored in any way unless they are by chance sent through the U. S. mail.

Every effort should be made to see that lawlessness is unpopular. Children's contacts with the lawless element should be made as rare as possible, and if inevitable, the duration should be shortened. This may be accomplished in part with youngsters by introducing alternative activities, such as controlled and organized outdoor fishing and hunting trips, shooting clubs, rifle clubs, and such competitive sports as baseball, tennis, and track. Wherever possible, the glamour should be taken out of law violations, and good sportsmanship glorified.

Program for the Individual Poacher

Although it may be discouraging at times, it is necessary to work continuously to rehabilitate the chronic poacher. If only a few are converted, it is well worthwhile; and these may, in turn, convert others--or at least the members of their immediate families.

Such rationalizations as "the game is ours," "we feed them all the time," "there is an over supply," and "everybody else is doing it" should be exposed for what they are-- shoddy attempts at self-justification for greedy and licentious appropriation of the nation's wildlife resource. This should be done as much and as frequently as possible. It can be repeatedly emphasized that legal hunting behavior today may mean that we will have game which we can legally hunt tomorrow. "Banquet behavior" should be something that is practiced in the field as well as in the home.

Photograph by Don Wooldridge
Courtesy Missouri Conservation Commission

Figure 15. An officer's most fruitful hours are spent with youngsters.

Program for the Community

Wildlife violations can rarely be explained on the basis of a simple need. They should be analyzed more deeply, and activities of the potential violator should be diverted into a more socially-approved channel. Communities should be sold on the idea that they can have as much or as little crime as they wish, and this includes wildlife violations. Crime is a function of the entire society, and the amount and character of it is determined primarily by a community's attitude.

Witness, for example, the widespread feeling against killing female deer a few years ago, even though biologists were convinced that it was sound; or the wave of opposition that swept across the United States when it was proposed that the Dinosaur National Monument be used as a dam site. If such sentiments were to be widespread and directed, then game violations, such as taking excess bag limits, killing game out of season, and using illegal equipment should be reduced considerably. If this particular point can be sold to community leaders, much will be accomplished toward preventing violations, particularly by the younger generation. The sportsmen of this country could well organize a movement which would lift the entire moral tone of the nation. Appeals to "pillars of society" and other influential people can do much toward accomplishing this. A play on community pride, spearheaded by influential leaders in the community, can accomplish a great deal; and that being the case, it is almost impossible to over-sell the value of the idea.

SUMMARY

Since even a large and effective wildlife enforcement group can police only a small per cent of present-day sportsmen, it appears that the answer is, in part, more and better cooperation brought about by education. Perhaps concentration will be on the younger generation, but certainly it must touch all ages, classes, colors, and creeds; and every true conservationist, professional and amateur, will work toward this end by both word and example.

CHAPTER VI

The Wildlife Law Enforcement Officer

RESPONSIBILITY AND CALLING

The effective arm of the wildlife law enforcement program is the individual officer, or warden. He is charged with the responsibility of enforcing laws passed to conserve the states' custodial wildlife resources for the people, and he is particularly concerned whenever these resources are threatened by the rapacity of uninformed or designing men.

His calling is an ancient one, and in modern times he has taken his place at the side of other law enforcers who hold paramount their duty to serve the people in the safeguarding of their interests. A brief historical sketch of various policing agencies will throw light on this phase of the program.

HISTORICAL SKETCH OF POLICING AGENCIES

Originally, our ancestors took turns standing guard over communal property. Later, some of the more enterprising individuals hired others to take their turns for them. Still later, these hired guards became full-time night watchmen. This function was later taken over by the police department. It is interesting to note that there are a few places in the United States today where there are night watchmen in addition to regular police.

Police Systems in England

The first laws in England were enforced by military guards. On another level the knights who roamed the country were law enforcement officers of a sort. However, they made as well as enforced their own laws. Later, the lords and barons made laws and hired law enforcement officers or guards to enforce them. These guards were known as Comes Stabuli or Masters of the Stable. The word was later corrupted to constable, which is still in use in America and England today.

In England, the head of the shire (comparable geograph ically to a county in the United States) was responsible for policing the area and maintaining law and order. The head of the shire, known as a reeve, was the chief police officer. The words "shire" and "reeve" were later contracted to "sheriff," or the chief police officer of the shire.

Photograph by Jim Sherman
Courtesy Iowa Conservation Commission

Figure 16. Proud of his service stripes.

In 1828, because he believed that the constable system in the England of his day was inadequate, Sir. Robert Peel banded together the first modern policing group in the English-speaking world. Parliament, under Peel's recommendation, authorized a police department to cope with the rising crime, which it was noted was increasing because of faster, four-horse carriage transportation. This meant, in effect, that a criminal was able to commit a crime in greater London and escape outside the city limits before he was apprehended by the constable, whose jurisdiction ended at the boundary line. English police officers, even down to the present in London, are sometimes referred to as Bobbies or Peelers.

Police Systems in North America

The first police system in North America was patterned after that of the Mother Country. In the 1870's the Royal Canadian Mounted Police came into being. In the West during the 80's the county sheriff, the U. S. marshall, and the vigilantes played roles that are familiar to present-day movie-goers, radio fans, and viewers of T. V.

The state police system was developed in the United States just after 1900. In 1908 the Federal Bureau of Investigation was organized, and as regards jurisdiction there is in the world today no comparable organization. [1]

Game Wardens

The earliest game protector in Maine was known as a "moose warden." As the title implies, his duty was to protect moose. Many early wardens were political appointees and received no pay other than from fines collected.

One of the differences between wildlife law enforcement officers and officers in most other phases of enforcement work is that the wildlife officer encounters people of almost all ages, colors, creeds, and social positions. There is an even wider diversity in wildlife cases than, for example, traffic violations, since the very young, the very old, and the physically handicapped normally do not drive automotive

---

1. New Scotland Yard, the police force of greater London, might be likened to the detective force of New York City proper.

vehicles; yet they frequently hunt or fish. It is essential to the success of the enforcement program that the qualifications of the wildlife officer be on a high plane. His personal and professional qualifications are discussed below.

Personal Qualifications

The man selected for professional training as a wildlife officer should possess or be able to develop the following personal qualifications. The more he meets these, the better is the foundation upon which his professional training is based.

A good officer has a liking for people and an understanding of human behavior. This is perhaps as essential as a knowledge of fish and game. He is able to cooperate with co-workers and with persons in other agencies. He can speak well in public and, if necessary, can conduct a public meeting.

He is intelligent, accurate, patient, and resourceful, and possesses great capacity for detail. His mind is clear and capable of logical and concise reasoning, and he is able to submit prompt, concise reports of his daily activities. His memory for names and faces is well developed.

He has no physical handicaps and keeps himself in excellent condition, because he knows he may be subjected to sudden and severe demands on his strength and energy. For example, in the Rocky Mountain area many officers are required to hike several miles a day with a pack that may weigh up to 60 pounds.

Not infrequently an officer will be in such a position that he must display a considerable amount of courage and poise in order to carry himself well through a particularly hazardous situation. For example, during the last five years a disturbing number of wildlife law enforcement officers have been assaulted, some of them fatally. [2]

The officer is a competent outdoors man. Being able to pitch camp, prepare meals, and take care of himself or others in an emergency is all in a day's work. He knows how to pack, handle, and care for horses and is able to

---

2.   Nelson Benedict and George Laycock. 1954. Murder in the woods. Field and Stream 58. January, p. 88.

Courtesy Washington Department of Game

Figure 17. Officers are trained in first-aid.

ride well over any terrain. In addition, he is a good automobile driver and mechanic enough to make minor adjustments on automobiles, trucks, and other automotive equipment under his jurisdiction. He is also an expert handler of shoulder and side weapons of all types and makes used in hunting and in self-defense.

PROFESSIONAL QUALIFICATIONS

Among his professional qualifications are those dealing with a basic point of view, or guiding philosophy; with education requirements; and with a code of ethics. These are outlined in the following sections.

Point of View

The underlying philosophy of modern law-enforcement procedures stresses compliance with the law, not because of fear of punishment but because of enlightened self-interest growing out of a program of public information. The professionally-trained wildlife officer of today therefore enters the service with a point of view that reflects this basic philosophy. He is not so eager to apprehend as to explain and caution. He would much rather have a patrol district frequented by sportsmen who observe good conservation practices because they understand the issues involved than one wherein conservation is practiced because of the proximity of the badge.

Education

Education and experience requirements vary from state to state. At present a few states require a degree in wildlife conservation from a recognized school. New York, Pennsylvania, Missouri, Michigan, and others require a three to six-months in-service training course. Requirements of other states vary from a high-school education and law enforcement experiences to a high-school education. At present the U. S. Fish and Wildlife Service requires game law-enforcement experience for beginning personnel.

If the officer has not graduated from an accredited wildlife conservation school, it is highly desirable that he study until he has learned to recognize all forms of fish and game and fur-bearers and non-game animals that range in the state or territory in which he is or hopes to be employed

Photograph by Don Wooldridge
Courtesy Missouri Conservation Commission

Figure 18. Training school for officers--an interesting and necessary interlude.

In addition to this, he should have a knowledge of the life history of these animals in order to make a contribution to game management practices and to be able to discuss his problems intelligently with his superiors and with the general public.

Code of Ethics

It is said of the armed forces that certain moral qualities make officers and gentlemen. This is equally true of conservation officers. A lack of this is indicated by dishonesty, unfair dealings, indecency, indecorum, lawlessness, injustice, or cruelty. Although it is recognized that everyone cannot be expected to perform perfectly at all times, there is a limit of tolerance below which the standards of an officer cannot fall without compromising the individual and the profession. Some of the things which an officer must observe at all times are: (1) avoid knowingly making any false official statements; (2) avoid dishonorable failure to pay debts; (3) avoid using insulting or defamatory language to or about another officer in his presence, or about his family or other people in or out of the service; (4) avoid being grossly drunk or conspicuously disorderly in public; (5) avoid public association with notorious people such as gangsters or prostitutes, unless in the line of duty; (6) avoid committing or attempting to commit a crime involving moral turpitude; (7) avoid failure without good cause to support his family; (8) avoid failure to carry out his duties as administered under the oath and as required by law; (9) avoid opening and reading the correspondence of another without authority; (10) being sufficiently familiar with the practice and procedure of criminal law so as to avoid exceeding his authority (if an officer acts outside scope of this authority, it reflects adversely upon both the department and himself); (11) avoid putting his hands on, or intimidating, any person except when he is arresting him or when he has, previous to the time of putting his hand on the person, made it very clear that he is giving assistance (an officer may be attacked for touching another person on the claim that this person thought he was being assaulted, or the officer may, under certain circumstances, be called into court for assault if the suspect was not under arrest); (12) accept no gifts or favors from anyone under his jurisdiction; (13) strive for greater professional attainment by study; (14) always accept and delegate orders in the proper

Photograph by Frank Elder
Courtesy Wildlife Management Department
Utah State Agricultural College

Figure 19. Collecting life history information on non-game fish.

chain of command, unless a compromise of personal morals is involved.

It should always be borne in mind that a good officer has many friends but few close associates.

Photograph by Frank Elder
Courtesy Wildlife Management Department
Utah State Agricultural College

Figure 20.   Trash fish today--trout tomorrow. Fish are killed with rotenone.

EMPLOYMENT

The bulk of all enforcement officers is employed by the states or by the Federal Government, with comparatively few working with private organizations. The number of enforcement personnel of the various states varies from as few as 15 in one western state to several hundred in an eastern state. The U. S. Fish and Wildlife Service employs game management agents who have other duties in addition to law enforcement (this is also true of most states). As the present trend sees increasing numbers of sportsmen afield, many more openings will exist in this area.

PROFESSIONAL DUTIES

The duties of a wildlife law enforcement officer are rigorous and exacting. At any moment, day or night, he may be called upon to do anything from chasing a stray deer out of an orchard to helping capture a dangerous criminal. Eight-hour days and weekends off are something the officer hopes for but rarely is able to take advantage of.

His duties fall into three main categories and deal with (1) management, (2) educational programs, and (3) law enforcement. The amount of time spent in each of these three major areas varies with the time of year, the locality being worked, and departmental policy.

Wildlife Management

The first phase of a law enforcement officer's work is concerned with wildlife management. This involves, among other things, the making of game counts; the settlement of damage claims, including an evaluation of the amount of damage done; the taking of control measures in the case of predators or other animals doing damage to crops; the supervision of hunts; the operation of checking stations; and the taking of bag and creel census.

Educational Programs

The second phase deals with education. Much of the work involves conducting public meetings to explain law and policy, particularly when a new law or policy has recently been put into effect. Education is frequently more effective and also more time-consuming when conducted on an individual basis. It is often necessary to repeat statements

Photograph by Frank Elder
Courtesy Wildlife Management Department
Utah State Agricultural College

Figure 21. Spreading fish poison is part of a day's work.

which appear to be fairly obvious to the officer. Education may, and many times does, deal with the various youth groups such as the 4-H, Boy Scouts, etc. Even though the state or federal agency may have one or more public relations men, the law enforcement officer is the local representative of the department and is looked to as such by a great many of the residents. It is his conduct and general behavior which determines how the department shall be judged.

Another phase of the educational program is developing and maintaining a cooperative organization with other groups and agencies which have a similar interest.

Law Enforcement

This third phase of an officer's duties may be divided into general considerations and those of a more specific nature. General considerations include knowledge of state wildlife laws and court rulings, use of the uniform, use of side-arms, and use of the official automobile.

Specific considerations include making the arrest, identifying, collecting, and preserving evidence; and appearing in court. The general considerations will be discussed here briefly; the others will be the subject of subsequent chapters.

KNOWLEDGE OF STATE WILDLIFE LAWS AND COURT RULINGS

The subject of law in its several aspects as applied to wildlife management is studied intensively by the enforcement officer as part of his professional training. In spite of this, there is constant need for him to continue to study new and old fish and game laws and court rulings. This is for the reason that such laws are continually being revised in the light of local conditions. It is important that the officer know where to look for such information and how to obtain it.

Code Books

Information on state fish and game laws may be obtained either from the code book, which is generally issued every two to four years, or from proclamations, which have the effect of law when published and which supercede code

Courtesy Federal Bureau of Investigation

Figure 22. The FBI rifle range at the United States Marine Corps base at Quantico, Virginia. Twenty-four Special Agents are firing in a kneeling position at 200 yards.

material. It has been aptly said that the best fish and game laws are those which say the least. Perhaps this is a national tendency, since many of the recent code books are considerably smaller than some earlier ones. This small size provides an unexpected benefit for a layman seeking information, since a few minutes of casual thumbing through a code book can give an idea of its general contents. However, the best way to find information on a specific subject is to work from the index. For example, in the 1954-1955 code book of the Utah Fish and Game Department, information on trapping muskrat may be obtained by turning to the index and noting the page and section of the code where information on muskrat begins. It is also necessary to study the current proclamation on trapping fur-bearing animals for dates of open season and for the place and manner in which muskrat may be taken.

A search for information on hunting bear is considerably more complicated in the Utah code book. Nothing is listed about bear in the index, and it is therefore necessary to turn to the definition of game animals. This section defines both big-game and other game, but at no place is there any mention of bear. This means, in effect, that there is a continuous open season on bear and no limit on either numbers or manner of taking.

The only factor that remains to be determined is whether or not a license is necessary in order to hunt bear. Under the section on licenses it is stated that a license is necessary in order to hunt game animals. Because the bear is not a game animal, it is not necessary to have a license to take or attempt to take bear (as of April 1, 1955).

The situation is somewhat different for anyone wanting to fish. The section under the license code specifies, by implication, that it is necessary to have a license in order to angle for fish. However, under the section defining fish it states that fish means all species of fish. Therefore, it is necessary to have a license to fish for non-game as well as for game fish.

Indexes

Before committing himself to a course of action involving law enforcement, the officer may find it necessary, or at least desirable, to be able to check on certain court rulings. Most county court houses have reasonably complete law libraries that can provide both interesting and profitable reading. These instructions, which discuss Utah and other Pacific states but apply elsewhere, should make the initial effort considerably easier.

The indexes to the older Pacific Reporter (volumes 1-300 of series 1), consist of 40 volumes entitled Utah and Pacific Digest. In volumes 1-39 appear criminal and civil proceedings and type cases, all arranged alphabetically. In volume 40 is a table of cases digested. To use this index, first select the volume which contains cases of the proper alphabetical type; for example, an officer who desires information concerning rulings on cases involving fishing violations would select volume 17, which contains cases dealing with Exchange of Property through Fixtures (Pro-Fix). He would then turn to the section desired, where he would find listed all fish cases for the entire 1st series of the Pacific Reporter, 1-300. A short summary of each case is given, along with the title of the case, volume, book, name, and page. For example, Doe v. State 129 P 320 is an abbreviation for Doe versus State, volume 129 of the Pacific Reporter, 1st series, page 320.

The indexes to the more recent Pacific Reporter (volumes 1-100 of the second series) consist of 15 volumes, with the proceedings and type cases arranged alphabetically as in the first series. These volumes are entitled Pacific Digest, 1-100 P 2nd, with the volume number and contents following. The procedure for finding cases in these volumes is the same as for the earlier ones.

There are separate books for volumes 101-220 of the 2nd series. Each index volume lists all cases in 10 Pacific Reporter volumes, and each index volume runs from A through Z for types of cases. The procedure here is to select an index volume with the type case desired for one of the 10 Pacific Reporter volumes.

Indexes for volumes above 220 are annual books. These are entitled Pacific Digest, 1951 Annual 221-233 P 2nd, etc., through 1954. The procedure for locating information in these index volumes is similar to that for the preceding set.

The index for the American Law Report, 1st series, 1-175, is entitled Permanent A. L. R. Digest, 1-175, and consists of 12 volumes. This index is set up in the same way as for the 40 volumes covering the 1st series of the Pacific Reporter, and the procedure here is similar to that of the Utah Pacific Digest.

The 2nd series of the A. L. R. consists of 35 volumes to date (July 1955), and the index for volumes 1-25 is a book

Courtesy Washington Department of Game.

Figure 23. Officers in full uniform.

entitled A. L. R. 2nd Series Digest which contains all type
actions from A-Z. The procedure here is the same as for
the annual indexes of the Pacific Digest.

THE UNIFORM

Wildlife officers should wear, in the best military
fashion, distinctive, good-quality uniforms, every item of
which should be prescribed in detail. A uniformed officer
commands quicker attention and more respect than one with
out a uniform. A uniform also aids in building up and maintaining professional prestige and morale. Both dress and
field uniforms should be kept neat and clean. If a side-arm
is worn, it should be displayed.

SIDE-ARMS

Officers in many state fish and game departments, and
some agents of the U. S. Fish and Wildlife Service game
management branch carry side-arms, ostensibly to protect
their lives while they are engaged in the discharge of their
official duties. Actually, the major value of carrying side-
arms is the psychological effect this practice has on the vio
lator. However, there are certain areas where the officer
may unmask an escaped felon while making a routine license
check. In such a case, violence may follow.

It should be remembered that the average American has
an inherent respect for a uniformed law-enforcement official, and a displayed side-arm is a part of the uniform. If
an officer carries a pistol, he must never use it in a misdemeanor charge to force a suspect to stop, even though the
fact that he does not use it may mean that the subject will
escape. In the case of a misdemeanor, firearms should not
be drawn or discharged for the purpose of frightening a
prisoner or a suspect. Such action may lay the officer open
to serious charges for which he may be severely criticized
or prosecuted. Only where it is necessary to use a firearm
to protect life or limb may one be used.

The urgent need of gun safety and the limits of liability
of a bonding company are emphasized in the case of an
Arizona game warden.[3] The case follows:

---

3.   Truog v. American Bonding Company of Baltimore, Pacific Reporter,
      Vol. 107, 2nd series, 203, Arizona.

Photograph by Margaret Fisler
Courtesy North Carolina Wildlife Resources Commission

Figure 24. Proficient use of side-arms is a must for officers.

While in the field, Deputy Game Warden Donnell shot at some animals and the bullet wounded Plaintiff Truog in the wrist. Truog sued the deputy warden, the state game warden, and the bonding company, the American Bonding Company of Baltimore, for damages. The Superior Court sustained the defendant's (bonding company) demurrer to the complaint and gave a judgment of dismissal to the defendant. The appeal is on the demurrer and judgment.

The plaintiff contended that the deputy warden was acting within his scope of duties by being out protecting the game and enforcing the laws by which the game was being hunted; thus the bonding company was liable for acts committed in this capacity. The court ruled that the warden could not have been protecting the game by shooting at it and this act in itself places the warden beyond the scope of his duties. An officer's bond does not protect him in his personal and private affairs, which shooting of game would come under. As to the officer's shooting being committed in discharge of his duty, the facts are not stated and are unknown. The Superior Court judgment was affirmed.

Side-arms may be worn in sight or concealed, depending on the state ruling and on the nature of the case that the officer is working on. As a general rule, when officers are in uniform and have side-arms on their person, it is more desirable that these be worn in sight. Plain-clothesmen, or undercover investigators, should not wear a gun in sight. It is quite obvious that a side-arm should be in excellent condition. The officer should practice enough to maintain high proficiency in drawing and using the weapon.

THE OFFICIAL AUTOMOBILE

It is believed that the main officer force of a conservation department should carry on most patrol duties in well-marked passenger cars. This means that an officer's presence in an area is easily ascertained. This removes much of the element of surprise which some officers believe to be highly important. On the other hand, a well-marked passenger car commands more respect than any other type of law enforcement vehicle, and many of the occasional violators and some of the habitual ones may be benefited. However, since this procedure aids the lawless element, who often makes it a practice to be well informed as to the officer's whereabouts, his routine, and the make of car that he drives, punitive rather than preventative measures become necessary.

In order to deal effectively with this group, an under-cover squad of plain-clothesmen should travel in unmarked and unlisted cars. Normally, these officers should be unknown to the local populace. The personnel of this squad might either be permanent or drawn as needed from among the uniformed officers. It is recognized, of course, that the practice of having both uniformed and non-uniformed officers will often increase the required total personnel.

RESERVE WARDENS

A word should be said here concerning the reserve wardens. Several states have a system of reserve wardens who operate with the regular wardens, generally without pay. The reserve warden systems of California and New Mexico will be discussed.

The California System

California reserve wardens are trained for 12-week periods, with one two-hour night session a week. Prior to the course, the program is advertised in local papers, and all applicants are screened by wardens and supervisory personnel. There is a general trend toward giving coverage primarily to common laws and practical wildlife problems. At the end of the course a comprehensive examination is given, and applicants who successfully complete the course are either organized into a patrol unit or are placed on the waiting list to fill future vacancies in an existing unit, all of this depending on local conditions and needs.

Patrol units are normally organized by county, with the bulk of the members residing in the largest city. Units consist of 25 members and have a uniform set of constitutions and by-laws. Officers of these patrol units are appointed by department law enforcement heads. Meetings are held monthly and generally cover work plans and wildlife problems. An outside speaker is often scheduled.

Reserve wardens are required to work at least eight hours a month. However, this rule may not be strictly enforced during the slack season. Work is by direction and practically always under direct supervision of a regular warden. Typical assignments entail assisting the regular warden with routine patrol, helping operate checking stations, manning exhibitions at county fairs, and conducting hunter-safety training classes.

Reserve wardens furnish their own uniform and side-arms and pay all of their own expenses. Uniforms are almost identical with those worn by regular wardens, the only difference being the small "R" on the badge. The local sportsmen's club generally purchases the badges and sometimes also underwrites the cost of insurance against charges of false arrest.

Citations may be issued by reservists when a regular warden is not immediately available. These are issued as a courtesy and not as an arrest. Violators are directed to appear in court when and where notified. However, all violations information is turned over to the regular warden, who handles the case in court. This method also allows the regular wardens to screen cases and avoid filing what is not considered to be a "good case."

Discipline of reserves is strict. Members may be dismissed for improper use of the badge, improper use of authority, failure to work, abusive conduct, or for any other good reason. One regular warden is usually delegated to the active supervision of the reserve patrol unit. However, work assignments may be made with any or all of the wardens in the territory.

Reserve wardens apparently join for one or more of several reasons. One of these is the fact that participation in reserve activities for a period of two years qualifies one for admittance to the civil service examination for regular warden. Another reason is a genuine desire to promote better conservation practices. Some are probably interested in gaining social prestige in sportsmen's affairs, and some prominent citizens use the reserve wardenship to fulfill their local civic obligations.

The New Mexico System

Here the reserves are organized into patrol units of not more than 25 men. They qualify by taking a six-weeks practical course given one night a week. In New Mexico the reservists wear no uniform, but they do wear shoulder patches and badges which are different from those of the regular employees. They work both on the direction of the regular warden and on that of their own elected captain. Violations are usually prosecuted by the regular warden. However, at times reservists do take their own cases into court. Although the organization and handling of the reserve warden system in New Mexico is perhaps somewhat more informal than in California, it seems to work quite well, possibly because of the fewer number of sportsmen in New Mexico.

CHAPTER VII

Tactics of the Arrest

One of the specific responsibilities of the wildlife officer is to prevent the violation of wildlife law; but when a violation does occur, he must be prepared to arrest the violator and take him into custody. This chapter will present those tactics of arrest which the wildlife officer should use.

DEFINITION OF ARREST

Arrest is defined as the taking of a person into custody by legal authority. This may be accomplished either by arrest on sight or on proper warrant. A person is actually under arrest when he has been physically restrained or is under complete control.

> It is not necessary. . .that there be an application of actual force or manual touching of the body, or physical restraint which may be visible to the eye. . . .[1]

The law in most states specifies that after an officer has advised a subject that he is authorized to arrest him and of his intention of doing so, then he may use a reasonable force to take him into custody. It should be noted, however, that in the case of a misdemeanor it is not permissible to use such weapons as side-arms, clubs, and blackjacks except in self-defense.

TYPES OF ARREST

The types of arrest discussed in the following sections are the non-warrant or sight arrest, the warrant arrest, the misdemeanor on complaint, and the citizen's arrest. The citation plan will be treated separately.

Non-Warrant Arrest

A wildlife officer may, without a warrant, arrest a person under the following circumstances: (1) when a

---

1. American Jurisprudence, Vol. 4. p. 5.

Photograph by Jim Sherman
Courtesy Iowa Conservation Commission

Figure 25. The walkie-talkie may help keep a violator under surveillance.

wildlife (or other) law offense has been committed or attempted in his presence; (2) when the person arrested has violated a wildlife law, although not in his presence; (3) when a wildlife offense has in fact been committed and the officer has reasonable cause for believing the person being arrested committed it; (4) when a charge is made upon reasonable cause, in the case of a felony, by the arresting officer; (5) at any time during the day or night when the officer has reasonable cause to believe that the suspect has committed a felony. A night arrest for a misdemeanor under similar circumstances is not permissible.

Warrant Arrest

A wildlife officer may make an arrest in obedience to a warrant delivered to him. A warrant of arrest may be described as a legal instrument, properly executed by competent authority, generally a magistrate, which commands the arrest and apprehension of the person listed therein. Any warrant may be addressed either to a particular police officer or to any police officer and may be legally served by any police officer to whom it is handed for service.

In the use of a warrant it is particularly important that the officer exhibit it to the arrestee in order that the latter may not have legal grounds for assaulting the officer. In no instance, however, should the officer permit the warrant to leave his hands.

After making an arrest under a warrant, it is necessary that the subject be taken immediately to the court, preferably to the magistrate who issued the order; however, this is not absolutely necessary. After the arrest has been completed, the law requires that the warrant be returned to the issuing official and shall bear on the reverse side of the warrant an endorsement setting forth the date, time, place of apprehension, and signature of the arresting officer.

It is true that relatively few warrants are used by fish and game law enforcement officers. Nevertheless, the warrant is a useful instrument and should be used when necessary.

Misdemeanor on Complaint

In the case of a misdemeanor which has been committed sometime in the past, the wildlife officer may go to the justice of the peace or to the city judge and request that a complaint be issued. A complaint of this kind may generally be issued any time within a year of the time of the violation. The county attorney usually prepares the complaint, and the magistrate issues to the officer a warrant or summons which declares that the defendant must come or be brought into court on a certain day (or forthwith, in case of a warrant) and answer the charges against him. This type of arrest cannot be made at night in the case of a misdemeanor except at the discrimination of the magistrate who so endorses the complaint.

Citizen's Arrest

A private citizen may arrest another for a public offense committed or attempted in his presence; when the person arrested has committed a felony, although not in his presence; or when a felony has been in fact committed and he has reasonable cause for believing this person is the one responsible. This is known as a citizen's arrest.

In the event a citizen is making an arrest, he may call upon a third party to assist him. Since it is necessary for the arresting party to bring the arrestee under control before he is actually under arrest, it is quite obvious that the arresting citizen should consider the circumstances before attempting the act. It is somewhat foolish, for example, for a single individual to attempt to take several people into custody who obviously have no intention of submitting voluntarily to arrest.

THE CITATION

Although a person may be arrested either with or without a warrant, many fish and game violations are handled on the citation plan. As commonly employed by fish and game officers, a citation is merely a notice issued by an officer directly or by mail to appear in court at a certain time; it is signed by the officer and acknowledged by the defendant. The accused is not under arrest and is therefore not handled as an arrestee.

If a person believed to be a violator is cited rather than arrested, then the officer may go about his other business instead of dropping all work and immediately taking the subject before a magistrate. This method also avoids the possibility, however remote, of the officer's being accused of false arrest.

The citation does not have legal standing, in that failure to appear in court does not carry a penalty with it; in some states, however, failure to appear, unless good cause exists, may bias the court against the subject.

Many fish and game violators are happy to sign citations stating their willingness to appear at a future date, because this is considerably more convenient and avoids the chance of a night in jail or a quick change in plans. Many criminals taken on fish and game violations are particularly anxious to use the citation method rather than be placed under arrest, because in this way they are not searched, their fingerprints are not taken, and their past record is not brought to attention.

In addition to obtaining an agreement to appear at a certain date, an officer who properly handles the situation may gain a statement of admission of guilt which can be used in the event the subject later changes his mind and decides to plead not guilty.

It is permissible to seize guns, fishing tackle, and other equipment used in the commission of the offense, even though the subject is not under arrest. This adds considerable inducement to the arrestee to appear in court at the proper time. When equipment is seized, it is at times possible to return it immediately and take a receipt for it, if this latter procedure is considered desirable. In many instances this receipt, describing the equipment in detail along with the circumstances of seizure, has received the same weight in federal court that the equipment itself would have received.

ARREST PROCEDURE

When making an arrest the wildlife officer should observe certain established procedures. Not only will he be enabled to complete the arrest, but he will avoid much of the risk of physical injury or the chance of a successful defense by the defendant that he was unaware of the officer's identity.

Officer Identification

It is often stated that when an officer approaches a suspect, it is necessary that the officer first identify himself, state his intention of arresting the subject, if such is the case, and specify the cause of arrest. Although there are admitted exceptions, this is the general procedure. This is important, first for the officer's protection, and second, in the event the officer is injured or killed in making the arrest.

The identification should be made in such a way that the suspect and bystanders, if there are any, will have no doubt as to the officer's official status. Unless it can later be shown that the officer quickly and properly identified himself, a successful defense may be built up around the subject's claim that he thought he was being held up.

Of course, when the subject is either in the act of committing an offense or is discovered making an escape, it is obviously not necessary to notify the accused of the intent to arrest, because it is self-evident. In cases where a badge is plainly visible or where the officer is in uniform, then the badge or uniform is evidence of official status.

Confident Approach

The question of when an arrest shall be made is one that has always plagued law enforcement officers and probably will do so for some time to come. But after the officer has reached the decision to make an arrest, he should proceed with confidence. In fact, when it is evident that the officer has a legal right to make an arrest, and it is obviously his duty to do so, then nothing should prevent him from going ahead. It is equally obvious that under no circumstances should he resort to brutality, profanity, abuse, or threats.

In the case of hardened criminals, the officer should never allow himself to be placed at a physical disadvantage; and unless the officer knows otherwise, the only safe procedure is to assume the subject being arrested is dangerous.

Character of Suspect

Good judgment in making an arrest is very important. When the character of the person being approached is known, it should be considered and should determine the officer's conduct. A person known to the officer personally or known by reputation to be a good citizen should not be treated in the same way as someone who has a criminal background. However, when there is a question in regard to the subject's character, it must be assumed that he may possibly be desperate and should consequently be approached accordingly. Some people never hesitate to impose on an indulgent officer who shows the slightest disposition to be lenient. It is possible for an officer to be firm, carry out his duties to the letter, and at the same time be courteous and considerate.

Resistance to Arrest

It should be emphasized that to bring about an arrest or to prevent the escape of an arrestee when only a misdemeanor is involved, neither an officer nor a private individual has the right to kill or seriously injure a person. Although it is legitimate to use whatever force necessary to bring about detention and arrest, this must fall short of serious injury. If it does happen that an officer kills a person in the process of arresting him for a misdemeanor, the officer very probably will be charged with manslaughter, unless he can prove self-defense or accidental death.

When strong physical resistance is encountered during the course of an arrest and the prisoner has been forceably subdued, the officer should immediately file a complaint charging the accused with interfering with an officer in the performance of his duty. In this way the officer protects himself from future charges by the subject. If the officer has suffered any physical injury, even to the extent of bruises, he should have a competent and unbiased physician make a complete physical examination and issue a certificate as to what was found.

Right to Resist

The right of a person to resist unlawful attempts to arrest should be recognized by the officer. It is entirely possible that the subject may claim, and rightly so, that he was under the impression the attempted arrest was unlawful; therefore, his resistance to arrest does not violate a law. It may be that a subject can claim and prove to the court that no crime had been committed and that he was actually resisting an unlawful attempt at arrest, in which case the arresting officer will find himself on the defensive rather than on the offensive. Moreover, a third person may aid a suspect defending himself against illegal arrest. An officer, of course, may at any time call in a third person, or fourth or fifth for that matter, to assist him in making a lawful arrest.

In addition to other factors which must be recognized when considering an arrest, there are the rights of the individual under the Consitution of the United States and of the state in which he resides. In making an arrest, it must be kept in mind that in the United States there is strong regard for the rights of the individual, his personal freedom, and his right to safeguard his home.

THE SEARCH WARRANT

A search warrant is defined as an order in writing, in the name of the state and signed by the court, that orders an officer to search certain named buildings and/or premises for a particular piece of personal property and to bring it before the court. A search warrant for a daylight search may not be used at night. Search warrants cannot be issued on "probable cause" only. They are issued only on the basis of a sworn deposition giving "reasonable cause to believe." A search warrant also has to be returned with endorsement and show or list materials obtained under it.

The Constitution protects a citizen, in general, against search and seizure of person and property within his residence, and this right has been jealously guarded by the courts. Usually an officer, when seeking a search warrant, is acting on the strength of hearsay evidence which is not admissible in court. Also, the informant may not wish to appear in the case. The officer must examine all evidence and be satisfied that it is adequate before he asks for a search warrant.

It is desirable that an officer take at least one additional officer with him, not only to guard exits but to act as a witness in the event the occupant of the building later accuses the officer of committing some criminal act. In the event contraband is believed to be concealed in the bed occupied by a presumably ailing female, the officer has no recourse but to send for a physician and a matron to make the search.

During the search care should be taken not to damage anything and to replace all material as it was found. If the occupant is agreeable, it may be more desirable to ask that equipment be handled by him; and the officer, in case there is no chance of being taken advantage of, may simply look on. When an officer takes property under a warrant, he must give a receipt for it, stating in detail what was removed. In the event that no one is present when the search is being made, the receipt should be placed from where the material was removed.

SEARCH OF AUTOMOTIVE VEHICLES

The question is frequently asked whether or not an officer can search automobiles or other means of conveyance without a warrant. Many states have taken the stand that it is permissible to search automobiles, occupants, and any equipment used by the occupants or contained in the vehicle without a warrant if there is "reason to believe," or as it is sometimes stated, "upon probable cause," that a violation has been committed or that the automobile contains evidence of same.

It is quite obvious that this must be more than mere suspicion on the part of the wildlife officer. It must be based upon well-founded evidence that the vehicle to be searched has been used in connection with a violation of wildlife law, and the mere fact that a hunter's automobile is moving out of a hunting area is not sufficient reason to believe that there has been a violation. The probable cause for such belief should be more concrete. In the event that officers are overzealous in stopping cars and carrying on intensive searches, it is entirely possible that they may be called into court on the charge of interfering with individual rights.

Some states require that an officer stopping automobiles, boats, or other means of conveyance be in uniform. However, whether or not the officer is in uniform, it is obvious that a badge or other insignia of identification should be prominently displayed; otherwise, the officer takes the chance of being misidentified as someone who is not authorized to stop motor vehicles, and he may therefore be subject to injury.

It is generally considered undesirable and, by some, unlawful to set up extensive road blocks on main highways and stop every automobile in the hope of picking up a few game violators. In instances where long strings of traffic are held up for some time while a search is being conducted, the damage to public relations may outweigh the benefits derived from the road block. It is more desirable to hold road blocks in the vicinity of hunts or as spot-checks on side roads.

While reasonable precautions should be taken to keep potential violators from dumping illegal game before they reach a road block, it is obviously quite difficult to do this in all cases. After a checking station has been established for several days, few or no experienced law violators will attempt to bring illegal game through the station; however, this is not necessarily true of the unintentional violator. Therefore, from the standpoint of enforcement, less benefit is derived from this extended set-up than from a short one.

THE AIRPLANE IN ENFORCEMENT

The airplane is becoming an increasingly important tool in wildlife law enforcement. The use of air-ground coverage greatly increases the efficiency of certain law enforcement operations. The ability of the plane to cover a vast area in a short space of time, maintain contact with a ground team, and direct the officers to trouble areas via the most expedient route makes this piece of equipment quite valuable.

The Iowa Conservation Commission lists plane uses under six major headings: law enforcement, transportation (executive flying), officer familiarization with his area, aid to other enforcement agencies, collecting management data, and such public service as rescue operations and controlling fires.[2] The law enforcement activities start with an autumn spot-check on illegal pheasant hunting. This is made at various points in the state's pheasant range, flying at an altitude of 2,000 to 3,000 feet. Suspicious or slow-moving

---

2. Aircraft report, of August 18, 1954, by pilot Frank Heidelbauer to Ray W. Beckman. Permission to use by James Harlan, Assistant Director, Iowa Conservation Commission.

Photograph by Jim Sherman
Courtesy Iowa Conservation Commission

Figure 26. Planning a raid.

cars are watched to see if subsequent actions would warrant directing a ground officer to the vehicle. During the legal hunting season, aerial patrols are utilized in checking early and late-hour shooters and other infractions.

During January and February the plane patrols for such illegal activity as spearing fish through the ice and trapping. Because of limited accessibility offered by roads, lanes, and trails, often through private property, the ground officer is not able to do in a matter of several weeks what the plane can accomplish in a few hours. Early spring patrol activities are primarily concerned with protecting migrating waterfowl, particularly the blue and snow geese concentrated in the Missouri River bottoms.

The value of a plane in preventing violations in an area is quite obvious, particularly since there is a great number of aircraft constantly traveling throughout areas where hunting and fishing occur. A specialized aircraft able to land and take off in very small space and even in wet places enables the officer to make arrests directly from the plane.

The Iowa Conservation Commission plans on inaugurating the use of car-top identification insignia in the aerial law enforcement work. This is done by placing a fluorescent, fire-red, fabric disc, three feet in diameter, on a square of heavy, green canvas. This insignia is attached to the top of the car by rubber shock cords.

AVOIDING ILLEGAL ARREST

While the officer is technically always subject to suit for illegal arrest, fish and game departments make every effort to protect him from malicious or false charges. This does not relieve personal responsibility, but it does afford aid and comfort. False-arrest insurance is available from Lloyd's of London.

In California the Warden's Association buys group insurance for the regular wardens; the sportsmen, or in some cases the reserve units themselves, do the same for the reserve wardens. The following case in California is cited as an example of possible consequences growing out of the arrest and prosecution of a suspect:[3]

---

3. White v. Towers, <u>Pacific Reporter</u>, Vol. 235, 2nd series, 209, California.

The plaintiff was a man who had been tried and acquitted on two counts of polluting waters, and had then entered civil action against the fish and game investigator who had arrested him. The charge was malicious prosecution. Judgment against the plaintiff was given in Superior Court on grounds that peace officers are immune from civil action for malicious prosecution. The plaintiff appealed.

The Supreme Court of California sustained the judgment by a 4 to 3 majority ruling that civil action for malicious prosecution would burden the peace officer with unfair restrictions to his job. It was stated that criminal prosecution for malicious prosecution or ouster from their job would deter the officers from most malicious prosecution. This immunity only applies while officers are within the scope of their authorized duties.

The plaintiff also contended the second action should not have been filed in Federal Court; however, the Supreme Court pointed out that the waters where the offense was alleged to have taken place were under both state and federal jurisdiction.

Three judges disagreed with the ruling on the grounds that only duly authorized deputies should be immune and not all personnel such as inspectors, clerks, etc. They also believed that this immunity would lead toward "statism."

Another case points to the fact that responsibility for avoiding improper arrest must be shared by the citizen:[4]

Officer Sanders attempted to question one W. P. Gisske at night on a city street near where two felonious crimes recently had occurred. The defendant refused to answer the officer's questions and was escorted by him to the police station. On the way, Officer Sanders searched Gisske for possible concealed weapons.

At the station the defendant was turned over to the sergeant in charge who booked him and had him placed in jail until the following morning. Gisske filed suit against Officer Sanders for false imprisonment. The findings and judgment were for the plaintiff. Sanders appealed.

The Appellate Court ruled that an officer surely has a right to question, in a pleasant manner, persons on the street if circumstances warrant the questioning. Under the circumstances above, the officer was justified in accompanying the defendant to the station and searching him for concealed weapons. It is the duty of the desk sergeant to determine if the person should be detailed or released. When the sergeant accepts the responsibility for the person, the officer is no longer obligated. Thus, he was not responsible for the imprisonment, false or not.

---

4. Gisske v. Sanders, Pacific Reporter, Vol. 98, p. 43, California; Court of Appeals, Second District, 1908.

If an officer were liable for improper arrest, when acting upon reasonable grounds when making an arrest, even if improper, it would be idle to maintain a police force in large cities. It is the duty of all good citizens, when called upon, to give all information available in his power to the proper police officers, even of a personal nature, when the circumstances warrant the asking of questions of this nature. The court found that the officer had acted lawfully within his given authority and reversed the judgment. [5]

ENTRAPMENT

One practice that wildlife officers must avoid being guilty of is that of entrapment. This is defined as "the planning of an offense by an officer and the procurement by improper inducement of the commission of the offense by one who would not have perpetrated it, except for the trickery or fraud on the part of the officer." [6] It is contrary to law and public policy for an officer to inspire, incite, persuade, or lure any person into the commission on a crime with the intent of prosecuting or punishing the act. This is not only contrary to law, but it constitutes a defense for the accused.

Regardless of whether or not a person actually did commit a crime, if the court finds that he was "entrapped," he will be acquitted. But in order for a defendant to avail himself of the defense of entrapment, it must be made to appear that the officer instigated the commission of the crime, and had it not been for such instigation, the defendant would not have committed the act at all. There is a very fine line to be drawn between setting a trap to "catch a man in the act," and entrapping him into committing the act. The first is legal and the second, illegal.

Cases involving entrapment usually arise when a "decoy" is used by enforcement officers. It is not the use of the decoy which provides the defense; but if the decoy is an enforcement officer who knows that a certain person is an habitual law violator and suggests and urges the commission of an offense which the person would not otherwise have committed, entrapment is then said to have taken place, and the person will be held not guilty. On the other

---

5. Miller v. Fano, Pacific Reporter, Vol. 66, 183.
6. Lee v. State, Pacific Reporter, Vol. 92, 2nd series, p. 621, Oklahoma.

hand, if the person plans the commission of an offense, and the decoy merely goes along on the expedition, there is no entrapment because the offense was thought out and undertaken by the defendant independently of the officer. This is actually what happened in "the famous Molly McGuires" cases in the Pennsylvania labor war in the coal regions, and which made the Pinkerton Detective Agency world famous for its peace-time activities.

SUMMARY

If the foregoing basic considerations are carefully followed by the wildlife enforcement officer when making an arrest, some of the dangers inherent in arrest situations will be minimized. Also, the careful officer will avoid any action that might serve to open a legal loophole through which the wildlife law violator can escape the just punishment for his offense.

CHAPTER VIII

Arresting the Dangerous Criminal

Conservation officers are rarely dealing with hardened criminals, but they are constantly coming in contact with people who are heavily armed and who are proficient in the use of these firearms. It sometimes happens that in a spirit of extreme belligerency or under the influence of alcohol one of these people turns his weapon on a hunter or on the wildlife officer himself, or the officer may find himself faced with the necessity of handling a known felon. It is in such extreme cases that the officer finds himself compelled to handle effectively a dangerous antagonist.

Since every officer should know how to deal with such cases should the occasion arise, much of the discussion that follows lists techniques used by law enforcement officers dealing with supposedly dangerous criminals. Although it is not possible to eliminate dangers inherent in these situations, many of them can be minimized by thoughtful consideration of the basic principles involved and by planning possible courses of action to cover hypothetical situations. In all cases circumstances and good judgment must dictate the course of action that is actually followed at the critical moment.

BASIC PRINCIPLES OF ARREST

The basic principles applicable to arrest vary but little from those of a successful military operation. They may be referred to as the four S's, namely: superiority, simplicity, speed, and surprise. Superiority of man power has scared even hardened criminals who have previously threatened not to be taken alive. The value of superiority in such equipment as weapons, radios, lights, field glasses, and automotive equipment is obvious. Simplicity of plan makes for an easy and unconfused completion of an arrest plan. Speed and surprise work together to complete a successful arrest.

ARREST SITUATIONS

Some of the possibilities which exist in arrest situations are: attempted flight on the part of the subject, attempt by the subject to kill or injure the officer, attempt by the subject to commit suicide, attempt to destroy or hide evidence, injury to innocent by-standers, attempted delivery of the subject by confederates, and public disturbances arising out of the arrest. A well-trained and thoughtful officer will consider these possibilities before attempting arrest.

HAZARDOUS-ARREST TECHNIQUES

The techniques in which wildlife officers are encouraged to become proficient deal with the approach, the body search, and the use of handcuffs. These techniques form the subject of the sections that follow.

The Approach

In every approach situation the officer should remember the necessity for alertness and for planning. To forget this is to court trouble.

Since there is always the possibility of trouble arising during an arrest, an officer should maintain an alert state of mind at all times. This is even true when the arrest is for a relatively minor misdemeanor, as well as for a more serious offense. The Federal Bureau of Investigation has suggested that alertness may be stimulated if the officer will go into every arrest situation with this thought: "This person may resist arrest and attempt violence."

An alert, forceful, and aggressive officer is in a position to convince his subject that he is in full command of the situation. Many subjects faced with such opposition submit to arrest without a show of force. On the other hand, a lethargic approach may give the person being arrested the advantage of a few precious seconds.

Whether officers are in teams or working alone, a definite plan of action should be worked out before approaching the subject. While the plan of approach must be complete, it should also be as simple and as flexible as possible to meet changing or unexpected conditions.

It is of the utmost importance that one man be in charge. It is his responsibility to direct the activities of

Courtesy Federal Bureau of Investigation

Figure 27. A Special Agent of the FBI draws and fires his .38 caliber revolver from hip position.

others, to give the commands to the person or persons being arrested, and to coordinate all activity.

When approaching a person known or thought to be dangerous, the officer should take advantage of any natural cover. Generally, when two officers approach a dangerous suspect, the line of attack should approximate a triangle with the subject at the apex. This excludes the possibility of the officers shooting each other or of the subject being able to eliminate quickly both officers.

Individual situations will dictate whether or not the suspect should be ordered to put up his hands, or whether the officer will approach with a drawn gun or will draw it later. In any event, the suspect's hands should be watched very carefully to determine whether or not he will reach for a weapon.

Body Search

Preliminary and final, complete body search of the suspect should always be made. In fact, a preliminary body search at the time of actual arrest is mandatory in cases involving dangerous suspects. When a search is made, it should be thorough and careful. Slipshod methods of searching may not reveal concealed weapons and may give the arresting officer a false sense of security. Some of the usual places where weapons are concealed are the groin area, shoe or boot tops, chest, back, and around the belt.

The preliminary body search can be accomplished in a number of ways, but probably the most foolproof method is the wall search. In this method the prisoner is required to face a wall, automobile, tree, or some other solid object, spread his hands far apart and place them on this object. He is then required to spread his legs and move them backward until he is spread-eagled into such a position of unstable equilibrium that he can take very little action against the officer. He should be required to keep his face toward the wall so that he cannot observe the officer's activity. The officer then places his left foot inside the prisoner's right foot and makes contact with him by placing his left hand on the subject's back near the belt. If the prisoner then attempts anything, a push of the hand or kick of the foot will force the subject to the ground and give the officer a chance to take counter measures.

When the subject is in the wall-search position, the officer can holster his gun and proceed to search him in comparative safety. He must, however, be constantly alert. After completing the search of the right side of the subject's body, the officer reverses the procedures for the left side. If there is more than one subject, each can be searched in turn. In going from one subject to another, the searching officer should never cross the line of fire of the man who is acting as guard.

As a practical matter, law enforcement agencies arrange that the search of female prisoners be conducted by females. However, situations may arise in which it is essential both for the protection of the officer and of the prisoner that if no other female is present, a preliminary search be conducted at the time of her arrest by a male officer. The occasions on which such circumstances arise are rare.

It is probably always desirable to effect a complete search of a prisoner after he has been taken to his place of detention. When a second search is made, it should be absolutely complete.

A receipt should be issued for all personal property, and the prisoner should sign this receipt, if he will. Personal property should be kept separate from any evidence which will not be returned.

Use of Handcuffs

In most cases the wildlife officer will restrain the dangerous suspect by the use of handcuffs. This is particularly true when he must transport his prisoner over long distances, when he is outnumbered and needs to partially immobilize his prisoners in order to transport them, or when an obstinate prisoner threatens to inflict physical injury on himself or on the officer.

When handcuffs are to be used, the suspect should be made to stand on the wall-search position and move first the left hand back of himself and then the right. In case he is to be transported a long distance, it is necessary to fasten the handcuffs in front of him. In this case the handcuffing can be made more effective by running the prisoner's pant's belt over the chain between the handcuffs and by fastening the belt in back. To prevent the prisoner from

Figure 28. Two Special Agents of the Federal Bureau of Investigation in training on the United States Marine Base at Quantico, Virginia, conduct a practice wall search.

applying handcuffs as a weapon, it may be necessary at times to fasten them behind the prisoner's back or to run the chain connecting the two links between his legs.

A subject must be treated as one who is innocent until proven guilty. While the prisoner is in custody the officer must provide him with food and other necessities of life. Care should be taken not to inflict injury on the suspect by placing the cuffs on so tightly that the circulation is retarded or cut off. In the event medical attention is required it must be provided as soon as possible. A prisoner is never handcuffed to a solid object.

When using handcuffs, the officer should always keep in mind that, at best, they are only a temporarily restraining device and that many experienced criminals are able to slip out of them very readily. Handcuffs cannot substitute for an alert mind, and the officer who relaxes mentally as soon as the cuffs are on places himself immediately at a disadvantage.

THE RAID

In the course of a wildlife officer's career he may be compelled by circumstances to conduct or participate in a raid. Usually a raid is ugly business at best, and a knowledge of raid tactics will stand the officer in good stead.

Definition

A raid by law enforcement officers is a sudden assault on an area, building, or individual with the object of apprehending some person or persons or of securing evidence or other material. Raids are generally planned, but on occasion they may be spontaneous. Under no circumstances should a raid be executed unless there is no question as to its legality.

Planning a Raid

Spontaneous raids should normally be made only when it appears that either evidence or individuals may be lost or escape if there is a delay. Planned raids are much more effective, but to insure their success the planning must be carefully done. A number of important factors enter into the picture. Each one will be briefly considered.

1. Is the raid necessary to the performance of duty? Is the raid legal?

2. What is the composition of the raiding party? Will there be superiority of man power? Is each member of the party an experienced officer, competent in the role he is to play? Is it absolutely understood who is in charge?

3. Is the party properly oriented? Does each member understand the plan of approach? Do the officers have a knowledge of the terrain, the number and location of buildings or other structures, the possible positions of lookouts and their scope of view, and the possible routes along which the quarry may try to escape? In fish and game violations, particularly, the raiding party should consider the positions of wild or domestic animals as well as routes which can be used to avoid these and other obstacles.

4. Is the available equipment adequate for the task? Are the weapons of the type best adapted to the situation? Are signals agreed on and penetrating enough to be heard above the noise of gun fire?

5. What hazards may be expected? How many persons are being raided? What weapons may they be expected to have available? What is the character and nature of each person? Will opposition probably continue to the bitter end, or will it probably cease at the first show of superior force? Is the possibility of trickery considered? What communication facilities may the suspects be able to make use of?

Normally, a raid should be conducted when there is a minimum of opposition and interference from outsiders or from uninterested persons. On extensive, well-planned raids, it may be desirable to prepare one or more alternate plans, drawn up in detail, in the event the original plan appears to be failing. For example, one plan may be carried into effect until the suspect surrenders, and a second put in operation when the suspect chooses to flee or to resist. In a large raiding party it may be desirable to have maps prepared so that each individual will have no question as to his routes and duties. Night-raiding parties should avoid wearing such shiny objects as luminous watch dials or anything that can reflect even a small amount of light.

As a final precaution, just before a raid is to be put into operation, all equipment should be carefully checked to

see that it is in proper working order and that no items
have been omitted. These items should include handcuffs,
which may be needed if stiff resistance is offered after the
suspect has been put under temporary custody. In the
event total darkness pictures are to be taken, the proper
infra-red equipment should be included.

STOPPING AUTOMOBILES

In seeking to arrest occupants of a moving automobile,
the officer should exercise caution in approaching the
vehicle. If possible, he should stop the car in question by
the use of siren and red lights. In most instances his car
should parallel the suspects' car no farther forward than a
point where his front seat is opposite the back of the front
seat of the subjects' car. With the two cars in this position,
it is awkward for the driver suspect to take action against
the officer.

When the suspects stop, if it is daylight, the officer
should park at a slight angle to the other car in order to
secure cover. If it is night, the officer should so park that
he can take full advantage of the car lights.

He should order the occupants out of the car, line them
up in the road, and then carefully approach the car to check
seats and floor for anyone who might be hidden there.
After he has removed the ignition key and locked the doors,
the officer may search the suspects. Needless to say, in
all cases the officer should keep his gun hand free.

FRESH PURSUIT

In connection with the foregoing section on stopping
automobiles, the officer should keep in mind the act of
fresh pursuit. This is a law, effective in some states,
which gives the officer the right to cross a state line to
make an arrest when in fresh pursuit of an alleged criminal.
In some states this act of fresh pursuit applies to felonies
but not to misdemeanors.

It is recognized that the officer must of necessity be
the aggressor, and it is up to him to decide just what amount
of force is necessary to effect the arrest. If, in the process of pursuing a subject, he sees the suspect leave his car
and take refuge in a private home, the officer may break in
doors and windows. This applies to a misdemeanor as well

Photograph by Jack Dermid
Courtesy North Carolina Wildlife Resources Commission

Figure 29. The best of modern equipment for air, ground, and boat contact.

as to felonies or to the more serious crime of homicide. However, it is customary and desirable for officers to state their intentions of breaking in if the suspect does not admit them.

IMMEDIATE HEARING

Once an arrest is made the prisoner should not be allowed out of sight for an instant, and the officer should be careful that some confederate does not pass weapons or other objects that might be used to inflict injury upon the officer. But he must not disregard the prisoner's right to an immediate hearing and he is obliged by law to take the arrestee forthwith to the nearest police station for booking.

CHAPTER IX
The Officer in Court

An officer may be required to appear in court either as a witness or as the prosecutor for his own case. [1] In either event, adequate preparations and complete familiarity with the details are absolutely necessary. Since a full treatment of case law is outside the scope of this book, only a few salient points will be introduced. Before going ahead, however, it seems desirable to present in a generalized manner a verbal picture of court procedure.

GENERALIZED PICTURE OF A TRIAL

Briefly and considerably oversimplified, a criminal case is tried according to the following pattern: The prosecuting attorney makes a statement in which he briefly summarizes what he expects to prove. The defense attorney makes (or is entitled to make) a statement outlining the defense and what he expects to prove or disprove. The prosecution then puts its witnesses on the stand for direct examination. Witnesses can be cross-examined by opposing attorneys, but counsel cannot cross-examine their own witnesses, nor can they question the validity of their witnesses' own testimony. After the direct evidence by the prosecution is in, the defense may place its witnesses on the stand. After the defense presents its case, rebuttal may be given by the prosecution. The defense may meet this rebuttal evidence by what is known as "sur-rebuttal." After all evidence is in, each side may address the jury. Finally, the prosecution closes the argument by summarizing the material to the jury. The jury is then charged by the judge and their verdict is returned. The sentence is pronounced by the judge in the event the defendant is found guilty. Motions for a retrial by the defense must be made within a specified time.

---

1. In this text only the officer's role as witness is discussed.

THE BRIEF

Although it is not expected that every prosecution will result in a conviction, at the same time the officer should have such grounds for instituting the proceedings as will justify him, in the opinion of the district attorney and of the judge who tries the case, in having brought the action. It is recognized that at times a prosecution is justifiable and desirable even when it is a moral certainty that a conviction will not be had. The legal instrument that permits the prosecutor to view these grounds is the brief.

By disclosing the strength and weakness of the prosecutor's position and the possible lines of defense, the brief enables him to determine if an arrest is justifiable under evidence submitted. Such a brief is particularly necessary when the defendant elects to fight the charges. For this reason, in every case, no matter how trivial, the officer should prepare a brief of the evidence for his own and for the district attorney's information.

The average district attorney handles dozens of cases a month and can give a misdemeanor charge only limited time. He may not be too familiar with fish and game laws, with fish and game conditions, or with practices prevailing in the field. If he can sit down with a brief of the case, illustrated with sketches and photographs, he is in a better position to grasp quickly the circumstances and possibilities of action. Furthermore, he will have the brief with him during the trial to refresh his memory and to oppose the defense better during cross-examination.

The brief, prepared by the officer, should list the code sections involved and the alleged offenses. It should give the "who, what, when, where, how, and why" of the crime, all set forth chronologically. It should give the position, observation, and action of the officer or officers. It should list witnesses and a brief of the testimony they can or will give. Photographs and sketches should be attached.

PREPARING TO APPEAR IN COURT

Previous to his appearance in court, the officer should review the violation and discuss with the prosecuting attorney what the approach to the case will be and what questions will be asked. This preparatory work will increase the effectiveness of his testimony.

Review of the Violation

A refreshed memory will help the trial to go along smoothly and will appear to present a vivid recollection of events as they occurred. While it is not expected that an officer will remember intricate sets of figures or complicated and long-drawn-out details, constant referring to notes may impair the value of his testimony. He should also bear in mind that if he refers to his notes in court, th opposing council may ask to see them and may cross-examine him on them.

For this reason the officer should coach himself until he is able to reconstruct mentally the crime and the evider pointing to it. In this respect it is helpful to arrange all th material chronologically and then review it thoroughly fro original notes, sketches, photographs, or from any other material he plans to use on the witness stand.

Preliminary Discussion

In the courtroom the officer-witness and the prosecuto should function as a team. A preliminary discussion befor the trial begins will afford opportunity to decide on the approach to the case and on the matter of questioning.

As regards the approach to the case, serious consider ation is given the types of witnesses, the particular judge, and the impaneled jury. In any approach selected, howeve it is always necessary to act with deference toward both th court and the jury.

Good courtroom technique requires that evidence be presented in a logical, concise manner in order to put ove1 a point. During this pre-trial meeting, the lawyer learns what the officer is going to testify to and how he will testify The witness learns what questions the lawyer is going to as and how he will ask them. He also learns how he should react to the questions he will undergo from both prosecutor and defense attorney.

The preliminary discussion will not only set the witnes at ease, but will help him to understand exactly what any given question will mean. Witnesses can be prepared for

ffirmative examinations, but they obviously cannot be
repared for all possible cross-examination questions.
ome of these questions are used to test the credence of
he witness and of his knowledge, but they may be used also
o test consistency of testimony.

The witness should be instructed not to become excited
nd to be sure the question is understood before he answers
t; not to guess at answers to questions, but rather to state
hat the answer is not known. A witness may answer a
uestion in part or ask for a restatement or for further ex-
lanation. The witness should also be instructed that if
ater it becomes evident to him that he has misinterpreted
nd misanswered an earlier question, he should so state
is position and reanswer the earlier question.

TESTIFYING IN COURT

A case that moves steadily forward because the wit-
esses for the prosecution present their testimony in a sim-
le yet firm and unshakable manner creates a more favor-
ble impression on the court as regards the charge against
he defendant than a case marked by vacillating witnesses
vho are uncertain in their testimony, poorly prepared by
ouncil, and ignorant or unmindful of accepted courtroom
rocedure. The observation of a few general procedures
vill improve the officer's ability to testify effectively.

General Procedure

All statements should be made in a conversational
one, but loud enough for the jury and the court to hear and
nderstand. Most answers should be directed toward the
ury. All speech should be courteous. The court should
lways be addressed as "Your Honor," and attorneys should
e answered by "Yes, Sir," or "No, Sir" to questions that
an properly be answered that way. At no time should the
fficer attempt to be witty or sarcastic. If a question is not
nderstood, the officer should state that it is not understood
nd ask for a restatement or rephrasing. An undue amount
f time need not be taken to answer questions; on the other
and, answers snapped back too quickly may lead to a lack
f confidence in his testimony and perhaps, worse still, may
ause the officer to make a misstatement which can later be
sed against him.

The truth should be told in all instances, even though it is favorable to the defendant. This does not mean that the officer should volunteer information which will militate against his own case, but it does mean that when he is asked he should be truthful. He should not hesitate to correct mistakes in testimony made earlier in the trial. The officer, when realizing that a mistake has been made, should state something to the effect that previously his testimony had been "so and so," and that it is now realized this was in error and the true statement is "so and so." When a time, distance, or speed cannot be defined exactly, it should be stated as "on or about," or "the speed was about."

It is important that the officer appear to be impartial and fair and not overly anxious to convict. The slightest bias should never be shown toward a defendant. The officer does not assume that the defendant is guilty until he is so stated by the court. On the other hand, he should assume that the evidence points to his guilt. The person charged should always be referred to as the "defendant."

Witnesses should not volunteer information over and above that asked or implied by a question, unless, of course, such information is in answer to a question as "Tell the court what happened on July 25th at 7:00 p.m. near Henrysville." This type of question naturally leads to a general discussion of events, time, and place.

A defendant is never on trial for past offenses, and reference to past criminal records should therefore not be made unless specifically requested by council. It should be understood that council may frequently try to bring out the past criminal record of an individual in order to prejudice the jury. Even though the testimony may be stricken from the record, it is commonly recognized that it cannot be so easily stricken from the minds of the jurors. In this connection, it is axiomatic that officers must go into court with clean hands. An officer with a record of law violation to his credit, even before he was appointed an officer, will frequently find his testimony completely discredited by a clever lawyer.

After the testimony is complete the officer should leave the court unless he has been asked by the court or prosecuting attorney to stay. Staying in court after testifying may create the impression that the officer is over-anxious to convict or overly concerned about the outcome of the case.

Cross-Examination

During cross-examination the officer should be particularly careful about walking into traps set by opposing council. Frequently, cross-examination will be used to divert the jury's attention from real issues and put the officer rather than the defendant on trial in the minds of the jury. The opposition may attempt to show that the witness is not worthy of belief because of his character or reputation, or that he is prejudiced, or that the testimony itself is in error because of incompetence or because it is immaterial.

Some of the tricks used on cross-examination include misquoting the witness or demanding a "yes" or "no" answer. As an example of the former trick, the defense may quote the officer as having testified in such a way and then, glibly assuming that the officer has indeed so testified, proceed with the questioning. It is important when this trick is tried that the officer immediately call it to the attention of counsel by saying, "Mr. So and So, I am sorry I have not made myself clear, but" and proceed to state the facts as they were previously stated.

The defense attorney may demand a yes or no answer when the question is such that neither one, without qualification, can possibly be a correct answer. In this case the officer has to state that the question cannot be correctly answered by either "yes" or "no" and that he is willing to give the facts as he understands them.

Another trick used on witnesses is for the defense attorney to shout, "Whom have you talked to about this case, and who told you to testify the way you have?" This question may catch a witness, who will answer without thinking, "No one." Actually, there are two questions, and the correct answer is generally that the officer has talked to his superior and that he is telling the truth to the best of his ability, and no one has told him to testify otherwise. In the event the questioner accuses the witness of talking to other people about the case, then the best answer is to list who has been talked to, such as the prosecuting attorney, superiors, and anyone else who may have entered the case.

The officer may also be accused of refreshing his memory, in which case it may be true and perfectly legitimate, and the officer should state that he has used the process known as "refreshing and recollecting." It may be that he has revisited the scene of the crime or discussed the affair with other witnesses, all of which is proper.

Statements of Time or of Possession

In cases involving wildlife law violations, the elements of time and possession generally play an important role in helping to establish innocence or guilt. The officer-witness should therefore know how to answer questions based on these elements.

Frequently the term "on or about" is used in referring to the time element. For example, "On or about 5:00 p.m. I saw John Doe shoot and kill a drake pintail." If shooting time for migratory waterfowl closed at 5:00 p.m., this type of statement would be inconclusive evidence since opposing council could contend that it might just as well have been before 5:00 p.m. as after. In case it was not permissible to have mourning doves in possession between the 5th and 15th of March of a particular year, the following statement is admissible: "On or about the 10th day of March, but between the 5th and 15th, I found John Doe in possession of 10 mourning doves."

Perjury

Perjury is committed by willfully and corruptly giving, in a judicial proceeding or course of justice and upon a lawful oath or in any form allowed by law to be substituted for an oath, any false testimony material to the issue or matter of inquiry. Perjury means that false testimony must be given willfully and corrputly and that it must appear that the accused did not believe it to be true. A witness may commit perjury by testifying that he knows a thing to be true when, in fact, he knows nothing about it at all or is not sure about it or is reasonably sure that it is not true.

A witness may testify falsely as to his belief, remembrance, impressions, opinion, or judgment and thereby commit perjury. If a witness swears that he does not remember certain matters when, in fact, he actually does, or testifies that his opinion is sure when, in fact, it is otherwise, he commits perjury if the other elements of the offense are present.

The oath must be one required or authorized by law and must be duly administered by one authorized to administer it. When a form of oath has been prescribed, a literal following of such form is not essential, it being sufficient if the oath administered conforms in substance to the prescribed oath. An oath includes an affirmative when the latter is authorized in lieu of an oath. [2]

It is no defense that the witness voluntarily appeared, or that he was incompetent as a witness, or that his testimony was given in response to questions that he could have declined to answer, or even that he was forced to answer over his claim of privilege. [3]

CONDUCT IN COURT

Insofar as possible, the officer-witness should be alert but easy and dignified on the witness stand. He should sit erect, with feet on the floor and with hands folded easily in the lap or on the arms of the witness chair. Under no circumstances should the officer allow himself to indulge in nervous mannerisms, or in any way react so that the jury will be disconcerted or annoyed by his acts or mannerisms. He should maintain an even temper and not be evasive or argumentative with either the opposing council or the court.

His personal appearance should be above reproach. Such items as shined shoes, clean, well-pressed clothes, and freshly-shaven face are absolutely necessary.

DEFENSE ATTORNEYS

Defense attorneys are sometimes said to fall into two general categories: the friendly type and the brow-beating type. In either case, when the officer is acting as a witness, he should recognize that opposing attorneys are in court to win cases, and he should not be taken in by either type. Frequently, the friendly attorney will attempt to lull the

2. United States Government. 1951. Manual for courts-martial. Washington, D. C.: U. S. Government Printing Office. p. 375.
3. Ibid., p. 376.

witness into a false sense of security and cause him to divulge things which he normally would not. The brow-beating attorney may try to intimidate the witness or to so abuse him that he will become enraged, lose his temper, and fight back, thereby prejudicing the jury against himself and the case. In extreme cases, a witness may ask the court to intervene in his favor.

It should be kept in mind that law cases are no longer largely contests between brilliant lawyers. Trials are now conducted in a much greater measure by judges than they were a few years ago. In dealing with a lay-judge it is not advisable to become too technical nor to appear in any way to reflect upon his legal knowledge.

CHAPTER X

The Preparation of Evidence

One of the responsibilities of the wildlife officer is to prepare enough evidence against the violator to justify taking him before the court with reasonable chances for a conviction. This preparation includes the identification, the collection, and the preservation of such kinds of evidence and in such a manner that the admissibility and effectiveness of the evidence in court will serve the ends of justice. In order for the officer to discharge this responsibility, he must exercise the qualities of a trained investigator.

THE OFFICER AS AN INVESTIGATOR

The officer's investigative role requires that he understand and know how to handle proof of a wildlife law violation. He must know, for example, what constitutes evidence; what evidence is admissible in court; when and in what manner to apprehend presumed law violators so that no legal obstacles to conviction can arise from that source; how to develop information; how to recognize evidence in the field; how to collect and preserve evidence to safeguard its admissibility; how to obtain evidence from witnesses and from others who may be able to help; how to detect discrepancies, dishonesty, or general lack of good faith; when to call upon experts for help; and how to testify, and other courtroom techniques. The previous chapter having dealt with the role of the officer in court, the present chapter focuses attention on his role as regards evidence.

NATURE AND KINDS OF EVIDENCE

Evidence is anything that can be shown or told in court to support the charge of violation. In its nature it may be classified as direct and circumstantial, or presumptive. In its several forms it may be called real evidence, documentary evidence, oral evidence, or opinion. Since the whole matter of evidence is too broad and technical to be covered completely in this text, the following treatment, while helpful to the student, to the officer in the field, and to the instructor of wildlife courses, is somewhat cursory.

135

Direct Evidence

Evidence which tends directly to prove or disprove a fact in issue is called direct evidence. It testifies to the very fact. For example, it is direct evidence if an officer testifies that he saw a sportsman shoot and kill a deer or that he saw a person in a boat throw ground, raw meat into the lake.

Circumstantial Evidence

Evidence which tends directly to prove or disprove not a fact of violation but a fact or circumstance from which, either alone or in connection with other facts, a court may, according to the common experience of mankind, reasonably infer the existence or nonexistence of another fact which is in issue, is called indirect or circumstantial evidence. It is established from cause to effect and leads to the fact that a violation was committed. For example, it is circumstantial evidence that a person killed a deer when it is found in his possession, although it is direct evidence that he is in violation if mere possession of it is illegal.

Circumstantial evidence, even when believed, does not always conclusively establish a fact; but it may, with other known facts, prove the elements involved. It tends to show that under the established set of circumstances the accused may have, or at least was in a position to have, committed the violation. Circumstantial evidence is not necessarily inferior to direct evidence. In all cases, the plausibility of the statement and the competency of the witness must be weighed.

Presumptions

As a general rule, the word "presumption" means justifiable inference. That is, when a lawyer or other person in court presumes a statement, it simply means that he justifiably infers the statement from the evidence at hand. In other words, it is nothing more than circumstantial evidence as weighed and measured in terms of its logical value.

As an example, possession of game out of season raises the presumption that the owner killed the game. A gun that is in good working order after a shot has been fired is presumed to have been in good working order at the time the shot was fired. On the other hand, an accused person

is presumed to be innocent until his guilt is proved beyond
a reasonable doubt.

Real Evidence

One of the forms that direct or circumstantial evidence
takes is that of real evidence. This kind of evidence includes physical objects such as bodies of game animals,
blood, weapons, empty shell cases, projectiles, glass fragments, and articles of clothing. However, to be admitted
in court as real evidence, such items must be proved relevant to the issue involved.

Documentary Evidence

Demonstrative or visual evidence is called documentary
evidence and includes, among others, writings, such as
confessions, field notes, photographs, sketches, and fingerprints. Each is herein described briefly.

Writings. A writing is the best evidence of its own
contents, and the original or its equal must be introduced to
prove its contents. For example, when the law specifically
makes it illegal to set traps at a certain time and place, then
a signed confession that the suspect then and there did knowingly and willfully set a line of traps with which he took game
constitutes documentary evidence that a violation was committed.

In order for this type of evidence to be admissible in
court, however, it is necessary to present evidence authen-
ticating the original document and then to introduce the original document in evidence. This means, of course, that the
wildlife officer must be able to prove that the suspect wrote
the confession, or that he understood what he was signing,
and that the suspect's signature is authentic.

A carbon copy of a document, as complete, as the original copy in all the essential respects, including relevant
signatures if any, or an identical copy made by a photographic process or other duplicating instrument is considered to
be a duplicate of the original and equally admissible with
the original. If admissible writings have been lost or destroyed, or when for some other reason they cannot be produced, then the contents may be proved by an authenticated
copy or by the testimony of a witness who has seen the
writing.

<u>Field notes</u>. One of the primary sources of documentary evidence available to the wildlife officer is found in the field notes he keeps as a matter of routine. His notebook should serve as a combination diary and case book. His daily entries should show the area and the weather, including precipitation, per cent of overcast, and direction and velocity of the wind.

Immediately after the officer makes an arrest he should make a complete entry in his notebook, listing the contraband game and equipment together with all identifying marks placed on the contraband. Notes should include the full name and address of the accused, plus any distinguishing marks or characteristics that will aid in future identification. The day and time, place where the offense occurred, particular act or acts which constitute the violation, names and addresses of accomplices or witnesses, and the exact location of the officer in relation to where the accused was at the time the alleged offense was committed, should all appear in the notes.

The extreme importance of initialing and dating all field notes at the actual time they are made was emphasized in a recent, widely-publicized, criminal case. The defense attorney repeatedly questioned the laboratory technician, who was testifying for the state, as to whether he was briefed and as to what evidence he had looked for. Over and over again defense asked to see the notes which had been made by the expert witness as he went along. As they were produced, the defense attorney noted that some were undated and charged, "So you are now simply relying on your memory, is that correct?"

Many cases are lost every year because of an officer's neglect or carelessness. He may have thought that evidence was conclusive when it was not, the evidence having been insufficient or inadmissible. The officer may have counted on the defendant's oral plea of guilty only to learn at the trial that the defendant had decided to plead not guilty.

Notes should be accurate, complete, legible, and understandable. They should contain only authorized abbreviations, because it may be necessary later to introduce the notebook into court. Personal remarks or conclusions should not be recorded.

Photographs. Photographs, in a state where these are admissible as evidence, may be more effective than oral testimony. In any case, they are valuable as documentary evidence, especially where the objects to be shown to the court cannot be brought in. Some states admit photographic evidence once it has been shown, while in other states photographs are not admissible as evidence except for the purpose of illustrating the testimony of the witness. In Salt Lake City, Utah, photographs taken by a camera that records the offense and registers the time are admissible evidence. However, such photographs must be taken by a photographer who can qualify as an expert witness, they must not misrepresent the object, and they must not tend to incite sympathy or prejudice. In addition, the object photographed must be relevant, material, and competent. [1]

It is important that the officer have reasonable skill in the use of photographic equipment and some understanding of the basic principles involved. Otherwise, it may be simple for the opposing attorney to demonstrate that the lack of knowledge has given a distorted impression of the previous happenings.

Photographs enlarged to an 8-by-10 size are generally acceptable and are the most usable in court. Wherever possible, the negative should accompany the print to court, to dispel any question concerning retouching. Complete information on the taking of the picture, as well as a clearly defined chain of custody, should accompany each photograph when it is offered as evidence. This information should include the name of the case, the day, the exact time, the location, and the compass directions; the light conditions, type and speed of film, lens stop, and type and brand of camera; and a note as to the particular reason for taking the picture. Any of these facts may be important during the trial, should the defense question or attack the photograph as evidence.

None of these data should be placed on the back of the photograph, because such practice constitutes inadmissible

---

1.   These conditions were stated by Judge Leland G. Larsen in an opinion on a fictitious case involving a speeding charge as reported in The Salt Lake Tribune, July 27, 1955. p. 12.

Figure 30. Gun vault, FBI Academy, United States Marine Corps Base, Quantico, Virginia.

hearsay evidence and furnishes the defense attorney with material for troublesome cross-examination and perhaps a valid reason for objecting to the introduction of such photographic evidence. Even though data should not be placed on the back of the photograph, there is no objection to marking each photograph with an identifying number.

Sketches. Another kind of documentary evidence is the sketch, a graphic representation of a law violation showing essential details. It may be used during court trial to refresh the memory of a witness, to obviate the necessity of going to the scene of the crime, or to crystalize what may otherwise be a lengthy verbal description. Sketches may be either rough drafts or finished drawings. They may be the ones made at the scene of the violation or ones made later to scale. In any case, the scale should be approximately correct and the measurements reasonably accurate. The investigator should know the degree of accuracy of the sketches and figures and be willing to state it. In many cases a finished drawing is made later for courtroom presentation, but it is based on the rough sketch which is kept with the investigator's notes. These notes are available for court presentation when and if necessary.

Fingerprints. Still another example of documentary evidence is the recording of fingerprints. In the case of bloody fingerprints on the handle of a knife found near the carcass of a deer, the only legal question involved may be the identification of the particular prints forwarded to, for example, the Federal Bureau of Investigation.

Oral Evidence

Oral Evidence, proceeding from exclamation or from word of mouth, includes everything pertinent to the case which the officer or other witness has seen or heard or otherwise observed through his own personal experience. Confessions, spontaneous exclamations, and dying declarations are examples of oral evidence.

Confessions. A confession is an acknowledgment of guilt, a voluntary admission by a person that he committed the violation with which he is charged. Although it is usually oral, a confession may be received directly from the pen. The general practice, in the case of an oral confession, is to reduce it to writing over the signatures of suspect and witnesses.

A confession must be given voluntarily if it is to be used as admissible evidence; one obtained by coercion, unlawful influence, or any other illegal inducement is not admissible. [2] However, the fact that a statement is declared inadmissible because it was not voluntarily given does not invalidate pertinent facts which were obtained in connection with the admission of guilt. For example, a person who has been forced to admit that he killed a deer out of season could not be convicted on his own statement, but he could be convicted if the carcass of the deer were found in his possession.

The fact that an oral confession was made may be established by the testimony of a witness who was present and heard the statement, this being true whether or not the confession was later reduced to writing. An accused person cannot legally be convicted on his own uncorroborated confession unless there is other evidence, either direct or circumstantial, that indicates the crime has been committed. [3] For example, a person who walks into the sheriff's office and confesses that he recently killed a fellow hunter cannot be convicted if this is absolutely the only evidence bearing on the alleged killing. The same would be true of a person confessing to a fish or a game violation. However, if the person were to present even such minute evidence as the scale of a fish or the feather of a bird which he stated was part of the illegal game, then the case could be processed. The corroboration rule does not apply to a confession made by the accused before the court in which he is being tried, nor does it apply to statements made prior to or in pursuance of the act.

Spontaneous exclamation. This is an utterance concerning the circumstances of a startling experience made by a person while he is in a state of excitement, shock, or surprise. The utterance is caused by the person's participation in or observation of the event and warrants a reasonable inference that the utterance was made spontaneously

---

2. United States Government, op. cit. p. 248.
3. Ibid., p. 249.

and instinctively as an outcome of the event, as opposed to a statement made after deliberation or by design.

Spontaneous exclamations are admissible as evidence contrary to the general hearsay rule. They are admitted as evidence on the theory that a person who has just committed an act is more likely to tell the truth at that moment than he is later, after he has thought it over. For example, if immediately after a man shoots a fellow hunter someone asks him why he did it, he may respond truthfully, whereas after he has recovered from the shock he may not. A spontaneous utterance may be proved by competent evidence or testimony of a person who heard the statement being made, even though he was not present at the occurrence which gave rise to it.

<u>Dying declarations</u>. In homicide trials, dying declarations of alleged victims, including the identity of the person or persons who caused the injury, are admissible as evidence. The reason for accepting this type of evidence is that the statement would obviously otherwise be unavailable; also, presumably those who believe that they are about to die tell the truth.

In order to establish admissibility of this evidence, it must be demonstrated that the victim believed, either by his actual statement or by other facts or impressions, that death was imminent. The fact that the victim later did or did not die is immaterial. On the other hand, the statement is not admissible if the victim had some hope of recovery but died shortly thereafter.

Dying declarations are not acceptable if they were obtained under duress, but they may be rightfully obtained in answer to leading questions or upon urgent solicitation. The declaration may be either oral or in writing and in favor of or against the accused. As an example, a declaration by a dying hunter to an officer or other witness that his companion shot him as the result of an argument over ownership of a deer may be used as admissible evidence in court to the prejudice of the second hunter.

Limitations of Oral Evidence

While this type of evidence is the most common, it may also be the least reliable. This is because of the

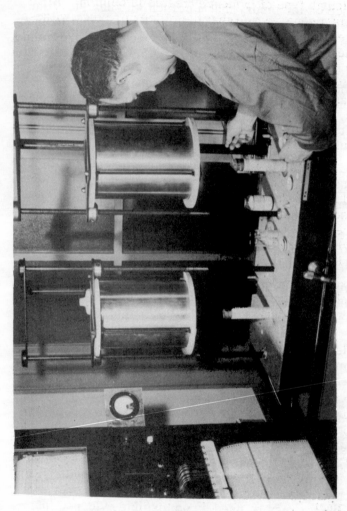

Courtesy Federal Bureau of Investigation

Figure 31. Technician places a specimen in the differential thermal analyzer used in connection with the examination of soils at the FBI Laboratory, Washington, D. C. The instruments on the left control furnace temperature and record temperature changes of the sample.

possibility of honest mistakes, improper observation, bias, or other incompetencies.

Opinion

The fourth type of evidence treated is opinion. Although it is a general rule that the officer or other witness must state facts and not opinions or conclusions, impressions under some circumstances, as based on personal observation, are required by the court. Examples of these are the distance that a shot was fired at a game animal, the speed of an automobile, the identification of a voice as that of a man, woman, or child, and, in many cases, an opinion as to whether a given individual was behaving in a manner which would cause him to be adjudged drunk.

To be admissible in court, opinions of a technical nature must be given by an expert witness. Such a witness is defined as one who is skilled in some art, trade, profession, or science, or as a person who has knowledge and experience in relation to matters at hand which are generally not within the knowledge of men of common education and experience.

An expert witness may express an opinion on a state of facts which is within his specialty and without specifying data on which it is based. However, his admissible expert opinion is regarded as evidence only when it pertains to the matter on which the opinion relates.

SOURCES OF EVIDENCE

If the wildlife officer is to be really effective, it is important that he develop a number of different sources of information. If he seeks this information from the right sources, he may gather evidence essential to the case which will be in addition to such real evidence as may readily be available to him at the scene of the violation.

The Informant

Probably the most important source is the informant. Such a person is one who gives information that may lead to the arrest and conviction of a suspect.

The Complainant

The complainant is anyone who notifies a law enforcement officer or agency of an actual or suspected offense. He is generally the witness or discoverer of the violation and the one who is willing to so state, without giving the information confidentially.

Witnesses

Witnesses usually are a good source of information. An investigator should make every effort to locate all known witnesses to a violation, and to obtain thorough and detailed interviews from as many of them as appears necessary.

Suspects

When properly questioned, suspects may be persuaded to give valuable information. Frequently this is the only source of information available to the officer.

Other Sources of Evidence

Other sources of information include the telephone companies, credit bureaus, finance companies, banks, city directories, hospital records, transportation companies, insurance companies, light and power companies, newspapers, state record divisions, and post-office departments

Identity of Informants

Information to wildlife officers may be confidential or given without restriction. When it is given as confidential, the officer should make every effort to properly safeguard the identity of the informant. The general rule governing the safeguarding of identity of confidential informants has been announced in the case of Wilson v. United States. [4] It reads:

> It is the right and duty of every citizen of the United States to communicate to the executive officer of the government charged with the duty of enforcing the law all the information which he has of the commission of an offense against the laws

---

4. Wilson v. United States, Pacific Reporter, Vol. 59, 2nd series, pp. 390, 392.

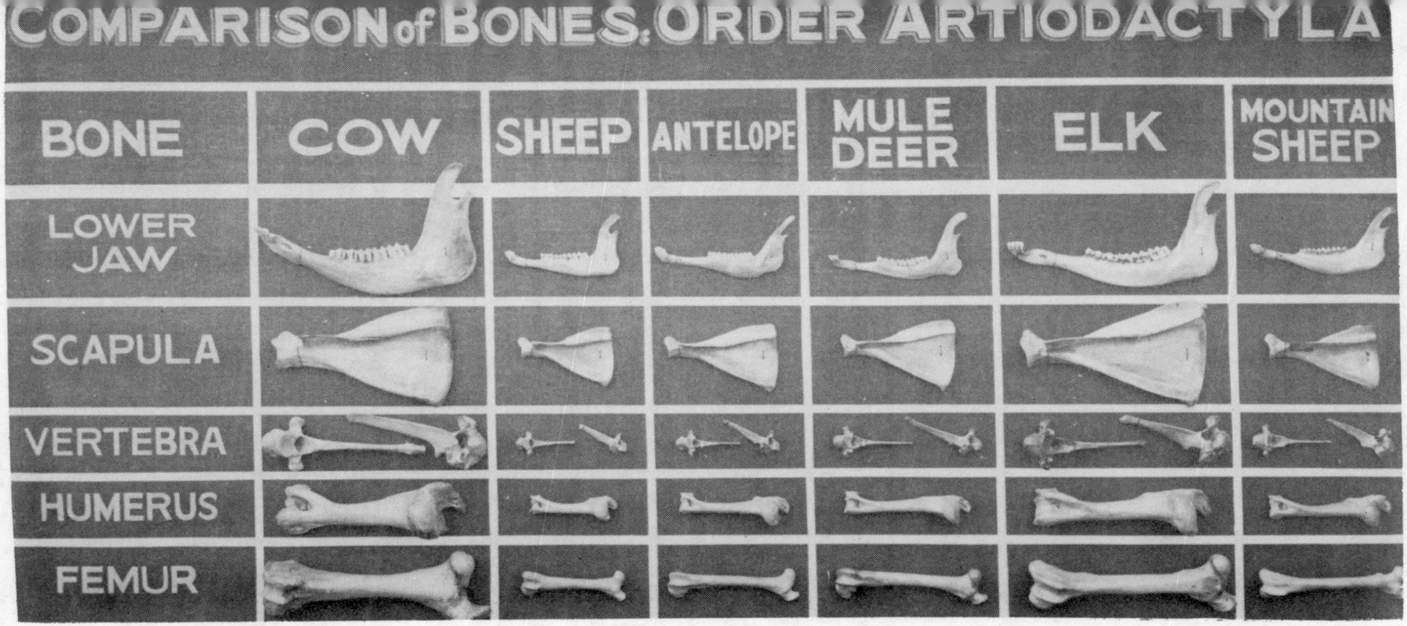
COMPARISON of BONES: ORDER ARTIODACTYLA
BONE
COW
SHEEP
ANTELOPE
MULE DEER
ELK
MOUNTAIN SHEEP
LOWER JAW
SCAPULA
VERTEBRA
HUMERUS
FEMUR

Courtesy Lee Yeager*

Figure 32. The bone board is an aid in either the field or the laboratory.

*Originally published 1953, Journ. Wildlife Management 17. 2:224.

of the United States, and such information is privileged as a confidential communication which the courts will not compel or permit to be disclosed without the consent of the government. Such evidence is excluded, not for the protection of the witness, but because of the policy of the law;. . .however. . .a trial court must dispose of the case before it. If what is asked is essential evidence to vindicate the innocence of the accused or lessen the risk of false testimony, or is essential to the proper disposition of the case, disclosure will be compelled.

INTERVIEWS AND INTERROGATIONS

A confession from the suspect, or information from material witnesses to a violation, when not forthcoming at the time of the violation, may usually be secured through questioning. In fact, a successful investigator depends in great measure upon his effectiveness in questioning the various people involved, or those who may contribute to the solution of the violation.

Investigators generally divide questioning into two broad classifications. (1) The interview, employing the indirect approach, is conducted to learn facts from persons who may have a knowledge of a violation but who are not themselves involved. It is a general discussion carried on in a conversational manner and permits the person to talk without being asked direct questions. (2) The interrogation, or direct approach to information, is used to obtain facts, admissions, or confessions from those who are directly implicated. However, an interrogation is not necessarily confined to individuals suspected of the offense. It may include persons who are suspected of being accessories to or who have a knowledge of the violation but are reluctant to admit it. These persons, with whom the indirect approach may have been unproductive, are restrained from giving information for such reasons as fear or dislike of the officer, fear of retribution, desire to protect someone else, or a general dislike of law enforcement agencies.

In general, throughout the following sections, the terms "interview," "indirect approach," and "direct approach" are used with reference to either the interview or to the interrogation. The context should make the meaning clear.

Methods of Procedure

Obviously, the most opportune time to conduct the interview is when a suspect is surprised in the act of committing a violation. An admission of guilt and a signed confession are probably the easiest to obtain under these circumstances. In other instances, the interview should be conducted as soon as possible after the violation has been committed.

The steps in an interview should be carefully planned in advance so that, if possible, all questions may be used directly or indirectly at one session. A favorable environment should be selected whenever possible, and adequate time should be allowed to complete a thorough interview.

The person being interviewed should be made to feel that he is in no way being forced. Generally speaking, the investigator, while trying to be friendly and business-like, makes an attempt to get the person into a talkative mood; and whenever the conversation is apparently wandering outside the realm of interest, the interviewer guides it back into more productive channels. Digression may be permitted when the interviewer feels that possible points will be touched upon that might otherwise be omitted. He must be circumspect in word and deed, trying to avoid a clash of personality, undue acts of familiarity, profanity, violent expressions such as "murder," "steal," or "thief," improbable stories, or distracting mannerisms, all of which are very likely to militate against the success of the interview.

In the case of dishonest or otherwise unreliable persons, it may be desirable to start an interview with the indirect approach. This may give the person being interviewed an opportunity to trip himself up through admissions, inconsistencies, known misstatements, etc. In this case, the interview would probably shift from the indirect to the direct approach.[5] Talkative persons should be confined to the general subject. The discussion should be changed to a more definite type when the suspect is obviously stalling for time.

---

5. United States Army. 1951. Criminal investigation. Washington, D. C.: U. S. Government Printing Office, Dept. of the Army Field Manual FM 19-20. p. 52.

When a person is not under arrest, the investigator probably has a moral obligation to begin an interrogation. by explaining to the person about to be questioned that his rights under the Fifth Amendment to the Constitution of the United States entitle him to remain silent on matters which can later be used against him. When the person is under arrest, the investigator has a legal obligation to explain individual rights.

In all cases, the officer sympathizes outwardly with the offender and may indicate that anyone else might possibly have done the same thing under similar circumstances. He urges the suspect to tell the truth, all the while avoiding threats or insinuations. He may use such general questions as "Why did you do it?", "Tell me all about it," "How did you do it?", "When did you do it?", "What gave you the idea?", "Who helped you out?". [6]

Frequently the interviewer assists some witnesses in recalling related facts. He should make an attempt to lead them toward accurate statements and toward recalling details, without actually putting words or ideas to them. Where possible, the investigator should provide indices to help a witness in describing such things as size, height, weight, speed, etc.

Precautions

Throughout the interview the interrogator must be careful to refrain from threats of violence or promises of reward or leniency. If the suspect admits or implies guilt, the investigator must not become condescending, emotional, or overanxious.

Whenever confessions are obtained after officers have inflicted bodily harm or indulged in prolonged questioning accompanied by deprivation of the necessities of life, such as food, sleep, and clothing, the validity of the confessions is questionable. Promises of immunity or clemency, or imposition of confinement all tend to invalidate otherwise admissible confessions. Promises of reward and threats of disadvantage do likewise. On the other hand, threats or promises directed toward the accused do not in any way

---

6. Ibid., p. 51.

affect the admissibility of the guilt if these threats or promises are in no way connected with obtaining the confession. If it can be demonstrated that a threat or promise directed at the accused, and bearing on the confession, had ceased to operate on the mind of the accused at the time he made a statement, then the admissibility of the statement is not threatened.

The fact that a confession was made during an investigation does not render the statement inadmissible. The admissibility of a confession, when it is challenged, must be established by an affirmative showing that it was voluntary. Statements of admission of guilt which are made voluntarily, that is without urging, interrogation, or request, are acceptable. In this case, the question in point is whether or not the statement was voluntary or forced.

Silence on the part of the accused during the interview cannot be assumed to be a confession. However, under some circumstances, silence may appear to be evidence of guilt, as for example, when a simple statement of denial would tend to clear the issue. In this case, even though it appears reasonable that the accused is guilty, mere silence cannot by itself be taken as evidence unless it is substantiated by other material indicating that the offense as accused has probably been committed.

Since a confession not made in open court cannot be relied upon unless it is supported by other evidence, every effort should be made to secure such additional evidence of guilt. Also, because the defendant may change his mind and claim that the confession was made under duress or as the result of promises or threats, or that he was confused and did not realize what he was signing, the officer should read back the confession to the defendant, in the presence of witnesses, and obtain the defendant's signature. Generally, no difficulty arises from a person making a confession if he is taken immediately before the court.

Evaluation of Information

An interviewer must make use of all his knowledge of human nature. He must be able to make people talk freely and judge whether or not they are telling the truth, withholding facts, or otherwise impeding the progress of the case.

Admissions may be influenced by such factors as hope of gain, politics, race, religion, hatred of an officer, old age, mental or physical handicaps, revenge, fear of social stigma, or of economic loss. For this reason, the interviewer should continuously evaluate the behavior of the person before him. Annoying mannerisms, emotional tension, evasiveness, a few seconds of hesitation before answering, body movements, a dry mouth, continuous fidgeting, cold sweat, all indicating the emotional state of the person, may give the officer a clue as to whether or not he is telling the truth. The officer should take care, however, not to place undue emphasis on any one of these items. A flushed face, for example, which might be interpreted as evidence of guilt, may indicate nothing more than anger or embarrassment.

Strategems

When there is strong reason to believe the suspect is guilty and when the regular method of approach to the interview has been unfruitful, other techniques may sometimes be employed to advantage. Since these depend for their success upon the investigator's ability to tell a convincing tale, they should be resorted to by only the most skilled officers.

One technique makes use of the "emotional" approach, designed to arouse the suspect to action. In this, the investigator may discuss the seriousness of the violation and the possible penalties involved, and may appeal to the suspect's pride, ego, or fear. Here, needless to say, a fine line exists between permissible appeal to the suspect's emotions and innuendo or threats which are not permissible and which may invalidate such evidence as may be obtained through this approach.

A second procedure is the "cold shoulder" technique.[7] The suspect is invited to the investigator's office. There the latter takes the attitude that it is agreeable with him if the suspect thinks he can "get by with it." In fact, he refuses to have anything to do with the suspect.

The "hypothetical story" may be used effectively. In this approach a fictitious violation, varying only in minute

---

7.   United States Army, op. cit., p. 53.

details from the actual offense, is related to the suspect.
The investigator later asks the suspect to repeat the hypothetical story back to him and compares it with the actual,
true story. In case the suspect relates the true story
rather than the hypothetical one, he is then confronted with
these inconsistencies. It should be borne in mind that there
are times when an innocent person might accidentally relate
the actual rather than the hypothetical story, but this possibility is indeed rare.

Another technique is the use of the "signed false statement." The suspect is asked to make a sworn written
statement. In case discrepancies appear, they are pointed
out to him to gain a true confession.

The playing of one suspect against another, when two
are believed to have knowledge of or to have participated in
a crime, is yet another technique sometimes used. The
suspects are interrogated separately and one may be told
that the other has confessed to the crime and has implicated
his partner. Some officers feel that this conduct is unethical
and causes the suspects to react against the officer. Among
other things it should be remembered that almost all professional criminals are well aware of such techniques and are
very unlikely to fall for such a flimsy trap.

It is not uncommon to use contrasting-investigator personalities, the one determined and almost insulting, the
other sympathetic and understanding. In this approach the
interview is so arranged that the suspect will play into the
hands of the sympathetic interrogator. A slight deviation
from this is where these two contrasting personalities are
used, one at a time. Just when the suspect is apparently
about to be abused, the sympathetic investigator comes in,
in somewhat of a rage, orders the first investigator out, and
then sympathizes with the suspect. All of this is done, of
course, in the hope that the suspect will break down and confess.

SAFEGUARDING EVIDENCE

The identification and collection of evidence of wildlife
violations is an exacting and ardous task. A great amount
of professional training and field experience is necessary
before competency in these areas is attained.

Since the effectiveness of the wildlife officer is measured to an appreciable degree by his ability to place sufficient admissible evidence in the hands of the prosecuting attorney to justify formal charges against the suspect, it is of the utmost importance that evidence so painstakingly gathered should be carefully safeguarded. Two ways in which this can be done are by substantiating confessions and by observing the chain of custody. The first has already been discussed; the second will be the subject of the following section.

Chain of Custody

Each person who handles a piece of evidence, from the time it is discovered until it is properly linked to the case, should so handle it that the continuous chain of custody will be provable. This includes a complete record as to who has had the material and where it has been stored. This record should include the date, name, time, place, and signature of each person. Each one releasing material should obtain a signature from the receiver. In the event it is sent through the mail, it should be registered. Technicians handling film should place an identifying mark on the edge of the negative and on the back of the final prints. Failure to keep intact this chain of custody may render vital evidence inadmissible.

AIDS TO AND RESTRICTIONS ON EVIDENCE

While the investigator is gathering evidence to support his charge that a suspect has violated a wildlife law, he should bear in mind some of the aids which the courts have provided for his use. He should also recognize the restrictions which, while safeguarding the rights of the suspect, make it more difficult for the officer to marshall sufficient evidence to support the charge.

Judicial Aids

Included among those aids which the officer may use in preparing his brief for the prosecuting attorney are judicial notice, official records, and prima-facie evidence; proof of character and character of the accused; modus operandi; and double jeopardy. Each one will be discussed in turn.

Judicial notice. Certain kinds of facts need not be proved by the formal presentation of evidence, because the court is authorized to recognize their existence without such proof. This recognition is termed a judicial notice. [8] That is, it is assumed to be known for a certainty or, in other words, it is common knowledge. Examples of such judicial notice are (1) the statutes of the several states or those of the Federal Government; (2) the day of the week a given date of the month was on; (3) the ordinary divisions of time into years, months, weeks, or other periods; (4) general facts and laws of nature, including ordinary operations in effects and general facts of history; (5) the political organization and the chief officials of the government of the United States, of its territories and possessions, of the District of Columbia, and of the several states of the United States; (6) the signatures and duties of persons attesting official documents,. or copies thereof, kept under the authority of any governmental agency of the United States; (7) the treaties of the United States, and executive agreements between the United States and any state of the United States or between the United States and any foreign country; (8) current political or de facto conditions of war and peace; (9) organic and public laws, including regulations having the force of law; (10) the seals of courts of record, and the seals of public offices and officers of the United States and its territories and possessions; (11) the public laws or regulations having the force of law in effect in any country or territory or political subdivision occupied by the armed forces of the United States. ·

Official records. An official record is a statement in writing made of a certain fact or event. For example, when an officer or other person, in the performance of an official duty imposed on him by law or custom, states facts or ascertains the truth of a matter, and the channels of information have been demonstrated to be trustworthy, this is deemed to be an official record. In this connection it may be presumed prima facie:

1. That a person who has performed such a duty performed it properly;

---

8.   United States Government, op. cit., p. 273.

2. That a foreign or domestic record which reflects a fact or is even required to be recorded by law, regulation, or custom was made by a person so required to make it, provided the record is authenticated as an original copy;

3. That foreign or domestic records which are thus authenticated and shown to be on file in a public office and which reflect facts or events of a kind generally recorded by public officials, such as births, deaths, marriages, etc., were made by persons who in official duty by law or regulation are accustomed to record such facts and to know or ascertain through appropriate and trustworthy channels of information the truth thereof.

Maps, photographs, X-rays, sketches, and similar projections of localities, objects, persons, and other matters are admissible as official records when verified by any person, whether or not he made or took them, if he is personally acquainted with the locality, object, person, or any other thing thereby represented or pictured, and if he is able, from his own personal knowledge or observation, to state that they actually represented the appearance of the subject matter in question.

Prima-facie evidence. This evidence, like presumptions, is set up by rules of law. Because the burden of proving absolutely everything involved in a case is almost impossible, legislatures have established that certain facts are self-evident, the burden of proof falling on the defendant.

To make a prima-facie case, the officer simply presents the facts which, according to law, constitute a violation; and after that, it is up to the accused to explain away these facts, unless he is willing to risk conviction. Conviction is not automatic, but the burden of proof is on the defendant rather than on the prosecutor. For example, a law may state that it is illegal to use or possess salmon eggs, and that possession is prima-facie evidence of guilt. Then, if a person is found in possession of salmon eggs, he is guilty under the law. In some states the possession of a deer jack-light is prima-facie evidence of jack-lighting.

Proof of character. Whenever the character of a person is admissible in a case, the opinion of a witness as to that person's character may be received in evidence if it is first shown that the witness has an acquaintance or relationship with the person in question so as to qualify him to form a reliable opinion. Another method of establishing character is by dealing with the general reputation which a person holds in a community in which he lives or pursues his business or profession. In this case, the testimony must come from a person who has actually lived in the community and has formed the opinion as a result of having been a member of the community. For example, admissible evidence in this case cannot be given by a person sent into a community with the specific job of investigating the character of the accused.

<u>Character of the accused</u>. The general rule in evidence is that an accused may not have evidence of his bad moral character introduced against him for the purpose of raising inference of guilt. In order to show a probability of innocence, an accused person may introduce evidence of his own good character as well as the fact that he is a moral, well-behaved, law-abiding citizen.

Evidence of particular traits of character are inadmissible as evidence unless there is a reasonable tendency to show that the particular trait indicates the improbability of the offender's having committed some particular offense. For example, it is assumed that a person who has never broken a fish and game law is less likely to have done so than a person who has a long list of proven fish and game violations against him. As a general rule, character traits which are not directly involved in the charge against the accused are used only for the purpose of raising an inference that the accused may have a disposition to act in a particular manner.

However, in some cases evidence of other offenses may have substantial value as tending to prove something other than facts to be inferred about the disposition of the accused. Some of these examples are listed below.

1. The evidence tends to identify the accused as the perpetrator of an offense. An example of this is where two game violations have been committed in an area. The character of the two acts is similar, and the accused has previously been convicted of one. It may reasonably be assumed that he is also involved in the second violation. Another example of this identification is where the accused leaves a piece of personal property at the scene of the offense. To connect the personal property with the accused is to connect him with the offense.

A third example relates to the suspect's method of operating when engaged in committing a violation. Here again, identification of a <u>modus operandi</u> employed may lead directly to the accused.

2. The evidence tends to prove a plan or design of the accused.

3. The evidence tends to prove guilty knowledge or intent, if such knowledge or intent is an element of the charged offense. In this case, a person charged with killing game on posted land but who claims he did not know it was illegal could be confronted with evidence that on a previous occasion he had been accused and convicted of a similar act. However, a previous assault charge can not be used to indicate a tendency toward assault if the assault on the first person was under different circumstances and presumably with different intent.

4. The evidence tends to prove a motive. For example, proof that a person had obligated himself to kill quail to be later sold to a certain party would be sufficient evidence of motive that this person would be interested in killing quail. Another example is that previous evidence of having falsified daily work sheets in order to cover up the fact that he had not, in fact, been at work at all on that particular day would be evidence tending to prove that the person was not where he had avowed himself to be, and that he could have, indeed, been hunting quail as was charged.

This judicial aid provides the officer with yet another valuable tool. The fact that he is able to connect the suspect in any of the afore-mentioned ways with the commission of the offense permits him to go before the court with a much-strengthened hand.

<u>Modus operandi.</u> One of the fundamental concepts in crime investigation is that certain criminals have methods of operation which are peculiar to their individual behavior. That is, they develop, perhaps subconsciously, patterns and habits which they tend to display each time they commit a crime.

The study and cataloguing of operations have become so specialized that certain city police forces are at times able to predict approximately when and where a certain type of crime will be attempted; therefore, in many cases, officers

are able to prevent the commission of crime. Many
criminals have some peculiarity which may identify a
crime as belonging to that individual. Such habits as chew-
ing gum, breaking up match sticks, or spitting; peculiarities
of speech or eating; and certain nervous mannerisms all
may point to some individual or at least to a group of individuals who have these habits, peculiarities, or mannerisms
in common.

In the field of wildlife violation, an example of how
modus operandi helps the officer to apprehend a violator
and later to supply the prosecution with additional admissible evidence is seen in the case of illegal hunting. An individual, while engaged in illegal hunting, may follow a constant pattern of driving along back roads just at twilight, of
shooting game from an automobile, and then of speeding
away, with the intention of returning later to retrieve it.
Having encountered such behavior previously, the officer can
so station himself that he is able to surprise the offender in
the act of violation. Later, the signed and dated entry of
this case in the officer's field notes may be incorporated
into the brief he prepares for the prosecuting attorney.

Double jeopardy. In fish and game violations, it is possible to prosecute a violator twice as the result of a particular act. This happens when two separate sets of laws govern the management of certain game animals, notably migratory waterfowl. Thus, not only are state laws passed
in connection with such waterfowl, but Congress, having
power to make treaties, has entered into agreements with
Canada and Mexico to help manage, on a reciprocal basis,
the migratory bird resource.

As a result, a person may be charged in a state court
with violating a given law for some specific act, and he may
again be taken before a federal court for the same act. Because the courts hold that this does not infringe upon his
constitutional rights concerning double jeopardy, the officer
may press a charge of violation in both the state and federal
court. This may happen when a legal loophole found by the
defense in the first instance has been plugged by the prosecution before the case goes to the second court. Because
of this legal ruling concerning double jeopardy, the officer's hand is strengthened in his efforts to manage wisely
the wildlife in his area, and he may press the accusation

against the suspect with a double-barreled charge, so to speak.

Judicial Restrictions

The judicial aids just discussed work in favor of the wildlife law enforcement officer. On the other side of the medallion are judicial restrictions; these may work in favor of the suspect.

In order that the law violator be not found innocent of the charge because of insufficient or inadmissible evidence, the officer should remain acutely aware of these restrictions on evidence. Among them are included testimonial knowledge, hearsay evidence, rules of privilege, corpus delicti, and reasonable doubt.

Testimonial knowledge. Ordinarily, a witness may testify only to what he has learned through his own senses. That is, an officer may testify that he heard a shot in a thicket. Later, when he investigated the thicket, he found the apparently freshly killed carcass of a deer and that the person now before the court is the one that was seen leaving the thicket. He cannot testify by his own knowledge that the person leaving the thicket was the one who killed the deer, although circumstantial evidence would justifiably permit this inference. Thus, a point of evidence on which the officer might have relied could be adjudged inadmissible.

There are many exceptions to this rule. One of the common ones is that a person may testify as to his own age, including the date of his birth, even though he obviously does not know this of his own knowledge.

Hearsay evidence. Normally, a witness may not give testimony which is not his own. In other words, he may not make statements which are not from his own observations, or which were made by someone else and repeated to him. However, all third party statements are not hearsay. It depends on the purpose of the testimony and why it is being introduced. For example, a person may testify as to a statement made by another individual, and it is fact and not hearsay that the conversation was carried on. Whether or not the third person was actually stating the truth, and whether his evidence is admissible as such, is another question. If the testimony is introduced only to show that there was a conversation about a particular subject carried on between the witness and a third party, then the testimony is admissible as such.

There are numerous exceptions to the rule that hearsay evidence may not be introduced. One of these was covered in part in the Montana Supreme Court case of the State v. Russell. [9] Hearsay evidence was used, but it was brought out by a preliminary question that it was wholly immaterial to the case, and it was claimed that the defendant was not prejudiced thereby. The defendant was convicted by the justice of the peace court for unlawfully taking fish from a stream by the use of fishberries ground up with meat.

The case was appealed to the District Court where Russell was again found guilty. From judgment and an order denying him a new trial, Russell appealed to the Supreme Court of Montana. The proceedings follow:

1. An attack was made upon the complaint by the defendant, but court held that the complaint was sufficient to charge the unlawful taking of fish from a stream of the state.

2. The defendant claimed that the trial court admitted certain hearsay evidence. A witness of the state had testified that he was prompted to make a report to the deputy game warden because the Wagner boys told him someone down the river was killing fish. This explanatory evidence was hearsay, but it was brought out by a preliminary question that it was wholly immaterial, and it was inconceivable that any substantial right of the defendant was prejudiced by it.

The Supreme Court held that the only fair deduction from the evidence produced by the state is that the defendant deposited in the Bitter Root River, in Ravalli County, fishberries ground up with meat which were eaten by the fish, with the result that they were stupefied and rendered easy prey; that while the fish were in this condition the defendant, by means of a landing net, took at least one fish from the river. Had the jury believed the evidence offered by the defense, a different verdict would have been required. The only conclusion from the verdict is that no credence whatever was given to the story told by the defendant and his companions. There was evidence in the record to justify the verdict.

Rules of privilege. Under certain conditions, the defendant has what is known as the rule of privilege, or

9.   State v. Russell, Pacific Reporter, Vol. 160, p. 655, Montana.

privileged communication. The oldest of these is in regard to the relationship between the attorney and his client. It is the privilege of the client to forbid his attorney to testify in regard to any confidential communication made by the defendant to the attorney. If this were not the case, defendants would be afraid to go to lawyers and discuss their problems because of the possibility of having the information used against them.

Husband and wife are competent witnesses in favor of each other. They are also competent witnesses against each other, but the general rule is that both are entitled to a privilege prohibiting the use of one of them against the other. This privilege does not exist when the husband or wife is injured by the offense with which the spouse is charged. Examples of this are: assault on one spouse by another, bigamy, polygamy, unlawful cohabitation, the use of the wife for immoral purposes, and forgery by one spouse under certain conditions. An existing privilege may be waived by both spouses.

In many states a doctor cannot, over the objection of his patient, be permitted to testify regarding confidential information, unless the court rules that it is in the interest of justice. In addition, no person accused of a crime may be compelled to give evidence against himself. [10] This is known as privilege against self-incrimination. A confession obtained under duress or promise of leniency may later be excluded from evidence on the basis that it is violating the right against self-incrimination.

The officer should probably be more concerned with rules of privilege relating to husband and wife testimony and to self-incrimination, although on occasion he may deal with the others. It is well for him to remember that in court he cannot count on evidence which at the scene of the violation a man's wife may furnish or promise to furnish against her sportsman husband. Neither can he expect the accused person to go before the court and voluntarily incriminate himself, even though he might have promised the officer at the time of the arrest that he would "go to court and tell the truth about the whole thing." The wise

---

10.   Constitution of the United States, Fifth Amendment, currently used so freely by communists.

officer knows that he must forge his chain of evidence without these links.

Corpus delicti. The corpus delicti, or substance of the crime, must be produced before there can be a conviction. From time immemorial, the courts have said that a crime cannot be proven merely by the confession of the accused. It has been said that this is the first rule in a law book. Officers should bear this in mind when they are collecting evidence for a trial and should never lean entirely and absolutely on a confession if it is possible to gather other material in addition. Such additional evidence may be in the form of confiscated game or weapons, or it may be nothing more than the statement of a witness.

Reasonable doubt. In spite of all the efforts of the wildlife officer to gather evidence enough to convict a suspect whom he strongly believes to be guilty, it often happens that the courts find him innocent. The evidence just would not support the charge.

It is necessary that the court (and/or jury) be satisfied beyond all reasonable doubt that the accused is guilty before a verdict of guilty may be brought in. This means not fanciful or ingenious doubts or unwarranted speculation but rather an honest, substantial, conscientious doubt as suggested by the evidence, or lack of it, in the case. It should be a misgiving, generated by insufficient proof of guilt, and not a doubt suggested by the ingenuity of the counsel, nor a doubt born of merciful inclination, or personal prejudice as in the case of an attractive woman. The rule of reasonable doubt extends to every element of an offense as charged. This means that if a person appears to be guilty of a lesser charge, he must be declared innocent as accused if there is a reasonable doubt, based on the evidence presented, that he is guilty. This does not mean that every fact advanced by the prosecution must be proved beyond a reasonable doubt; it rather means that there is an over-all sufficient amount of evidence to warrant a conviction, and that on the whole the court is satisfied beyond a reasonable doubt that the accused is guilty.

THE QUESTION OF INSANITY

There are times when it is necessary to consider the sanity of an individual who has been apprehended for a wildlife violation. The question of insanity may come either before or at any time during the trial.

A person is said to be insane if he lacks mental responsibility. He is not mentally responsible for a crime or wildlife violation if at the time of the alleged offense he was suffering from mental defects, disease, or derangement to the extent that his impairment deprived him of his ability to distinguish right from wrong.

Mental diseases as such do not amount to insanity. Nor does insanity constitute proper defense for a person of low intellect who commits an offense under the delusion that he is righting a wrong as long as he knew at the time of the act that it was contrary to law and he was not acting under an irrestible impulse. On the other hand, an accused is not responsible for an act if, as a result of a mental disease, he believed that his act was legally and morally correct. A mere defect of character, will power, or behavior is not grounds for declaring the suspect even temporarily insane.

However, even though the suspect may have been entirely sane at the time the alleged offense was committed, he should not be brought to trial if he is considered mentally irresponsible at the time of the trial. This ruling rests upon the principle that the accused should possess sufficient mental capacity to understand the nature of the proceedings against him and to intelligently conduct or cooperate with his own defense.

Normally, the accused is initially presumed to be sane and to have been sane at the time of the violation. Only when there is substantial evidence that the accused was insane at the time of the offense or is insane at the time of the trial is the question of his sanity an essential issue. Such evidence may be introduced by the prosecution, by the defense, or on behalf of the court and is usually based on previous observation of the suspect's behavior or other evidence or on the demeanor of the accused in court. Once the issue has been raised, the burden of proving the sanity of the accused is on the prosecution.

In general, a medical board having at least one member trained in psychiatry passes on the sanity of an individual, although lay witnesses may state their opinion of his general mental condition, as judged by the bounds of common experience. If it is found that the accused is mentally responsible, then the trial proceeds as usual; however, if he is judged as having been mentally irresponsible for his acts at the time of the alledged violation, the court will enter a finding of not guilty as to the charges and specifications. If there is reasonable doubt as to the mental capacity of the accused at the time of trial, the court will adjourn until such time as the proper mental capacity of the individual has been established.

Because of the possibility that a suspected violator, in order to escape the onerous experience of arrest and public trial, may feign mental irresponsibility for his unlawful actions, the wildlife officer should be constantly alert to clues which will support his belief that the suspect is in normal command of his mental faculties. On the other hand, if because of evidence relating to "proof of character" the officer has any grounds for believing the suspect to be mentally incompetent, he should avoid placing himself in the untenable position of pressing formal charges against him and setting the legal machinery in motion for court action. His case will simply collapse if defense or the court raises the question of insanity.

As regards those cases where the question of insanity is not an issue, or where it has been resolved in favor of the prosecution, the officer must strive to build up a sufficiency of evidence against the suspect, utilizing every possible lead that his professional training and that present-day techniques of scientific crime detection and analysis provide. This leads to a discussion of the crime laboratory and its services.

CRIME LABORATORY UTILIZATION

Modern developments in the science of crime detection and analysis center around the crime laboratory, a necessary adjunct to the facilities of any large city police department. It is in here that highly-skilled technicians, using ingenious instruments and proven methods, lay bare the life story of the most minute particles of matter believed connected with a law violation. The wildlife law enforcement officer should know when and how to make use of the many services of the laboratory.

At the scene of some violations there are certain items which can be collected that later prove to be relevant and material evidence. There are certain definite procedures which should be followed when these materials are to be forwarded to a crime laboratory for expert analyses.

Blood and Similar Matter

In fish and game cases, blood or other body fluids are frequently deposited on the terrain. Although many things such as rust, paint, mud, food, sealing wax, grease, or vegetable matter may have the appearance of blood, their actual identity can be determined by chemical analysis.

Anything believed to be human or game-animal blood should be preserved. Blood or bloodstained material, before being sent to the laboratory, should be allowed to dry thoroughly without the benefit of artificial light, fans, or direct sunlight. If it has dried thoroughly prior to packaging, sterile containers are not necessary. Samples of liquid blood should be shipped to the laboratory air mail special-delivery, in a sterile container.

Certain determinations can be made at the scene of the violation by examining bloodstains. For example, it is possible to determine the direction of the fall of blood by noting the shape and height of the circular disk formed by the drop of blood. The direction in which blood has fallen is indicated by the shape of the stain. [11] Blood which falls at an angle makes an elongated or pear-shaped stain. The narrow end of the stain points in the direction in which the blood fell or was propelled. That is, the neck points toward the direction the blood loser was traveling. The height from which the blood was fallen vertically is indicated by the amount of spattering which has occurred as an etch of the circular stain.

Another consideration is the amount of clotting. Bloodstains normally clot in 10 to 20 minutes at ordinary temperatures. When blood first clots, the cells form a jelly-like mass with a liquid serum. Bloodstains dry in varying lengths of time, depending on temperature and humidity. A drop of blood normally requires from one to two hours to dry completely. It is believed that a bloodstain of average depth which covers an area of two to two and one-half

---

11.   United States Army, op. cit., p. 67.

inches in diameter would require more than an hour to dry completely under ordinary conditions. Bloodstains dry on the outer edge first and more quickly on non-absorbent material than on absorbent. The color of a dry bloodstain is affected to some degree by the type of background and length of exposure to sunlight. [12]

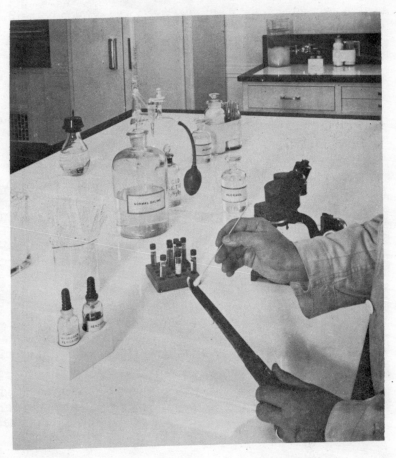

Courtesy Federal Bureau of Investigation

Figure 33. Conducting a test on a knife to determine the presence of blood in the Serological Section of the FBI Laboratory, Washington, D. C.

12. Ibid.

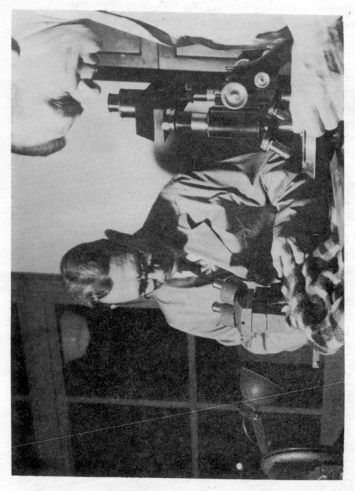

Courtesy Federal Bureau of Investigation

Figure 34. Technician (left) examines clothing under a microscope in an examination of fibers. On the right the technician examines hair under the comparison microscope. FBI Laboratory, Washington, D. C.

Hair Identification

In every case, hair or fiber from the scene of the violation should be carefully preserved. It should be picked up with forceps, placed in a folded sheet of paper, sealed with pressure-sensitive tape, and forwarded to a laboratory for analysis. Care should be taken to avoid dislodging any foreign particles adhering to hair or fiber.

Hair or fur fibers frequently may be identified by microscopic examination of the surface structure. In the event the officer should desire to make the identification himself by comparison with known specimens, he may refer to a publication such as Hardy and Plitt. [13] Hair surface structures may also be studied by making plastic impressions. The process is similar to that used in impressioning fish scales.

Fingerprints

All latent fingerprints submitted to a laboratory should, if at all possible, be accompanied by the fingerprint record of the suspects. When the presence of 12 or more points of similarity has been demonstrated, it has been the practice of the United States courts to accept this as a means of identifying fingerprints. In the case of unusual ridge characteristics, as few as six or seven points are considered sufficient. Single fingerprints of a limited number of outstanding criminals and of criminals who may specialize in certain types of crimes are indexed in the Identification Division of the Federal Bureau of Investigation.

It is essential that the officer have a thorough knowledge of the basic principles of fingerprinting if fingerprints are to be properly taken and prepared for transmittal to a law enforcement agency, such as the Federal Bureau of Investigation. This may appear to be an insurmountable obstacle to the officer, but the conscientious and far-sighted one will go ahead with it until he has mastered the techniques and understands the principles involved. Two manuals dealing with this subject which are recommended for

---

13.   J. I. Hardy and Thora M. Plitt. 1940. An improved method for revealing the surface structure of fur fibers. U. S. Fish and Wildlife Service Wildlife Circular 7. pp. 1-10.

study by the members of the wildlife law enforcement service are available at the Superintendent of Documents, U.S. Government, Washington, D.C. [14]

Fingerprint identification is based on the fact that no two fingerprints are ever identical and that they may not be obliterated permanently by the destruction of all of the surface tissue. Some of the areas in the vicinity of the crime which may be searched for prints are those of entrance and exit; any place where the suspect may have had a tendency to place fingers, such as doorknobs or frameworks; any place where there is dust; and any shiny, smooth surface, such as window glass. Prints may be developed with powder of various chemicals, such as iodine fumes and silver nitrate, or they may be photographed. Prints may be lifted by the use of commercially available lifting tapes or by scotch tape in the event these are not available.

Firearms and Ammunition

Firearms identification is the science of identifying bullets, cartridges, and weapons. This science is based on the premise that no two things are exactly alike. Few, if any, field officers are capable of making all of these identifications; and if they were, they probably could not be qualified as an expert in court. Therefore, it is desirable that these items be sent to the state crime laboratory or to the F.B.I.

The cartridge case, as well as the projectile, has marks peculiar to the gun from which it is fired. In addition, it is desirable to have a sketch of the area, showing the exact location of the projectile, cartridge case, and weapon. When the gun is to be handled, it should be picked up carefully so that any fingerprints present will not be obliterated. It may be possible to recover projectiles from game-animal carcasses and later to compare these with bullets fired from guns of suspects.

Firearms, projectiles, empty cartridge cases, and live ammunition should be transmitted by wrapping them securely in a box. This prevents scratching or shifting; the container should be properly labelled on the outside. In the event live

---

14.   Army Field Manual, FM 19-20, and Technical Manual, TM 10-632.

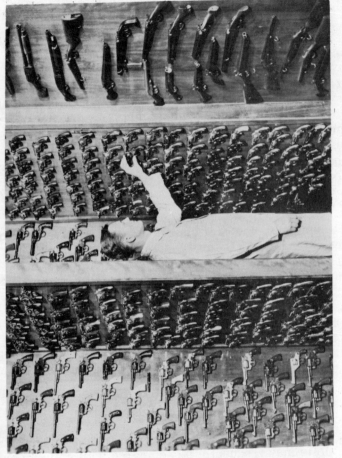

Figure 35. A portion of the firearms reference collection in the FBI Laboratory.

ammunition is to be shipped, it should be labelled as such and must be sent via railway express, as it cannot be sent through the mails. Normally, up to five rounds of ammunition should be included if that much is available. In all cases, as much information as is available concerning the make of weapon, caliber, and serial number should be included. Weapons should be tagged, and projectiles, ammunition, and cartridge cases should be individually marked.

If at all possible, weapons should be transmitted unloaded. As a precaution against a mistake, a final check should be made just before these are shipped. In the event it is impossible to unload them or it is highly desirable that they be left loaded, then they should be transmitted by railway express and a letter of transmittal should give this information. The wooden box in which they are shipped should be appropriately marked on the outside, and the guns should be properly labelled.

Glass Fragments

All suspicious pieces of glass at the scene of a violation should be retained. Laboratory examination may indicate the type of glass, the manufacturer, where the glass came from, and, in the event it was broken by a blow from a stick or bullet, the direction and angle of impact. If there is a series of holes in a sheet of glass, the sequence in which they were made may also be established. Automobiles or trucks traveling narrow, brushy lands may frequently have headlights, tail lights, or running lights broken out, and these fragments of glass may better help to identify the automotive vehicle used in the offense.

Soil Samples

The soil from the suspect's shoes or from the tires of an automobile may frequently be compared with soil samples removed from the scene of the violation. Some of the things a soil examination may indicate are the geological origin, area of origin, and similarity between the soil from the suspect's person or automobile and that from the violation area. Soil containers should normally be not less than a pint in size and preferably larger. The container should be sealed with tape, properly labelled on the outside, and transmitted by registered mail, along with complete information as to the area covered, the depth at which it was

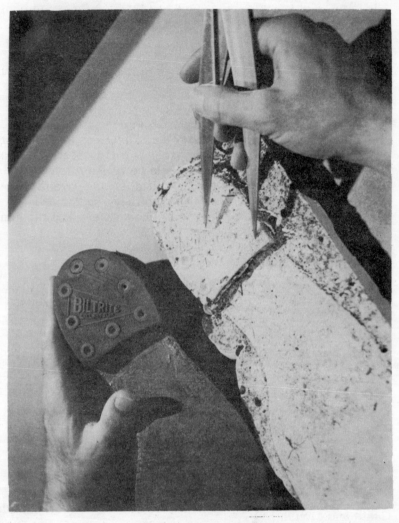

Figure 36. An examiner in the FBI Laboratory comparing the heel of a suspect's shoe with that of a cast made at the scene of a crime.

Courtesy Federal Bureau of Investigation

Figure 37. An examiner is shown comparing a plaster cast, made at the scene of a crime, against the FBI Laboratory reference file of tire impressions.

taken, whether or not it was the A, B, or C soil horizon, and the amount of litter on the ground in the area.

Casts and Moulds

Casts of shoe prints or tire tracks may be sent to the laboratory for identification or for comparison with other material. Particles of soil or other matter adhering to a shoe or tire may also be sent for examination and comparison. Casts should be properly marked, just previous to setting if possible, wrapped in soft material, packed in a rigid outer box, and transmitted by registered mail or by railway express.

Generally, casts and moulds are made originally from plaster of paris, which may be the grade used either by commercial artists or by dental laboratories. Substitutes include casein glue, cement, plastic, paraffin, or occasionally tallow. Plaster of paris is particularly well suited for such things as impressions of tires, shoe prints, and other marks which are in soft earth or snow. Moulds are simply the negative made from a positive cast. For example, the impression of a tire is recreated from a plaster of paris mould of the track.

The instructions for making plaster of paris casts are from <u>Army Field Manual</u>, FM 19-20. [15] The thickness of the material needs to be at least one inch plus the depth of the cast. The material is mixed in a glass, rubber, or plastic container. If the plaster of paris is caked or packed, it should be fluffed and run through a sieve. It should be mixed thoroughly and the container shaken to remove air bubbles. Thin mixtures produce better detail but take longer to set. In the event the mixture is too thick, it must be discarded rather than thinned.

Mixtures begin to set up immediately after preparation. If coloring is to be added, it should be put in the water before the plaster. The setting process may be hurried by adding salt or alum in the proportion of one-half teaspoon of salt per pint, or one teaspoon of alum per quart of water. The setting process may be slowed by adding a teaspoon of sugar or one part of borax solution to 10 parts of water. Borax also assists in making a sharper and harder cast. Potassium sulphate solution may be added, one part to 10 parts of water, to prevent expansion of the cast when that is desirable. Plaster casts harden in 20-50 minutes. During the setting-up process, the mixture becomes warm. When it begins to cool, this is evidence that it has hardened sufficiently to be removed. Casts should be marked as evidence as soon as they begin to cool rather than when they have become completely hard.

Impressions in such soft substances as sand or dust should be stiffened with a sprayed shellac, commercial art fixitive, or plastic before they are cast. The dry fixitives

15. United States Army, <u>op. cit.</u>, pp. 217-222.

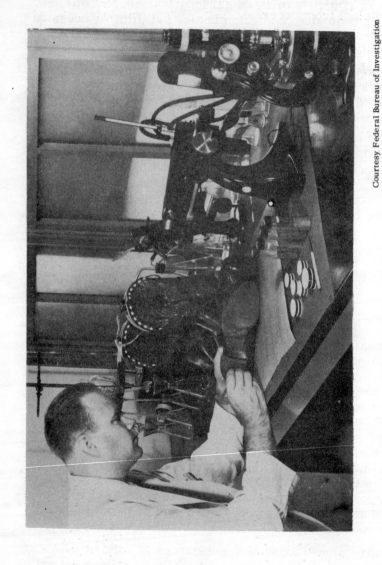

Figure 38. In the Petrography Unit of the FBI Laboratory soil is being removed from a suspect's shoes for mineral analysis.

should be coated with some light oil, such as machine oil, before the plaster is poured into them. Prints in snow should be coated with fine talcum to prevent the snow from being melted from generated heat. When reinforcement material is required, it should be added after about half of the plaster has been poured into the area to be cast.

Completed casts may be further hardened by dipping them in a cold alum bath; previous to this they never should be washed or scrubbed, since this removes detail. Casts should be cleaned only by an expert. Material for making casts and moulds may be obtained from paint stores or from law enforcement equipment-supply houses.

CHAPTER XI

The Future of Law Enforcement

Wildlife administrators are facing a new day and a multitude of new problems. The rapid turn-over of state directors is not entirely the result of an occupational hazard; it is in many ways the outcome of their own incompetence and inability to foresee and solve the problems involved in a complex organization. The directors of tomorrow, like safety engineers, must foresee and forestall the hazards of their job and their department. Some directors are now demonstrating that it is entirely feasible for highly trained technical men to be top administrators. A few of tomorrow's problems that should be solved today are discussed here.

Unless the moral holiday is stopped in some vacation areas, it may be necessary to have special legislation to prevent the excessive use of alcohol on fishing and hunting expeditions.

If the number of violations involving minors persists, it may be advantageous to more freely use the charge of "contributing to the delinquency of a minor" on parents.

Although it is desirable to change fish and game laws as little as possible, in order to keep the public acquainted with current laws, nevertheless it is very desirable to re-draw all poorly stated or antiquated laws promptly. In view of the present confusion and lack of agreement among authorities, it would appear well to encourage further research by competent university people and others on the aspects of sportsmanship, motives, attitudes, and rationalization which are involved in wildlife violations.

Sometimes a law is so unrealistic or so poorly drawn or so out-of-date that it is almost self-evident that it will be violated. Such a law should be removed from the books as soon as possible. It is desirable, however, that it be enforced as long as it is on the books. Otherwise, an attitude of abiding by only the "practical laws" may be adopted by the enforcement personnel and by the public.

JUDGES AND JURIES

In recent years the courts have come under considerable fire for their attitude toward fish and game laws.
Some judges feel the attitude of the court in many cases reflects that of the people, and that changing the attitude of
the court is not that of changing a relatively few judges but
of changing the vast populace who support these particular
judges.

Kelly[1] quotes a judge as believing the kid-glove treatment used on violators is simply a reflection of public attitude. He states that this is undoubtedly true but asks if it
should be. Kelly further states:

> A judge's office makes him a teacher of responsibilities.
> His authority gives him a firm hand in molding public behavior.
> He is a leader, not a follower. Suppose a fifth-grade teacher
> permitted herself to reflect the instincts of her pupils?[2]

It has been said that the administration of criminal law
in the United States is a disgrace to our civilization.[3] In
England, where criminal law originated, many reforms have
been made, but relatively few of those have occurred in
America. Many jurists believe that the present Justice of
the Peace Courts are inadequate. The sentencing ability of
judges has been objectively criticized. It has been suggested
that youth and adult correction authorities have a responsibility that should be considered more seriously. The
present-day use of excessive fines is considered by many to
be unsound from the rehabilitation standpoint. This should
be studied intensively and objectively. At present many
states consider the use of adverse publicity, that is, the publicizing of fish and game violations, as an effective enforcement tool. This is undoubtedly true for the stalwart citizen,
who feels that he must not at any price have his name published in the paper as a law violator. However, this is little
or no deterrent to the chronic violator. There are, on the
other hand, several reasons why it is undesirable to publicize the names of fish and game violators, and the offense
and punishment: such a system points to the wide diversity

---

1.   Claude Kelly. 1953. What our courts must learn: game laws are no
     joke! Utah Fish and Game Bulletin 10.6. p. 8.
2.   Ibid.
3.   Edwin H. Sutherland, op. cit., p. 277.

of punishment that is meted out for the same crime and leads to discontent and a sense of unfair practice, which is generally charged to the fish and game department; the punishment, including fines and jail sentences, is in many cases actually incorrect because of the failure to state the suspension of either part or all of the fine or of the jail sentence, again leading to what appears to be a wide diversity of punishment for identical crimes. Possibly the most important objection to publicly announcing lists of violators and their punishment is that it frequently causes a contest to develop between officers, which may turn them into man-hunting cops rather than conservation officers.

Fish and game departments will help much by keeping wildlife laws simple and to the point. There should be as few changes as possible from year to year, but at the same time unenforceable or out-of-date laws should be removed. Because sporting equipment--particularly guns--are frequently highly prized by the owner, it is desirable that an officer taking possession of equipment should make his position quite clear. Normally, guns or other equipment cannot be confiscated by conservation officers but only by the court. When equipment is confiscated it is generally later sold at public auction. There have been times in the past when a great deal of animosity has been incurred because overly-confident officers have not adequately explained the legal procedure. It may be desirable to go further and set definite advance dates, for example, the first Monday in every third month, for confiscation sales. In this way there can be no reasonable charge of inadequately publicizing the sale.

ENFORCEMENT PERSONNEL

It has been said that an enforcement unit is no stronger than its weakest link. Whether or not a service is respected depends to a very large degree on what the public thinks of the individuals who enforce the laws. All too frequently the public judges an entire service by some thoughtless or discourteous act on the part of one or two individuals. Unfortunately, many fish and game departments have set salaries and entrance standards of enforcement officers below that of other employees. As a result, the quality of enforcement personnel has not been what it should be, in spite of the fact that most people consider the enforcement officer to be the Conservation Department representative.

In view of the difficult assignment given most officers, it would seem desirable to select the top men in the field. It has been said that education is so important to the solution of problems in human relations that the blame for many malpractices can be directly attributed to this lack of proper training or education.

It is inconceivable, other things being equal, that an enforcement officer can be more capable than a biologist when the biologist has had four or more years college training and the enforcement officer has had little or none. Yet in spite of this, the enforcement officer is frequently expected to recognize and deal with all phases of wildlife management, to enforce laws, and to carry on an educational program all at the same time. It is far more desirable to have a small number of adequately trained, highly competent officers, rather than the frequent practice of increasing duties and assignments without increasing either salary or professional standards. Enforcement officers are first of all law enforcement officers, but they should also be wildlife specialists and individuals with considerable knowledge of human psychology and group behavior. Their pay scale and performance records should be based on all of these attributes. Unfortunately, in some cases, enforcement officers consider themselves as policemen only and look to other law enforcement groups for salary and training comparisons. This leads to friction and to a rift between divisions of the Conservation Department. It is surprising how much some enforcement officers believe that the only reason a law has failed is that it has inadequate teeth in it, and that given the proper laws no enforcement problems would exist. This age-old and time-worn philosophy should be refuted as often as it comes up.

Officers must be made to realize that in order for them to be effective agents they cannot themselves be lawless. This is particularly true when they go before court. An officer whose private life is above reproach will inspire the confidence and trust of the public. On the other hand, one who allows favors to friends, who uses alcohol on the job, who has the manhunting attitude toward sportsmen, will never succeed in any very large degree. It is well recognized that the public demands of its servants more exacting and exemplary conduct than it expects of private citizens. The enforcement officer of tomorrow should be well-trained and adequately educated, and there should be sufficient personnel to properly carry on enforcement as well as limited management and educational work. Training and education of conservation officers should be on a comparable basis with the other professional conservationists, such as the research biologist. A merit system with a standard job sheet and a performance sheet is a must for a conservation department. The machinery should be so set up that competent, ambitious men can be promoted and the incompetent, or unwilling, be readily and summarily dismissed. It should be recognized that eventually college-trained men will fulfill most or all of the enforcement positions. This offers a tremendous opportunity to future conservation personnel. It does so because of two reasons: first, the enforcement group comprises by far the largest single unit of conservation personnel in the United States; and second, because this group is the most heterogeneous age group. It also offers a much better chance for administrators to make deserved in-service promotions.

Enforcement work, as well as all other phases of conservation, should be entirely divorced from politics.

Officers should be given well-marked, preferably passenger, cars which will be recognized by the public. Administrators may want to seriously consider using marked cars for all conservation employees in order to demonstrate to the public the extent of conservation personnel activities. All officers should be required to have both field and dress uniforms which are comparable with those used by the more progressive state highway patrol officers. Undercover men wearing civilian clothes and driving unmarked, unlisted cars can carry on such activities as are required of this particular group. It should be recognized that the average American citizen has an inherent respect for the high-grade, uniformed police officer; and that, in itself, will do much toward creating the proper respect for fish and game laws.

NEW LAWS--OLD LAWS

Poorly defined and ill-marked boundaries of hunting or fishing units are an invitation for trouble to enforcement officers and administrators alike. All boundary lines should

be clearly and adequately defined and should be set where
they are easy to find. New laws, or ones that have been
troublesome in the past, should be publicized frequently in
a popular fashion, locally and statewide. It should be recognized that the best laws are those which say the least. Kelly[4]
points out that some conservation administration problems
stem from making frequent and difficult changes in the law.
He further quotes a young circuit judge as saying that administrators have encouraged wardens to concentrate on
minor and technical infractions. This, the judge believes,
is why some courts take a dim view of game laws and of
those who administer them. Kelly concludes by saying that
we need simpler laws and we need sound enforcement, but
more than anything else we need to teach the public to practice conservation and respect conservation laws.

OFFICERS OF TOMORROW

The gun-toting, man-hunting warden of yesterday is
going and in his place will come a competent enforcement
officer trained in all phases of wildlife management. This
man, believing in the value of a technical college degree,
will build an integrated program of enforcement, management, and public education. He will wear a distinctive, high-
class uniform and will ride in a well-marked fish-and-game-
department automobile. There will be better law enforcement and better laws than there have ever been before. This
will have been made possible by a more informed and sympathetic public. This officer will command and receive the
same respect as his brother peace officers in other phases
of public service.

By 1970, there may be as many as 70,000,000 sportsmen roaming the fields of the United States in search of fish
or game. They will find a reduced habitat, but they will also
find better use being made of available habitat. Areas previously not occupied will be stocked with game--for example,
the chukar partridge in the western United States. Fishing
and hunting gear will be improved, but creel limits, at least
on trout, will be lower; the emphasis will be on the sport
rather than on the accumulation of a large game bag.

The sportsman of 1970 will find many more high dams
than did his father or grandfather. He will also find a

4. Claude Kelly, op. cit. p. 8.

greater emphasis on general soil conservation and good land use. Rare species, such as the grizzly bear, will continue to be in trouble except in isolated areas. Vanishing species, such as the whooping crane, may be nothing more than a regrettable memory.

Colleges, teaching recognized courses in wildlife conservation, will offer wildlife law enforcement as an integral part of their curriculum. All in all, the sportsman of 1970 will bring home much less "bacon" than did his father, but he will be a better-adapted and happier sportsman than was his fond and frequently disconsolate parent.

Appendix A
Definitions and Legal Terms*

A POSTERIORI. From the effect to the cause; from what
comes after.

ABET. To encourage or set another on to commit a crime.
This word is always applied to aiding the commission
of a crime. To abet is to assist; to cause; to hire; to
command. Abetting imports a positive act in aid of the
commission of an offense. The abettor must stand in
the same relation to the crime as the criminal; approach it from the same direction; touch it at the same
point. (See Aid and Abet.)

ABIDE. To accept the consequences of; to rest satisfied
with. With reference to an order, judgment, or decree of a court, to perform, to execute.

ABROGATE. To repeal; to make void; to annul.

ABROGATION. The destruction of or annulling a former
law, by an act of the legislative power, or by usage.

ACCESSORY. He who is not the chief actor in the perpetration of an offense or present at its performance,
but in some way is concerned with it either before or
after. Any thing which is joined to another thing as an
ornament, or to render it more perfect. For example,
the halter of a horse, the frame of a picture, the keys
of a house, and the like, each belong to the principal
thing.

ACCESSORY AFTER THE FACT. Normally any person
who, knowing that a crime has been committed,

---

*In part from:

Ballentine, James A. 1948. Law Dictionary with Pronunciations.
2nd ed. Rochester, New York: Lawyers' Cooperative Publishing
Co. 1494 pp.

Bouvier, John. 1914. Bouvier's Law Dictionary and Concise Encyclopedia. Third revision. Kansas City, Mo.: Vernon Law Book Co.;
and St. Paul, Minn.: West Publishing Co. 3504 pp. 3 vol.

United States Government. 1951. Manual for Courts Martial. Washington, D. C.: U. S. Government Printing Office, Supt. of Documents.
665 pp.

185

thereafter receives, comforts, or assists the offender in order to hinder or prevent his apprehension, trial, or punishment is considered an ACCESSORY AFTER THE FACT. These acts need not necessarily be designed to effect personal escape or detection but may include those acts which are performed to conceal the commission of the offense. Thus, a person is an ACCESSORY AFTER THE FACT if he knowingly conceals illegally-killed game in order to help the perpetrator escape detection by a conservation officer. It should be noted, however, that mere failure to report an offense does not make one an ACCESSORY AFTER THE FACT.

ACCESSORY BEFORE THE FACT. One who, although absent at the time the crime is committed, yet procures, counsels, or commands another to commit it.

ACCIDENT. An event which takes place without one's foresight, or expectation, an event that proceeds from an unknown cause, or an unusual effect of a known cause. An event happening without human agency, or if happening through human agency, an event which is unusual and not expected.

ACCOMPLICE. In criminal law. One who is concerned in the commission of a crime, though not as a principal. A person so connected with a crime that at common law he might himself have been convicted either as principal or as an accessory before the fact. An accomplice may be one of the principal actors, or an aider and abettor, or an accessory before the fact, and includes all persons who participate.

ACCUSATION. A charge made to a competent officer against one who has committed, or believed to have committed, a crime, so that he may be brought to justice and punishment.

ACKNOWLEDGMENT. The act of one who has executed a deed, in going before some competent officer or court and declaring it to be his act or deed.

ACQUITTAL. Ordinarily, in criminal jurisprudence, the word means a discharge after a trial, or an attempt to have one, upon its merits; but under statutes it may refer to a discharge for other reasons. A release or discharge from an obligation or engagement. The absolution of a party charged with a crime or misdemeanor--a verdict of not guilty.

ACT. A thing done or established; a deed or other written instrument evidencing a contract or an obligation; a statute; a bill which has been enacted by the legislature into a law, as distinguished from a bill which is in the form of a law, presented to the legislature for enactment.

ACTION. An ordinary proceeding in a court of justice by which a party prosecutes another party for the enforcement or protection of a right, the redress or prevention of a wrong, or the punishment of a public offense; a judicial remedy for the enforcement or protection of a right.

ACT OF GOD. Any accident due to natural causes directly and exclusively without human intervention, such as could not have been prevented by any amount of foresight, pains, and care reasonably to have been expected. Any irresistible disaster, the result of natural causes, such as earthquakes, violent storms, lightning, and unprecedented floods, such a disaster arising from causes, and which could not have been reasonably anticipated, guarded against or resisted.

ADMISSIBLE. Pertinent and proper to be considered in reaching a decision. Used with reference to the issues to be decided in any judicial proceeding.

ADULT. A person who is at least 21 years old. In the civil law, a boy of 14, a girl of 12.

AFFIDAVIT. A statement or declaration reduced to writing, and sworn to or affirmed before some officer who has authority to administer an oath of affirmation.

AFFIRM. To declare solemnly instead of making a sworn statement. Persons having conscientious scruples against making oath are permitted to affirm.

AFFIRMATION OF JUDGMENT. A judgment of an appellate court which is a determination by that court that the proceedings under review are free from prejudicial error. If there is a decree partly in favor of and partly adverse to one who appeals from the adverse portion, an affirmance does not affirm the portion which was in his favor.

AGGRAVATED ARSON. See arson.

AID AND ABET. To constitute oneself as an aider and abettor there must be an intent to aid or encourage the persons who commit the crime, and there must be a sharing of intent with the perpetrator of a crime. One is liable as a principal in a crime if the offense is committed as a common venture or as a natural or probable consequence of the offense directly intended. A person may be guilty of an act committed by those with whom he voluntarily associates himself if the execution of the unlawful design was planned by the accused; this, even though the consequences were more far-reaching and serious than was anticipated by the principal. A person who plans a crime which is actually carried out by his associates is a principal in the act and is guilty of whatever illegal acts his associates may carry on during the course of the illegal act or acts which he planned and which were carried out by the associates.

A person, on the other hand, who merely witnesses a crime without intervention does not become a party to the commission of the crime unless he has a duty to interfere and his non-interference was designed to and did operate to encourage and aid the perpetrator of the crime. A conservation officer, for example, is guilty as a principal in a game violation if he idly stands by and watches a violation being committed and the violator escaping without interference.

A person who counsels, commands, or procures another to commit an offense which is subsequently perpetrated in consequence of such counsel, is a principal whether he is present or absent at the commission of the offense. This is true even though the offense is effected by a different means other than those suggested by the counselor. For example, a person might suggest to another that he should, in a specified manner, proceed to a given area and shoot pheasants (out of season). If the perpetrator of the crime proceeds to an area and acquires possession of pheasants by illegal methods, even though it is other than by shooting as suggested by the counselor, then the counselor as well as the perpetrator is guilty of the crime of taking pheasants illegally.

The offense committed by those persons who, although not the direct perpetrators of a crime, act to render aid to the actual perpetrator thereof.

ALIAS SUMMONS. A new summons issued in the same form and to serve the same purpose as one previously issued, and usually issued where the original summons has been returned, and hence has become <u>functus officio</u>, without having been served on any or all of the defendants.

ALIAS WARRANT. A warrant to the issuing official unserved and one which may later be reissued.

ALIAS WRIT. A writ issued to take the place of a similar writ which has been lost or returned or for some other reason has not taken effect or has become <u>functus officio</u>.

ALIBI. Literally present in another place other than that described. When a person, charged with a crime, proves (<u>se eadem die fuisse alibi</u>) that he was, at the time alleged, in a different place from that in which it was committed, he is said to prove an alibi, the effect of which is to lay a foundation for the necessary inference that he could not have committed it.

ALLEGATION. The assertion, declaration, or statement of a party of what he can prove.

AMBIGUITY. Duplicity, indistinctness or uncertainty of meaning of an expression used in a written instrument. The word "uncertainty" in a suit refers to the uncertainty defined in pleading and does not include ambiguity.

AMBUSH. The noun means the act of attacking an enemy unexpectedly from a concealed station; a concealed station where troops or enemies lie in wait to attack by surprise; an ambuscade. The verb "to ambush" means to lie in wait; to surprise; to place in ambush.

AMENABLE. To be amenable means to be liable to answer; responsible; answerable; liable to be called to account.

ANGER. A strong passion or emotion of displeasure or antagonism, excited by a real or supposed injury or insult to one's self or others by the intent to do such injury; resentment; wrath, rage, fury, passion; ire; gall, choler, indignation; displeasure; vexation; grudge; spleen.

ANIMAL. Any member of the group of living beings typically capable of spontaneous movement and rapid response to external stimulation (as distinguished from a plant). Animals, in contrast to plants, are able to move about and to take and ingest food. Strictly speaking, animals include human beings; however, in wildlife work the term frequently is used in a way which excludes the human race, and in many cases it refers only to vertebrates (animals with backbones).

Any animate being endowed with the power of voluntary motion.

ANIMALS DOMITAE NATURAE. Those animals which have been tamed by man; domestic. Those animals which are naturally tame and gentle or which by long continued association with man have become thoroughly domesticated and are now reduced to such a state of subjection to his will that they no longer possess the disposition or inclination to escape.

ANIMALS FERAE NATURAE. Those animals which still retain their wild nature. A man may have an absolute property in animals of a domestic nature, but not so in animals ferae naturae, which belong to him only after he has taken legal possession. Such animals as are of a wild nature or disposition and so require to be reclaimed and made tame by art, industry, or education, or else must be kept in confinement to be brought within the immediate power of the owner.

ANIMUS. Mind; intent; intention; disposition.

ANSWER. A plea interposed by a defendant to a declaration or complaint or any material allegation of fact therein, which, if untrue, would defeat the action. The traverse may deny all the facts alleged, or any particular material fact; but it is not the office of a plea or answer to raise an issue of law where such issue should be determined on demurrer.

APPARENT. Webster defines the word as clear, or manifest to the understanding; plain; evident; obvious; appearing to the eye or mind.

APPEAL. Any complaint to a superior court of an injustice done by an inferior one. This is the general use of the word.

APPEAL AND ERROR. The methods of exercising appellate jurisdiction for the review by a superior court of the final judgment, order, or decree of some inferior court.

The most unusual modes of exercising appellant jurisdiction are by a writ of error, or by an appeal, or by some process of removal of a suit from an inferior tribunal. An appeal is a process of civil law origin, and removes a cause, entirely subjecting the facts as well as the law to a review and a retrial. A writ of error is a process of common law origin, and it removes nothing for re-examination but the law.

APPEARANCE. Coming into court as party to a suit, whether as plaintiff or defendant. It may be of the following kinds:

Compulsory--That which takes place in consequence of the service of process.

Conditional--One which is coupled with conditions as to its becoming general.

De bene esse--One which is to remain an appearance, except in a certain event.

General--A simple and absolute submission to the jurisdiction of the court.

Gratis--One made before the party has been legally notified to appear.

Optional--One made where the party is not under any obligation to appear, but does so to save his rights.

Special--That which is made for certain purposes only, and does not extend to all the purposes of the suit; as to contest and jurisdiction, or the sufficiency of the service.

Subsequent--An appearance by the defendant after one has already been entered for him by the plaintiff.

Voluntary--That which is made in answer to a subpoena or summons, without process.

APPELLANT. He who makes an appeal from one court to another.

APPELLATE JURISDICTION. The jurisdiction which a superior court has to rehear causes which have been tried in inferior courts.

APPREHENSION. The capture or arrest of a person on a criminal charge. The word strictly construed means the seizing or taking hold of a man and detaining him with a view to his ultimate surrender.

APPROPRIATE. To appropriate means to allot, assign, set apart, or apply to a particular use or purpose.

ARGUMENT. An effort to establish belief by a course of reasoning.

ARMED. Furnished or equipped with weapons of offense or defense. A person who has in his hand a dangerous weapon with which he makes an assault, is certainly armed.

ARRAIGNMENT. Calling the defendant to the bar of the court, to answer the accusation contained in the indictment.

ARREST. The taking, seizing, or detaining of the person of another either by touching, or putting hands on him, or by any act which indicates an intention to take him into custody, and subjects the person arrested to the actual control and will of the person making the arrest. Touching is not necessary; it is sufficient if the person imprisoned understands that he is in the power of the officer, and submits. The taking of a person into custody by a legal authority. This can be accomplished either by arrest on sight or on a proper warrant. To deprive a person of his liberty by legal authority. The taking, seizing, or detaining the person of another, touching or putting hands upon him in the execution of process, or any act indicating an intention to arrest.

A restraint of the person, a restriction of the right of locomotion which cannot be implied in the mere notification, or summons on petition, or any other service of such process, by which no bail is required nor restraint of personal liberty.

ARRESTEE. The person arrested.

ARSON. To set fire to an inhabited dwelling or other structure of another person.

Aggravated Arson--In this case the essential element is the danger to human life. It is immaterial that no one in fact is injured.

ASSAILANT. A person who assails, or who assaults, the aggressor. In a fight the person who commits the first assault is the assailant.

ASSAULT. An unlawful offer or attempt with force or violence to do a corporeal hurt to another. Force unlawfully directed or applied to the person of another under such circumstances as to cause a well-founded apprehension of immediate peril.

Aggravated assault--One committed with the intention of committing some additional crime. Simple assault is one committed with no intention to do any other injury.

AT LARGE. Within the comprehension of the statutes inflicting a penalty on one who suffers animals to be "running at large," the term means strolling without restraint or confinement, or wandering, roving, or rambling at will; unrestrained.

ATTEMPT. An endeavor to accomplish a crime carried beyond mere preparation, but falling short of execution of the ultimate design in any part of it.

An attempt to commit an offense is an act or acts done with the specific intent to commit a particular crime which would have been completed except for some interference other than that which was voluntarily caused by the perpetrator. There must be a specific intent to commit some particular crime by an overt act which directly tends to accomplish the unlawful purpose. This act must be more than mere preparation. It must consist of devising or arranging means necessary for the commission of the offense, and goes beyond the preparatory stages in that it is a direct movement toward the commission of the offense. For example, the purchase of a gun with the intent of violating a game law is not an attempt to violate a game law; however, actual use of the weapon in attempting to kill game out of season is an illegal act even though the shot may go astray.

It is not an attempt when every act by the accused is completed without committing any offense. However, an accused may be guilty of attempt even though the crime turns out to be impossible because of something beyond his power or knowledge. For example, the person knowingly raises a gun and levels it at a game animal, out of season, and pulls the trigger with obvious and admitted intention of killing the game animal. However, the gun misfired and the animal is not killed. Still there is an attempt to commit an illegal act.

If, on the other hand, a person raises a gun, aims it at a game animal during a closed season, and pulls the trigger, he is not guilty of an attempt if he knew at the time he pulled the trigger that the gun would not fire because it was empty, or for some other reason.

ATTEST. A witness. To attest means to bear witness to; to affirm to be true or genuine.

ATTORNEY. The word, unless clearly indicated otherwise is construed as meaning attorney-at-law. When used in connection with the proceedings of courts, it often has a fixed and universal significance, on which the technical and popular sense unite.

ATTORNEY GENERAL. The chief law officer of a state or nation, to whom is usually intrusted the duty of prosecuting all suits or proceedings wherein the state is concerned. He may also advise the chief executive and other administrative heads of government in legal matters.

AUTOPSY. A medical or surgical examination of a dead body made in order to determine the cause of death. Sometimes spoken of as a "post mortem."

BAIL. One who becomes surety for the appearance of the defendant in court. Money or other security furnished in behalf of a defendant to allow him his physical liberty, pending his appearance for a hearing, a trial, or a sentence.

BAILIFF. A person to whom some authority, care, guardianship, or jurisdiction is delivered, committed, or intrusted. A sheriff's officer or deputy. A court attendant, sometimes called a tipstaff.

BAIL PIECE. A process authorizing the rearrest of a defendant who has defaulted an attendance at a hearing where bail has been provided for his liberty.

BATTERY. Any unlawful beating or other wrongful physical violence or constraint inflicted on a human being without his consent. An unlawful touching the person of another by the aggressor himself, or any other substance put in motion by him.

BEAST. Any four-footed animal which may be used for labor, food, or sport; as opposed to man; any irrational animal.

BELIEF. Conviction of the mind, arising not from actual perception or knowledge, but by way of inference, or from evidence received or information derived from others.

BENCH WARRANT. A warrant issued by proper authority o a court of record requiring the arrest of a person, and his appearance before the issuing authority. An order issued by or from a bench, for the attachment or arrest of a person. It may be issued either in case of a contempt or where an indictment has been found.

BEST EVIDENCE. The best evidence of which the nature of the case admits, not the highest or strongest evidence which the nature of the thing to be proved admits of: e.g., a copy of a deed is not the best evidence; the deed itself is better.

BIAS. A particular influential power which sways the judgment; the inclination or propensity of the mind towards a particular object.

BILL OF RIGHTS. That portion of the federal constitution and the constitution of each state which consists of the guarantees of such rights as are to a large extent declaratory of fundamental principles and the foundation of citizenship; those providing against excessive fines or cruel punishment.

BONA FIDES. Good faith, honesty, as distinguished from mala fides (bad faith).

BOND. An obligation in writing and under seal.

BRASS KNUCKLES. A weapon used for offense and defense, worn upon the hand to strike with as if striking with the fist. When first known and used, the weapon was originally made of brass, but it is now made of other heavy metal. It still retains the name of brass knuckles.

BREAKING AND ENTERING. What would be a breaking in burglary, it has been held, is equally a breaking by the sheriff to serve process. Even the right to lift a door latch has been denied. Other cases hold that the door may be opened in the ordinary manner such as by lifting the latch, turning the knob or turning a key left in the lock.

BRIBERY. The receiving or offering of any undue reward by or to any person in order to influence his behavior and to induce him to act contrary to his duties or to the known rules of honesty and integrity. Offering or receiving a present, with the intent and hope of causing dishonest behavior.

BRIBE. A gift or promise, which if accepted, is of some advantage as an inducement for some illegal act or omission.

BRIEF. A detailed statement of a party's case. An abridgment of a plaintiff's or defendant's case. Tidd says a brief should contain an abstract of the pleadings; a statement of the facts of the case, with such observations as occur thereon. The great rule to be observed in drawing briefs consists in conciseness with perspicuity.

BURDEN OF PROOF. The duty of proving the facts in dispute on an issue raised between the parties in a case.

CANON LAW. A body of Roman ecclesiastical law, relative to such matters as the church of Rome either had, or pretended to have jurisdiction over.

CARE. Charge or oversight; implying responsibility for safety and prosperity.

CASE. A question contested before a court of justice. An action or suit at law or in equity.

CAT. A domestic animal which if kept as a household pet is a thing of value. As such it is the proper subject of a civil action, it is property subject to taxation and is such an animal as is included in statutes against cruelty.

CAUSE. In Civil Law. The consideration or motive for making a contract.

CENSUS. A decennial official count by the government of the United States of the inhabitants and wealth of the country. In fish and game work it generally means an estimate derived from a presumably reliable sample.

CERTIFICATE. A writing made in any court, and properly authenticated, to give notice to another court of anything done therein. A writing by which testimony is given that a fact has or has not taken place.

CERVUS. A stag.

CHAIRMAN. The presiding officer of a deliberative body.

CHALLENGE FOR CAUSE. Those for which some reason is assigned.

CHALLENGE-PEREMPTORY. Those made without assigning any reason, and which court must allow.

CHANGE OF DOMICILE. A change of one's abiding place with no intention to live elsewhere than in the new abode. The residing permanently or indefinitely in the new abode.

CHANGE OF RESIDENCE. An actual removal to a residence outside of the state coupled with an actual intention to change one's residence from the state to residence out of the state.

CHANGE OF VENUE. This is permission of a court having jurisdiction in a case which allows the case to be tried in some other court, usually in another county, where, for a number of reasons it appears that a fair trial cannot be had at the originally scheduled place.

CHARACTER. The possession by a person of certain qualities of mind or morals, distinguishing him from others. In evidence--the opinion generally entertained of a person derived from the common report of the people who are acquainted with him; his reputation. The moral character and conduct of a person in society may be used in proof before a jury in three classes of cases: first, to afford a presumption that a particular person has not been guilty of a criminal act; second, to affect the damages in particular cases, where their amount depends on the reputation and conduct of any individual; and third, to impeach or confirm the veracity of a witness.

CHARGE. To charge a jury means that the court shall instruct the jury as to the essential law of the case, although, unless requested to do so by either party, the judge is not compelled to reduce the charge to writing, yet it is the better practice.

A duty or obligation imposed upon some person. A lien, incumbrance, or claim which is to be satisfied out of the specific thing or proceeds thereof to which it applies. To impose such an obligation; to create such a claim.

CHARTA DE FORESTA. A collection of the laws of the forest, made in the reign of Henry III.

CIRCUIT COURT. A court presided over by a judge or by judges at different places in the same district.

CIRCUMSTANCES. The particulars which accompany an act. The surroundings at the commission of an act.

CIRCUMSTANTIAL EVIDENCE. Facts inferred from circumstances rather than those seen or otherwise established.

CITATION. A writ issued out of a court of competent jurisdiction, commanding a person therein named to appear on a day named and do something therein mentioned, or show cause why he should not.

CITE. To summon; to command the presence of a person; to notify a person of legal proceedings against him and require his appearance thereto.

CIVIL. In contradistinction to barbarous or savage, indicates a state of society reduced to order and regular government; thus, we speak of civil life, civil society, civil government, and civil liberty. In contradistinction to criminal, to indicate the private rights and remedies of men, as members of the community, in contrast to those which are public and relate to the government: thus, we speak of civil process and criminal process, civil jurisdiction and criminal jurisdiction. It is also used in contradistinction to military or ecclesiastical, to natural or foreign. The word is frequently used as an adjective to qualify a wrong or breach of duty and to import that the wrong or breach of duty may be the subject of a civil action, as distinguished from a criminal prosecution.

CIVIL ACTION. In Civil Law. A personal action which is instituted to compel payment, or the doing some other thing which is purely civil.

CLAIM. The assertion of a demand, or the challenge of something, as a matter of right; a demand of some matter, as of right, made by one person upon another to do or to forbear to do some act or thing, as a matter of duty.

CLEAN HANDS. The maxim, "He who comes into equity, must do so with clean hands," signifies that equity deals only with conscionable demands and usually the maxim has reference only to the plaintiff's rights against the defendant and only when his equity has an immediate and necessary relation to the equity for which he sues.

CODE. A body of law established by the legislative authority of the state, and designed to regulate completely, so far as a statute may, the subject to which it relates. A system of law; a systematic and complete body of law.

COLD STORAGE. The term as used in the trade, means a storage space where the temperature is kept at a low degree, but above the freezing point; while a freezer is a place for the preservation of meat or poultry where the temperature is kept below the freezing point.

COLLUSION. An agreement to defraud a third party of his rights by the forms of law, or to secure an unlawful object.

COMMITMENT. A writ issued by a judge, magistrate, or justice of the peace by which the body of a person is committed to prison, and requiring the jail custodian to retain the person until properly released by law.

COMMON FISHERY. A fishery which is distinguished from a several or exclusive fishery by the number of persons who have a right to resort to the place for fishing; it is one which is not exclusive to one person, but is open to a number of persons, generally to the public.

COMMON LAW. Laws which have gained their standing by usage and custom, sometimes dating back to the unwritten law of England.

That system of law or form of the science of jurisprudence which has prevailed in England and in the United States of America, in contradistinction to other great systems, such as the Roman or civil law. Those principles, usages, and rules of action applicable to the government and security of persons and of property, which do not rest for their authority upon any express and positive declaration of the will of the legislature. The body of rules and remedies administered by courts of law, technically so called, in contradistinction to those of equity and to the canon law.

COMMON PLEAS. The name of a court having jurisdiction generally of civil actions. Such pleas or actions are brought by private persons against private persons, or by the government, when the cause of action is of a civil nature. In England, whence we derived this phrase, common pleas are so called to distinguish them from pleas of the crown.

COMPETENCY. The legal fitness or ability of a witness to be heard on the trial of a cause. That quality of written or other evidence which renders it proper to be given on the trial of a cause.

There is a difference between competency and credibility. A witness may be competent, and, on examination, his story may be so contradictory and improbable that he may not be believed; on the contrary, he may be incompetent and yet be perfectly credible if he were examined.

The courts are the sole judges of the competency of a witness, and may, for the purpose of deciding whether the witness is or is not competent, ascertain all the facts necessary to form a judgment.

COMPETENT. Able, fit, qualified; authorized or capable to act. (See Competency.)

COMPETENT EVIDENCE. That evidence which the very nature of the thing to be proven requires, as the production of a writing where its contents are the subject of inquiry.

COMPLAINT. In Criminal Law. The allegation made to a proper officer that some person, whether known or unknown, has been guilty of a designated offense, with an offer to prove the fact, and a request that the offender may be punished. It is a technical term, descriptive of proceedings before a magistrate.

To have a legal effect, the complaint must be supported by such evidence as shows that an offense has been committed and renders it certain or probable that it was committed by the person named or described in the complaint.

A sworn legal statement usually made before a court which charges a person with the commission of a crime. The word complaint is sometimes used synonymously with the word information. (See Information.)

CONCLUSIVE EVIDENCE. That which cannot be controlled or contradicted by any other evidence. Evidence which of itself, whether contradicted or uncontradicted, explained or unexplained, is sufficient to determine the matter at issue. Evidence upon the production of which the judgment is bound by law to regard some fact as proved, and to exclude evidence to exclude it.

CONFESSION. In Criminal Law. The voluntary admission or declaration made by a person who has committed a crime or misdemeanor, to another, of the agency or participation which he had in the same.

CONFIDENTIAL COMMUNICATIONS. Those statements with regard to any transaction made by one person to another during the continuance of some relation between them which calls for or warrants such communications. At law, certain classes of such communications are held not to be proper subjects of inquiry in courts of justice, and the persons receiving them are excluded from disclosing them when called upon as witnesses, upon grounds of public policy. Secrets of state and communications between the government and its officers are usually privileged.

CONFISCATE. To appropriate to the use of the state.

CONSPIRACY. A conspiracy is an act of two or more
persons who have agreed by conserted action to accomplish an unlawful act or some purpose not in itself unlawful but by unlawful means, and the doing of some act
by one or more of the conspirators to effect the object
of that agreement. This agreement need not be in any
particular form, not even in formal words. It is sufficient that the parties arrive at an understanding as to
what is to be accomplished and what part will be played
by each of the conspirators. The overt act of conspiracy must be an independent act by one of the persons
involved, but it need not be a crime in itself; but it
must be a manifestation that the conspiracy is being
executed. A telephone call to a conservation officer
that something is taking place in some far corner of a
county followed by an illegal act of hunting in the opposite by one of the conspirators is in itself an overt act
and therefore becomes part of a conspiracy. A person
may be guilty of conspiracy although himself being incapable of committing the crime. Thus a man 80 years
old who could not kill and carry away an illegally-killed
deer could plan for two youths to commit this act, and
all three would, under the circumstances, be equally
guilty.

CONSTITUTION. The fundamental law of a state, directing
the principles upon which the government is founded,
and regulating the exercise of the sovereign powers,
directing to what bodies or persons those powers shall
be confided and the manner of their exercise.

CONSTITUTION OF THE UNITED STATES OF AMERICA.
The supreme law of the United States. It was framed
by a convention of delegates from all the original 13
states, except Rhode Island.

CONSTRUCTIVE ESCAPE. Such an escape as takes place
when the prisoner obtains more liberty than the law all
allows, although he still remains in confinement.

CONTEMPT. A wilful disregard or disobedience of a public
authority.

CONTEMPT OF COURT. A despising of the authority, justice, or dignity of the court; such conduct as tends to
bring the authority and administration of the law into
disrespect or disregard, or to interfere with or prejudice parties litigant or their witnesses during litiga-
tions.

CONTINUANCE. The adjournment of a cause from one day to another of the same or subsequent term.

CONTRADICT. To prove a fact contrary to what has been asserted by a witness. A party cannot impeach the character of his witness, but may contradict him as to any particular fact.

CONTROL. To control, according to Webster, means to check, restrain, govern, have under command, and authority over. According to the Century Dictionary, it means to hold in restraint or check, subject to author ity, direct, regulate, govern, dominate.

CONVICTION. The confession of a person who is being prosecuted for crime, in open court, or a verdict returned against him by a jury, which ascertains and publishes the fact of his guilt.

The word applies simply and solely to the verdict of guilty.

In practice, that legal procedure which ascertains the guilt of the party and upon which the sentence or judgment is founded.

CORPUS DELICTI. From the Latin word, it literally means the body of the crime. In practice it may be a dead bod of a person, horse, house burned, carcass of a deer, the elements of the crime, or anything in fact that establishes the essence of the crime. In all cases it is necessary to prove the corpus delicti to establish that a crime has actually been committed.

COURT. A place where justice is judicially administered; persons officially assembled under authority of law, at the appropriate time and place, for the administration of justice. A time when, a place where, and persons by whom judicial functions are to be exercised, are essential to complete a court, in contemplation of law.

A body, in the government, to which the administration of justice is delegated.

COURT CALENDAR. A court's list of the matters which are ready to be heard and the times which the court has designed for their hearing.

COURTS OF THE FOREST. Courts held for the enforcement of the forest laws. The lowest of these was the Woodmote, or Court of Attachments. The next was the

Swainimote. The highest was the Court of the Chief
Justice. There was also a Survey of Dogs held by the
Regarders of the Forest every three years for the
lawing of dogs.

CRAZY. In ordinary language we speak of insane people as
crazy, and vice versa; mad, demented.

CREDIBILITY. Capacity for being believed or credited.
Worthiness of belief. The credibility of witnesses is
a question for the jury to determine, as their competency is for the court.

CREDIBLE WITNESS. One who, being competent to give
evidence, is worthy of belief. In deciding upon the
credibility of a witness, it is always pertinent to consider whether he is capable of knowing thoroughly the
thing about which he testifies; whether he was actually
present at the transaction; whether he paid sufficient
attention to qualify himself as a reporter; and whether
he honestly relates the affair fully as he knows it, without any purpose or desire to deceive or to suppress or
to add to the truth. Determining the credibility of a
witness is the duty of the jury.

CRIME. An act committed or omitted in violation of a public law forbidding or commanding it.

CRIMINAL. Relating to or having the character of crime.

CRIMINAL CHARGE. A charge which, strictly speaking,
exists only when a formal, written complaint has been
made against the accused and a prosecution initiated.
Popular usage sometimes substitutes the word accusation, but in legal phraseology it is properly limited to
such accusations as have taken shape in a prosecution.
A person is legally charged with crime only when he is
called upon in a legal proceeding to answer to such a
charge.

CRIMINAL INTENT. The intent to commit a crime; malice,
as evidenced by a criminal act.

CROSS-EXAMINATION. The examination of a witness by
the party opposed to the party who called him, and who
examined, or was entitled to examine him in chief.
The purpose of the cross-examination is to test the
truthfulness, intelligence, memory, bias, or interest
of the witness; and any question to that end within reason
is usually allowed.

CULPABLE NEGLIGENCE. This is defined as a degree of
carelessness greater than simple negligence. It is an

act or omission accompanied by a culpable disregard for foreseeable consequences to others. Leaving poison baits out where domestic animals or even children might reasonably be expected to pick them up is in this category.

CUMULATIVE PUNISHMENT. A punishment greater than a convicted person would suffer for a first offense. Such punishments of second and subsequent offenses are provided for by statute in England and in many states of the Union, and are held to be constitutional.

CUSTODY. The bare control or care of a thing, as distinguished from the possession of it. The mere fact of putting one's property into the charge or custody of another person does not divest the possession of the owner So one having the mere custody of the property of another may commit larceny of it.

DANGEROUS WEAPON. A weapon capable of producing death or great bodily harm. An unloaded gun, at some distance from the person alleged to have been assaulted, is not a dangerous weapon.

DECISION. A judgment given by a competent tribunal.

DECOY. To decoy is to entice; to tempt; to lure or allure. There can be no such thing as forcibly decoying a person, since fraud or deception is the moving element.

DE FACTO. Actually; in fact; in deed. A term used to denote a thing actually done. In fact, as distinguished from "de jure," by right.

DEFECT. A lack or absence of something essential to completeness. The want of something required by law.

DEFENDANT. The person or persons charged with the commission of a crime. A party sued in a personal action. The term does not in strictness apply to the person opposing or denying the allegations of the demandant in a real action, who is properly called the tenant. The distinction, however, is very commonly disregarded; and the term is further frequently applied to denote the person called upon to answer, either at law or in equity, and as well in criminal as civil suits.

DELINQUENT CHILDREN. Those who have committed offenses, or who are falling into bad habits, or are incorrigible.

DEMURRER. In Pleading. An allegation, that, admitting the facts of the preceding pleading to be true, as stated by the party making it, he has yet shown no cause why the party demurring should be compelled by the court to proceed further. A declaration that the party demurring will go no further, because the other has shown nothing against him.

DE NOVO PROCEEDINGS. A case in which the appeal is argued anew upon the merit of the matter, rather than an attack upon the record.

DEPUTY. A person subordinate to a public officer whose business and object is to perform the duties of the principal.

DIRECT EVIDENCE. Straightforward; not collateral. Evidence is termed direct which applies immediately to the fact to be proved, without any intervening process as distinguished from circumstantial, which applies immediately to collateral facts supposed to have a connection, near to remote, with the fact in controversy.

DISMISS. To remove. To send out of court. Formerly used in chancery of the removal of a cause out of court without any further hearing. The term is now used in courts of law also.

DISQUALIFIED WITNESS. No party to or person interested in the event of, any action or proceeding in which the opposite party has succeeded to the interest of a deceased person, shall be examined as a witness in his own behalf, in regard to any personal communication or transaction with the deceased.

DISTRICT ATTORNEY. Public officers elected or appointed, as provided in the several state constitutions or by statute, to conduct suits, generally criminal, on behalf of the state in their respective districts. They are sworn ministers of justice, quasi judicial officers representing the commonwealth.

District attorneys of the United States are appointed for a term of four years in each judicial district, whose duty it is to prosecute, in such district, all delinquents, for crimes and offenses cognizable under the authority of the United States, and all civil actions in which the United States shall be concerned, except in the Supreme Court, in the district in which the court shall be holden. He must appear upon the record for the United States plaintiff, in order that the United States should be recognized as such on the record.

DOCKET. A formal record of judicial proceedings; a brief writing. A small piece of paper or parchment having the effect of a larger one. An abstract.

DOCUMENTARY EVIDENCE. Written evidence includes such things as confessions, licenses, permits, tags, checks, registration cards, and statements by the officer, or by observers. It is frequently necessary to identify these statements by oral testimony in court.

Under physical evidence are such tangible materials as weapons, bullets, fingerprints, clothing, confiscated game, and fishing gear. It should be emphasized that it is very important to properly identify all physical evidence by marking it at once, so that it may be later properly identified when introduced at the trial.

DOCUMENTS. The deeds, agreements, title-papers, letters, receipts, and other written instruments used to prove a fact.

DOMESTIC ANIMALS. Those animals which by habit or training live in association with man. This class of animals includes cattle, horses, sheep, goats, pigs, poultry, cats and dogs. Such animals, like other personal and movable chattels, are the subject of absolute property. The owner retains his property in them even if they stray or are lost.

DOMICILE. That place where a man has his true, fixed, and permanent home and principal establishment, and to which whenever he is absent he has the intention of returning.

DOUBLE JEOPARDY. The second jeopardy of a person who has been previously in jeopardy for the same offense. The test is not whether the defendant has already been tried for the same act, but whether he has been put in jeopardy for the same offense.

DOUBT. The uncertainty which exists in relation to a fact, a proposition, or other thing; an equipoise of the mind arising from an equality of contrary reasons. Some rules, not always infallible, have been adopted in doubtful cases, in order to arrive at the truth. (1) In civil cases, the doubt ought to operate against him who, having it in his power to prove facts to remove the doubt, has neglected to do so. In cases of fraud, when there is a doubt, the presumption of innocence ought usually to remove it. (2) In criminal cases, whenever a reasonable doubt exists as to the guilt of the accused, that doubt ought to operate in his favor. In such cases, particularly when the liberty, honor, or life of an individual is at stake, the evidence to convict ought to be clear and devoid of all reasonable doubt. The term reasonable doubt is often used, but not easily defined. Failure to explain reasonable doubt in a charge is not error.

DURESS. Personal restraint, or fear of personal injury or imprisonment.

EMINENT DOMAIN. The superior right of property subsisting in a sovereignty, by which private property may in certain cases be taken or its use controlled for the public benefit, without regard to the wishes of the owner. The power to take private property for public use.

EVIDENCE. That which tends to prove or disprove any matter in question, or to influence the belief respecting it. Belief is produced by the consideration of something presented to the mind. The matter thus presented, in whatever shape it may come, and through whatever material organ it is derived, is evidence.

The instruments of evidence, in the legal acception of the term, are:

1. Judicial notice or recognition. There are diverse things of which courts take judicial notice, without the introduction of proof by the parties, such as: the territorial extent of their jurisdiction, local divisions of their own countries, seats of courts, all public matters directly concerning the general government, the ordinary course of nature, divisions of time, the meanings of words, and generally, of whatever ought to be generally known in the jurisdiction. If the judge needs information on subjects, he will seek it from such sources as he deems authentic.

2. Public records: the registers of official transactions made by officers appointed for the purpose; as, the public statutes, the judgments and proceedings of courts, etc.

3. Judicial writings: such as inquisitions, depositions, etc.

4. Public documents having a semi-official character: as, the statute-books published under the authority

of the government, documents printed by the
authority of Congress, etc.

5. <u>Private writings</u>: as, deeds, contracts, wills.
6. <u>Testimony of witnesses</u>.
7. <u>Personal inspection</u>, by the jury or tribunal whose
   duty it is to determine the matter in controversy:
   as, a view of the locality by the jury, to enable
   them to determine the disputed fact, or the better
   to understand the testimony, or inspection of any
   machine or weapon which is produced in the cause.

<u>Real evidence</u> is evidence of the thing or object which
is produced in court. When, for instance, the condition or appearance of any thing or object is material to
the issue, and the thing or object itself is produced in
court for the inspection of the tribunal, with proper
testimony as to its identity, and, if necessary, to show
that it has existed since the time at which the issue in
question arose, this object or thing becomes itself
"real evidence" of its condition or appearance at the
time in question.

<u>Extrinsic evidence</u> is external evidence, or that which
is not contained in the body of an agreement, contract,
and the like.

<u>Presumptive evidence</u> is that which shows the existence
of one fact, by proof of the existence of another or
others, from which the first may be inferred; because
the fact or facts shown have a legitimate tendency to
lead the mind to the conclusion that the fact exists
which is sought to be proved.

<u>Presumptions of fact</u> are not the subject of fixed rules,
but are merely natural presumptions, such as appear,
from common experience, to arise from the particular
circumstances of any case. Some of these are founded
upon a knowledge of the human character, and of the
motives, passions, and feelings by which the mind is
usually influenced.

<u>Circumstantial evidence</u> is the proof of facts which
usually attend other facts sought to be proved; that
which is not direct evidence. For example, when a
witness testifies that a man was stabbed with a knife,
and that a piece of the blade was found in the wound,
and it is found to fit exactly with another part of the

blade found in the possession of the prisoner, the facts are directly attested, but they only prove circumstances; and hence this is called circumstantial evidence.

Circumstantial evidence is of two kinds, namely, certain and uncertain. It is certain when the conclusion in question necessarily follows: as, where a man had received a mortal wound, and it was found that the impression of a bloody left hand had been made on the left arm of the deceased, it was certain some person other than the deceased must have made such mark; but it is uncertain whether the death was caused by suicide or by suicide or by murder, and whether the mark of the bloody hand was made by the assassin, or by a friendly hand that came too late to the relief of the deceased.

Circumstantial evidence warrants a conviction in a criminal case, provided it is such as to exclude every reasonable hypothesis but that of guilt of the offense charged to the defendant, but it must always rise to that degree of convincing power which satisfies the mind beyond reasonable doubt of guilt. This can never be the case when the evidence, as produced, is entirely consistent with innocence in a given transaction.

Secondary evidence is that kind of proof which is admissible when the primary evidence cannot be produced, and which becomes by that event the best evidence that can be adduced.

Prima facie evidence is that which appears to be sufficient proof respecting the matter in question, until something appears to controvert it, but which may be contradicted or controlled.

Conclusive evidence is that which, while uncontradicted, establishes the fact: as in the instance of conclusive presumptions; it is also that which cannot be contradicted.

Res gestae. But where evidence of an act done by a party is admissible, his declaration made at the time, having a tendency to elucidate or give a character to the act, and which may derive a degree of credit from the act itself, are also admissible, as part of the res gestae.

Dying declarations are an exception to the rule excluding hearsay evidence, and are admitted, under certain limitations in cases of homicide, so far as the circumstances attending the death and its cause are the subject of them.

Opinions of persons of skill and experience, called experts, are also admissible in certain cases, when, in order to the better understanding of the evidence or to the solution of the question, a certain skill and experience are required which are not ordinarily possessed by jurors. A non-expert witness on the question of the sanity of one accused of crime after stating such particulars as he can remember--generally only the more striking facts--is permitted to sum up the total remembered and unremembered impressions of the senses by stating the opinion which they produced.

EXAMINATION. In Criminal Law. The investigation by an authorized magistrate of the circumstances which constitute the grounds for an accusation against a person arrested on a criminal charge, with a view to discharging the person so arrested, or to securing his appearance for trial by the proper court, and to preserving the evidence relating to the matter.

EXECUTE. To complete; to sign; to sign, seal, and deliver.

EXHIBIT. To produce a thing publicly, so that it may be taken possession of and seized.

EXPERT TESTIMONY. There are several things on which laymen may not testify because of their lack of experience or special training. A ballistics expert, for example, is qualified to testify as to whether or not a bullet was or was not fired from some particular weapon. A doctor is better qualified to form an opinion as to the cause of death. A ditch-digger may be better qualified to testify as to the cause of a bank cave-in. An expert witness must be qualified before the court; he may then state facts, and opinions as based on the facts presented. It is always up to the jury to weigh the evidence and draw their own conclusions.

EXPERT WITNESS. One who has acquired such special knowledge of the subject matter about which he is to testify, either by study of the recognized authorities on the subject or by practical experience, so that he can give the jury assistance and guidance in solving a problem for which their equipment, good judgment, and average knowledge is inadequate.

One who is skilled in some art, trade, profession or science, or a person who has knowledge and experience in relation to matters at hand which are generally not within the knowledge of men of common education and experience. An expert witness may express an opinion on a state of facts which is within his specialty. An expert witness may be qualified by the court or he may be accepted without being qualified if there is no objection from either side. An expert may state his relevant opinions based on personal experience or observation or study without specifying data on which it is based. However, on cross-examination, he may be required to bring forth data upon which his opinion is based. An expert witness may also be asked to testify on a hypothetical question if this question is based on facts and evidence at the time the question is asked. When, at a later date, no such facts are actually introduced, the opinion based on them should be excluded from admissible evidence. An admissible expert opinion is regarded as evidence when it pertains to the matter on which the opinion relates.

EXTORTION. The communication of threats to another with the intention of obtaining something of value. For example, to gain an acquittance, or an immunity. The offense is complete when the communication has been completed. The success or failure of the venture is immaterial in determining guilt. The threat may be communicated by word of mouth or in writing. It may be in the form of a threat or unlawful injury to the person, or his property or any member of his family, or any other person held dear to him, or a threat to expose or impute any deformity or disgrace to the individual threatened, or to any member of his family or other person held dear to him, or a threat to expose any secret affecting the individual or others previously mentioned.

EXTRADITION. The surrender by one sovereign state to another, on its demand, of persons charged with the commission of crime within its jurisdiction, that they may be dealt with according to its laws. The surrender of persons by one federal state to another, on its demand, pursuant to their federal constitution and laws.

A process of requisition by which a defendant charged with a crime in one state, and apprehended in another state, is returned to the place of jurisdiction. Violations of fish and game laws in many states are considered as non-extraditable offenses.

EYE-WITNESS. One who saw the act or fact to which he testifies. When an eye-witness testifies, and is a man of intelligence and integrity, much reliance must be placed on his testimony.

FALSE ARREST. Any unlawful, physical restraint by one person of the liberty of another, whether in prison or elsewhere.

FALSE PRETENSE. An intentional, false statement concerning a material matter of fact, in reliance on which the title or possession of property is parted with. If possession is obtained by fraud, the offense is that of obtaining by false pretenses, provided the means by which it is acquired are false. A false pretense must be false when made and it must be knowingly false in that it is made without an honest belief in its truth. A false pretense is a false representation of past or existing facts. For example, one who pretends that he is about to perform a certain act but who at the time of the representation has no honest intention of doing so makes a false representation. A person who states that he will appear in a particular court at a given time but at that time has no intention of doing so, is guilty of false pretense.

False representations and statements, made with a fraudulent design to obtain "money, goods, wares, and merchandise," with intent to cheat.

FALSE STATEMENT. The term false statement refers to statements which are wilfully false or fraudulent. Wilful false is generally, though not invariably, the determining mark of crime.

FEAR. In robbery, the fear which moves the victim to part with his goods. If a transaction be attended with such circumstances of terror as in common experience are likely to create an apprehension of danger and to

induce a man to part with his property for the safety
of his person, he is put in fear.

FEDERAL COURTS. For the purpose of enforcing federal
law applicable to the whole country and therefore applicable to the District of Columbia, the courts of the
District are held to be federal courts.

FELONY. Whether a criminal act is a felony or a misdemeanor is usually made to depend upon the character
of the punishment provided by statute. An offense
which occasions a total forfeiture of either lands or
goods, or both, at common law, to which capital or
other punishment may be superadded, according to the
degree of guilt. A more serious crime than a misdemeanor; sometimes separated from the latter on the
basis of the monetary values involved.

This is the most serious grade of crime and includes
murder, man-slaughter, treason, burglary, rape,
robbery, arson, kidnapping, and most of the other
more serious illegal acts.

FERAE NATURAE. A term used to designate animals not
usually tamed, or not regarded as reclaimed so as to
become the subject of property. Such animals belong
to the person who has captured them only while they
are in his power. Wild animals; wild beasts. Animals
denominated ferae naturae include deer in the forest,
pigeons in the air, and fish in the public waters or in
the sea.

FERAL. Untamed, unbroken, undomesticated, or uncultivated; hence, wild; savage; bestial. Having escaped
from domestication or cultivation and become wild.

FINE. Pecuniary punishment imposed by a lawful tribunal
upon a person convicted of crime or misdemeanor.

FIREARMS. As sometimes used in statutes prohibiting
parades of unauthorized bodies with firearms, any gun
which to the ordinary observer appears to be an efficient weapon capable of being discharged is held to be a
firearm whether it has in fact been rendered harmless
or not. A weapon that propels a projectile by firing a
powder charge. Whether or not a weapon that fires a
projectile by spring or compressed air force is a firearm is something that must be determined by state or
local statutes.

FISH. An animal which inhabits the water, breathes by means of gills, and swims by the aid of fins. Fish may be either egg-laying or live-bearing. Fish themselves are normally <u>ferae naturae</u>--the common property of the public, or of the state--in the United States. Any of the numerous cold-blooded, strictly aquatic, water-breathing animals with backbones. When limbs are present they are developed as fins and the body is typically scaled or may be partially scaled or naked. Under certain terminology, any of the class Pisces of zoological nomenclature.

FISHERY. The right to employ lawful means for the taking of fish. It differs from a fishing place or the right to use a particular shore or beach as the basis for carrying on the business; the latter being vested in the shore owner and entirely distinct from the right to take fish from the water.

FISHING. Taking or attempting to take fish.

FISHING EXPEDITION OR FISHING EXAMINATION. The improper calling for and examination of documents of àn adversary, or the questioning of an adverse witness, on bare suspicion and with no reason to believe that evidence pertinent to the issues will be disclosed.

FISH, ROYAL. Fish which when brought ashore were the property of the king; such fish were confined to sturgeons, whales, and porpoises. (The latter two are mammals.)

FLIGHT. The evading the course of justice by a man's voluntarily withdrawing himself.

FOREST LAW. The old law relating to the forest, under which the most horrid tyrannies were exercised, in the confiscation of lands for the royal forests.

FORGERY. Forgery may be committed either by falsely writing or by knowingly uttering a falsehood which was made in writing. It is the altering, with intent to defraud, of a signature or any part thereof or of any writing which would, if genuine, apparently impose a legal liability on another, or change his legal right of liability or prejudice him. It is the uttering, offering, issuing, or transferring, with intent to defraud, of a writing known by the offender to have been fraudently made or to have been altered. It should be noted that it is not forgery to make a false statement or to alter a letter if it does not, by this alteration, impose a

legal liability on another or change a legal right or
liability to his prejudice. For example, a letter of
introduction. Forgery is not committed by the genuine
making a false statement for the purpose of defrauding
another. For example, a check bearing the signature
of the maker, although drawn on a bank in which the
maker has no money or credit, and even with intent to
defraud the payee or the bank, is not a forgery, for the
instrument, although false, is not falsely made. Likewise, if a person makes a false signature to an instrument and signs another name but puts the word "by"
with his own signature after the original signature,
thus indicating authority to sign, the offense is not
forgery even if no such party exists. False statements
of facts in a genuine document do not constitute forgery,
as, for example, when a conservation officer states
that he was in the field eight hours on a particular day
when in fact he was actually playing billards at "Joe's
Place." The primary aspects of forgery involve altering a signature or writing and composing a legal
liability as a result thereof. The altering of an instrument already invalid is not forgery because the instrument already had no legal standing. However, the making of another's signature on a statement with intent to
defraud, even though there is little or no resemblance
to the genuine signature, is forgery.

In order to constitute a forgery by altering a writing,
the alteration must affect a material change in the
legal tender of the writing. An alteration in the charge
on a complaint which reduces it to a lesser offense is
an example. As regards to the intent to defraud, it
need not be directed toward anyone in particular nor
need it be to the advantage of the offender. Furthermore, it is actually immaterial whether or not anyone
is actually defrauded.

FRAUD. An endeavor to alter rights, by deception touching
motives, or by circumvention not touching motives.
FUGITIVE FROM JUSTICE. One who, having committed a
crime, flees from the jurisdiction within which he was
committed, to escape punishment.
FUR. The hairy covering or coat of certain mammals
which is normally fine, soft, and thick, and has an un-
dercoat as well as an outer coat. This is distinguished

from the ordinarily thin, coarse hair of certain animals such as the mountain lion.

Skins valuable chiefly on account of the fur. Skins is a term appropriated to those valuable chiefly for the skin. The word hides is inapplicable to fur skins.

GAME. Wild animals, excluding fish. Generally only mammals. Any animals so defined by law or proclamation having the effect of law.

This term, as it is presently used, generally means all wild animals excluding fish. However, more specifically, it frequently applies to only birds and mammals. In many states all wild animals (wildlife) are either listed as fish or as game. This is broadly interpreted to mean that all cold-blooded (Poikilothermic) animals fall under the category of fish; and all warm-blooded animals fall under the category of game. Strictly speaking, a game animal or a game fish is any animal so defined by the legal code of any particular state or territory. All others are excluded. The word includes all animals of both land and sea which are hunted for sport. Fish, deer, pheasants, partridges, and even wild bees, are held to be within the meaning of it.

GAME LAWS. Laws regulating the killing, taking, or possession of game. The English game laws are founded on the idea of restricting the right of taking game to certain privileged classes, generally land-holders, and are said to be directly descended from the old forest laws.

GILL NET. A fish net so constructed that the fish is usually caught by its gills when it attempts to escape from the meshes of the net. Such nets are regulated as to their use in some jurisdictions and forbidden in others.

GUILT. That which renders criminal and liable to punishment. In general, everyone is presumed innocent until guilt has been proved; but in some cases the presumption of guilt overthrows that of innocence; as, for example, where a party destroys evidence to which the opposite party is entitled.

GUILTY. The state or condition of a person who has committed a crime, misdemeanor, or offense.

GUN. In the usual sense, a weapon which throws a projectile or missile to a distance; a firearm, for throwing a projectile with gunpowder. A firearm is sometimes defined as a weapon which acts by the force of gunpowder.

HABEAS CORPUS. Meaning literally that "you have a body." A writ of habeas corpus is an order of the court directed to the jailer or other police officer detaining a certain person to produce the detained person in court and to otherwise justify his being kept in custody.

A writ directed to the person detaining another and commanding him to produce the body of the prisoner at a certain time and place, with the day and cause of his capture and detention, to do, submit to, and receive whatsoever the court or judge awarding the writ shall consider in that behalf. A writ which has for centuries been esteemed the best and only sufficient defense of personal freedom, having for its object the speedy release by judicial decree of persons who are illegally restrained of their liberty, or illegally detained from the control of those who are entitled to the custody of them.

HEARING. The examination of a prisoner charged with a crime or misdemeanor, and of the witnesses for the accused.

The action brought before court or other official bodies having jurisdiction in a case, in which the testimony of the prosecutor, the defendant, and their witnesses are heard.

HEARSAY EVIDENCE. That kind of evidence which does not derive its value solely from the credit to be given to the witness himself, but rests also, in part, on the veracity and competency of some other person.

A statement offered as evidence to prove the truth of a matter, but which is not made by the author as a witness to the act. This applies to written or oral statements, by the use of symbols, or any other substitute for words which is offered as the equivalent of a statement. Hearsay does not become competent evidence even though it is received by court without objection. This simply means that a fact cannot be proven by showing that someone stated it as a fact. Hearsay is someone else's statement repeated.

HOSTILE WITNESS. A witness who is subject to cross-examination by the party who called him, because of his evident antagonism toward the party as exhibited in his direct examination.

HUE AND CRY. See: Statute of Hue and Cry.

HUNTING. The act of pursuing, taking, or attempting to take wild game.

HUNTING LICENSE. A license required in most, if not all of the states, under statutes which usually prescribe the fee to be paid therefor and make the procuring of such a license a prerequisite to hunting wild game in the state.

ILLEGAL. The word is synonymous with the word "unlawful."

IMPEACH. To impeach is defined by Webster's New International Dictionary as to bring or throw discredit on; to call in question; to challenge; to impute some fault or defect to.

IMPLICATION. An inference of something not directly declared, but arising from what is admitted or expressed.

IMPORT. To import goods is to bring them into a country from a foreign country. In a constitutional sense, articles brought from one state of the Union into another state of the Union are not imported.

INCOMPETENCE. The word connotes the converse of reliability in all that is essential to make up a reasonably safe person, considering the nature of the work and the general safety of those who are required to associate with such person in the general employment.

INCOMPETENT. An incompetent is defined in Webster's New International Dictionary as one who is incompetent; as one incapable of managing his affairs because mentally deficient or undeveloped; as children and idiots are incompetents in the eyes of the law.

INDIAN. No precise definition of the word has been attempted by the courts or by Congress. On the ground that the word is descriptive of race, it has been decided that a white man or a negro, who is adopted into an Indian tribe, does not thereby become an Indian.

INDICTMENT. An acquisition made by the grand jury, recommending that the defendant or defendants be tried in court.

INFORMATION. Strictly speaking, an information is an acquisition made in writing against an individual by the prosecuting attorney, and direct to the court without the matter having been passed upon by the grand jury. (See Complaint.)

IN PERSON. Without counsel in the conduct of one's action or defense.

INSANITY. A diseased or disordered condition or malformation of the physical organs through which the mind receives impressions or manifests its operations, by which the will and judgment are impaired and the conduct rendered irrational.

INSTIGATE. According to the Standard Dictionary, to instigate means to stimulate or goad to an action, especially a bad action. One of the synonyms of the word is "abet," which in law means to aid, promote, or encourage in the commission of an offense.

INTENT. In a legal sense, the word is quite distinct from motive and may be defined as the purpose to use a particular means to effect a certain result, while motive is the reason which leads the mind to desire that result.

INTENTION, INTENT. A design, resolve, or determination of the mind.

INVALID The word is defined by Webster as meaning having no force or effect or efficacy; void, null.

INVESTIGATE. To make inquiry, judicially or otherwise, for the discovery and collection of facts concerning the matter or matters involved. Authority to a legislative committee to make an investigation includes the power to call witnesses and to compel them to testify under oath.

JEOPARDY. The situation of a prisoner when a trial jury is sworn and impanelled to try his case upon a valid indictment, and such jury has been charged with his deliverance.

JOHN DOE WARRANT. A warrant for the arrest of a person which describes him by a fictitious name because his real name is unknown.

JUDGE. One who publicly is charged with and performs judicial functions; one who presides at the trial of causes involving justiciable matters in which the public at large is interested. A public officer lawfully appointed to decide litigated questions according to laws. An officer so named in his commission who presides in some court. In its most extensive sense the term includes all officers appointed to decide litigated questions while acting in that capacity, including justices of the peace.

JUDGMENT. The final consideration and determination of a court of competent jurisdiction upon the matter submitted. The sentence of the law upon the record; the application of the law to the facts and pleadings. The last word in a judicial controversy; the final consideration and determination of a court of competent jurisdiction upon matters submitted to it in an action or proceeding.

JUDICIAL NOTICE. A term used to express the doctrine of the acceptance by a court for the purposes of the case, of the truth of certain notorious facts without requiring proof. It is the process whereby proof by parol evidence is dispensed with, where the court is justified by general considerations in assuming the truth of a proposition without requiring evidence from the party setting it up.

JURISDICTION. The authority by which judicial officers take cognizance of and decide causes.

JURISPRUDENCE. The science of the law. The practical science of giving a wise interpretation to the laws and making a just application of them to all cases as they arise.

JURY. A body of laymen, selected by lot, or by some other fair and impartial means, to ascertain, under the guidance of a judge, the truth in questions of fact arising either in civil litigation or a criminal process. At common law, a jury must consist of 12 men. A body of men who are sworn to declare the facts of a case as they are proven from the evidence placed before them.

JUSTICE OF THE PEACE. A public officer invested with judicial powers for the purpose of preventing breaches of the peace and bringing to punishment those who have violated the laws. Usually elected by popular ballot and not necessarily a person with formal legal training.

JUSTICE'S DOCKET. A book required to be kept by a justice of the peace wherein it is his duty to enter the titles of all causes commenced before him, the time when the first and subsequent process was issued against the defendant, and the particular process issued the judgment rendered by the justice, and the time of rendering the same, the time of issuing execution and the officer to whom delivered.

JUSTIFIABLE TRESPASS. An intentional trespass which the law has authorized; as, an entry into a house through an open door to serve a civil process.

JUVENILE COURTS. Courts which have recently been created by statute, as a product of the solicitude of the law for the welfare of infants, to deal with dependent, neglected and delinquent children.

LAW. A statute; a bill; a legislative enactment; a constitutional provision; the whole body or system of rules of conduct, including both decisions of courts and legislative acts. That which is laid down; that which is established. A rule or method of action, or order of sequences. The rules and methods by which society compels or restrains the action of its members. The aggregate of those rules and principles of conduct which the governing power in a community recognizes as those which it will enforce or sanction, and according to which it will regulate, limit, or protect the conduct of its members. The aggregate of rules set by men as politically superior or sovereign, to men as politically subject.

In its relation to human affairs there is a broad use of the term, in which it denotes any of those rules and methods by which a society compels or restrains the action of its members. Here the idea of a command is more generally obvious, and has usually been thought as essential element in the notion of human law.

LAWFUL. Legal. That which is not contrary to law. That which is sanctioned or permitted by law. That which is in accordance with law. The terms "lawful," "unlawful," and "illegal" are used with reference to that which is in its substance sanctioned or prohibited by the law. The term "legal" is occasionally used with reference to matter of form alone; thus, an oral agreement to convey land, though void by law, is not properly to be said to be unlawful, because there is no violation of law in making or in performing such an agreement; but it is said to be not legal, or not in lawful form, because the law will not enforce it, for want of that written evidence required in such cases.

LAWYER. An attorney or counsellor at law; a barrister; a solicitor; a person licensed by law to practice the profession of law.

LEADING QUESTION. A question which puts into the witness's mouth the words to be echoed back, or plainly suggests the answer which the party wishes to get from him. In that case the examiner is said to lead him to the answer. It is not always easy to determine what is or is not a leading question. Certain questions cannot be put to a witness unless he is a hostile witness. But, questions may be put to lead the mind of the witness to the subject of inquiry; and they are allowed when it appears that the witness wishes to conceal the truth or to favor the opposite party, or where from the nature of the case the mind of the witness cannot be directed to the subject of inquiry without a particular specification of such subject. In cross-examination; the examiner generally has the right to put leading questions; but not perhaps when the witness has a bias in his favor.

LEGAL. According to the principles of law; according to the method required by statute; by means of judicial proceedings; not equitable.

LETHAL. Capable of producing death or great bodily harm.

LETHAL WEAPON. A gun, sword, knife, pistol, or the like, is a lethal weapon, as a matter of law, when used within striking distance of the person assaulted; and all other weapons are lethal or not, according to their capacity to produce death or great bodily harm in the manner in which they are used.

LICENSE. A right, given by some competent authority, to do an act, which without such authority would be illegal. A permission to do some act or series of acts on the land of the licensor, without having any permanent interest in it; it is founded on personal confidence, and not assignable.

MAGISTRATE. A public civil officer, invested with some part of the legislative, executive, or judicial power given by the constitution. A word commonly applied to the lower judicial officers, such as justices of the peace, police judges, town recorders, and other local judicial functionaries.

MAGNA CHARTA. The great charter of liberties which was wrung from King John by the barons in the year 1215, and later confirmed in parliament by Henry the Third, son of John. It contained some new grants, but was principally a declaration of the principal grounds of the fundamental laws of England.

MALA FIDE. In bad faith.

MALICE. In Criminal Law. The doing a wrongful act intentionally without just cause or excuse. A wicked and mischievous purpose which characterizes the perpetration of an injurious act without lawful excuse.

MALICIOUS ARREST. A wanton arrest made without probable cause. The term is applied when the arrest on which an action for malicious prosecution is based was under civil, and not under criminal process.

MALICIOUS PROSECUTION. A wanton prosecution made by a prosecutor in a criminal proceeding, or a plaintiff in a civil suit, without probable cause, by a regular process and proceeding, which the facts did not warrant, as appears by the result.

MALINGERING. Feigning illness, disability, mental derangement, or intentionally inflicting self-injury on oneself; all for the purpose of avoiding an act or duty as requested by an officer or by the court.

MALTREATMENT. In order for a charge of maltreatment of a prisoner to be brought against an officer the act must be real and without justifiable cause although not necessarily of a physical nature. Abuse may be by derogatory words, assault, striking, or depriving the prisoner of certain benefits and the necessities of life within a reasonable time.

MAMMAL. The highest class of animals with backbones, including man and all other animals that nourish their young with milk. Mammals are "warm-blooded" and except in one group the young are born alive.

MANSLAUGHTER. The unlawful killing of another, but without malice. It may be voluntary, as when the act is committed with a real design and purpose to kill, but through the violence of sudden passion which in tenderness for the frailty of human nature the law considers sufficient to palliate the offense. It is involuntary when the death of another is caused by some unlawful act not accompanied with any intention to take life.

MARTIAL LAW. That government and control which military commanders may lawfully exercise over the persons and property of citizens and individuals not engaged in the land and naval service. Military law applies to those rules enacted by the legislative power for the government and regulation of the United States armed forces.

MID-CHANNEL. If there be more than one channel of a river, the deepest channel is regarded as the navigable mid-channel for the purpose of territorial demarcation; and the boundary line will be the line drawn along the surface of the stream corresponding to the line of deepest depression of its bed.

MIDDLE OF THE STREAM. In international law, and by the usage of European nations, the term, as applied to a navigable river, is the same as the middle of the channel of the stream.

MISCONDUCT. A transgression of some established and definite rule of action, where no discretion is left, except what necessity may demand; it is a violation of definite law; a forbidden act. It differs from carelessness.

MISDEMEANOR. A term used to express every offense inferior to felony, punishable by indictment, or by particular prescribed proceedings. In its usual acceptation, it is applied to all those crimes and offenses for which the law has not provided a particular name.

A grade of crime less serious than a felony, but more serious than a summary conviction offense in some states.

MITIGATION. The reduction of damages or punishment by reason of extenuating facts or circumstances.

MODUS OPERANDI. Method of operation. The techniques used by a criminal in the commission of a crime. The type of operation that is peculiar to an individual.

MOOT QUESTION. A mooted or undecided point of law.

MORAL CERTAINTY. That degree of certainty which will justify a jury in grounding on it their verdict. The phrase is one the use of which is not likely to assist a jury in charging upon the question of reasonable doubt. It is an artificial form of words having no precise and definite meaning.

A probability sufficiently strong to justify action upon it.

MORAL CONSIDERATION. A consideration which is good only in conscience. The idea that in every case where a person is under a moral obligation to do an act, as to relieve one in distress by personal exertions, or to spend money, a promise to that effect would bind him in law, is not supported by principle or precedent.

MORAL EVIDENCE. Evidence not only of that kind which is employed on subjects connected with moral conduct, but all the evidence which is not obtained either from intuition, or from demonstration. In the ordinary affairs of life, we do not require demonstrative evidence.

MORAL INSANITY. A term sometimes employed to denote such mental disease as destroys the ability to distinguish between right and wrong as to a particular act, and sometimes to denote a mere perversion of the moral sense. It is sometimes used as being synonymous with irresistible impulse.

MORAL OBLIGATION. Where courts generally recognize the existence of a moral obligation as a sufficient consideration, it refers to promises that are enforceable because they are based on obligations which were formerly valid but have since become barred, as by limitations or bankruptcy.

MOTION. An application to a court by one of the parties in a cause, or his counsel, in order to obtain some rule or order of court which he thinks becomes necessary in the progress of the cause, or to get relieved in a summary manner from some matter which would work an injustice. It is said to be a written application for an order. An application made to a judge, chancellor, or court for the purpose of obtaining a rule or order directing some act to be done in favor of the applicant. It is usually a proceeding incidental to an action.

MOTION FOR DIRECTED VERDICT. A motion made by either plaintiff or defendant, after all the evidence is in, requesting the court to instruct the jury to return their verdict in favor of the moving party. A motion for a directed verdict in favor of the defendant is tantamount to a demurrer to the evidence.

MOTION FOR JUDGMENT ON PLEADINGS. A motion made by either party to an action in the nature of a general demurrer to the pleadings of the adverse party, and which, for all purposes of the motion admits the truth of all the allegations contained in those pleadings.

MOTION FOR NEW TRIAL. A motion the office of which is primarily to afford the court an opportunity to correct errors in the proceedings before it without subjecting the parties to the expense and inconvenience of an appeal or petition in error.

MOTIVE. The inducement, cause, or reason why a thing is done. It is an inducement, or that which leads or tempts the mind to indulge the criminal act; it is resorted to as a means of arriving at an ultimate fact, not for the purpose of explaining the reason of a criminal act which has been clearly proved, but from the important aid it may render in completing the proof of the commission of the act when it might otherwise remain in doubt. It is not indispensable to conviction for murder that the particular motive for taking the life of a human being shall be established by proof to the satisfaction of the jury.

MURDER. The unlawful killing of a human being with malice aforethought.

MUTILATE. To deprive of some essential part, as to tear off a portion of a railroad ticket.

NAVIGABILITY. The test of navigability is whether the river, in its natural state, is used, or capable of being used, as a highway for commerce, over which trade and travel are or may be conducted. Navigability is not destroyed because the watercourse is interrupted by occasional natural obstruction or portages; nor need the navigation be open at all seasons of the year, or at all stages of the water.

NAVIGABLE. Rivers must be regarded as public navigable rivers in law which are navigable in fact, and they are navigable in fact when they are used, or are susceptible of being used, in their ordinary condition, as highways for commerce. And it has been held that a stream of sufficient depth and width, in its natural state, to be used for the transportation of timbers or logs, is subject to the public right of user.

NAVIGABLE IN FACT. Navigability in fact is the test of navigability in law, and whether a river is navigable in fact is to be determined by inquiring whether it is used, in its natural and ordinary condition, as a highway for commerce.

NAVIGABLE STREAM. A river capable of floating to market the products of the country, and upon which boats, barges, rafts, or logs may be borne, is a navigable stream both in fact and in law. The criterion of navigability is the use to which the stream may be put.

NAVIGABLE WATERS. Formerly, the term was confined to those waters which were affected by the ebb and flow of the tides, but in the development of this country the meaning has been enlarged so as to apply to all waters which are in fact navigable.

NEGATIVE TESTIMONY. Testimony which either denies that certain alleged facts are true, or that certain things occurred, or which denies all knowledge of the matter. Testimony which is positive in form may amount merely to negative testimony.

NEGLIGENCE. The word ordinarily used to express the foundation of civil liability at common law for injury to person or property, when such injury is not the result of premeditation and formed intention. The question arises as to whether the basis of an action for negligence is the negligent act of the defendant or the injury resulting therefrom. It would seem that it is the injury and not alone the negligent act which gives rise to the right of action.

NEW TRIAL. A re-examination of an issue of fact in the same court after a trial. When there has been no trial upon issues of fact, a new trial will not be granted, as where the case has been submitted on the pleadings by stipulation leaving the court to decide under the law and upon the facts stated.

NO AWARD. A name which was given to a plea which denied that an award which was sued upon was ever made.

NO BILL. An indictment which was not found by the grand jury was indorsed "no bill" or "ignoramus" (we do not know).

NOLO CONTENDERE. Literally means "I will not contest it." In practice the term does not mean that no defense will be given to the charge nor does it mean that the defendant is pleading guilty. A plea usually made only in federal courts.

A plea sometimes accepted in criminal cases, not capital, whereby the defendant does not directly admit himself to be guilty, but tactly admits it by throwing himself upon the mercy of the court and desiring to submit to a small fine, which plea the court may either accept or decline. The difference in effect is that, after the latter, not guilty cannot be pleaded in an action of trespass for the same injury, whereas it may be pleaded at any time after the former.

NON EST INVENTUS. From the Latin meaning, "He is not to be found." A warrant which has been placed in the hands of an officer and cannot be served, because of the inability of the officer to locate the defendant, is usually returned <u>non est inventus</u>, which is sometimes abbreviated to NEI.

NONRESIDENT. One who is not residing or living in the state, or one who has no home or abode within the state, or one who has no intention, when leaving, of returning to a home or abode in the state

NOTARY, NOTARY PUBLIC. An officer appointed by the executive or other appointing power, under the laws of different states. Notaries are of ancient origin; they existed in Rome during the republic.

Their duties differ somewhat in the different states, and are prescribed by statute. They are generally as follows: To protest bills of exchange and draw up acts of honor; to authenticate and certify copies of documents; to receive the affidavits of mariners and draw up protest relating to the same; to attest and take acknowledgments of deeds and other instruments; and to administer oaths. Ordinarily notaries have no jurisdiction outside the country or district for which they are appointed; but in several states they may act throughout the state.

NOT GUILTY. The name given to a plea of the general issue in trespass and certain other civil actions. The plea of a defendant in a criminal prosecution, the effect of which is to deny the truth of the allegations of the indictment or information.

OATH. Any form of attestation by which a person signifies that he is bound in conscience to perform an act faithfully and truthfully. It involves the idea of calling on God to witness what is averred as truth, and it is supposed to be accompanied with an invocation of His vengeance, or a renunciation of His favor, in the event of falsehood. An outward pledge given by the person taking it that his attestation or promise is made under an immediate sense of his responsibility to God.

OATH OF OFFICE. An oath, the form of which is prescribed by law and which in most of the states is required as a qualification for a public office. The constitutions or laws of the states frequently provide that every state officer shall, before entering on the discharge of his duties, take a prescribed oath.

OBJECTION. Where evidence is objected to at a trial, the nature of the objections must be distinctly stated, whether an exception be entered on the record or not, and, on either moving for a new trial on account of its improper admission, or on arguing the exception, the counsel will not be permitted to rely on any other objections than those taken at nisi prius.

OFFENSE. The doing that which a penal law forbids to be done, or omitting to do what it commands. In this sense, it is nearly synonymous with crime. In a more confined sense, it may be considered as having the same meaning with misdemeanor; but it differs from it in this, that it is not indictable, but punishable summarily by the forfeiture of a penalty.

OFFICER. A person who holds an office, either public or private.

ORDER. A written order of a court or judge embodying a determination of some preliminary matter pertaining to the proceedings, which is not implicated with the essential rights of the litigants.

OUT OF THE STATE. As used in a proviso tolling the statute of limitations while the defendant is "out of the state," the expression has been held to apply not only to a resident who is absent for a time from the state, but also to a person who resides altogether out of the state.

PENAL STATUTE. A statute which imposes a penalty for transgressing its provisions. Such a statute is one that imposes a penalty or creates a forfeiture as the punishment for the neglect of some duty, or the commission of some wrong, that concerns the good of the public, and is commanded or prohibited by law.

PEREMPTORY. Final; positive; conclusive.

PEREMPTORY CHALLENGE. A challenge to proposed jurors which a defendant in a criminal case may make as an absolute right, and which cannot be questioned by either opposing counsel or the court. The motive which may influence a defendant or his attorney in the exercise of such right is not the subject of inquiry, nor comment in the presence of the jury.

PEREMPTORY DEFENSE. A defense which denies the right of the plaintiff to sue.

PEREMPTORY EXCEPTION. An answer which merely raises an issue of law, the legal effect of which is the same as that of a demurrer.

PEREMPTORY PLEA. A plea which sets up the defense that the plaintiff has no right to sue.

PERJURY. The wilful assertion as to a matter of fact, opinion, belief, or knowledge, made by a witness in a judicial proceeding as part of his evidence, either upon oath or in any form allowed by law to be substituted for an oath, whether such evidence is given in open court, or in an affidavit, or otherwise, such assertion being known to such witness to be false, and being intended by him to mislead the court, jury, or person holding the proceeding. The wilful and corrupt false swearing or affirming, after an oath lawfully administered, in the course of a judicial or quasi judicial proceeding as to some matter material to the issue or point in question. Some cases add the requirement that the false statement must be made after deliberation, others say that it must be knowingly false.

PERMANENT ABODE. A home, which a party may leave as interest or whim may dictate, but which he has no present intention to abandon.

PERMIT. The word is derived from the Latin word permittere, which means to concede, to give leave, to grant. To permit is to grant leave or liberty to by express consent; to allow expressly; to give leave, liberty, or license to; to allow to be done by consent or by not prohibiting.

PHOTOGRAPH. A photograph of a document is but a copy of that document, and its admission in evidence as a document is governed by the rules pertaining to copies.

PHYSICAL IMPOSSIBILITY. In the law of contracts, the term means practical impossibility according to the state of knowledge of the day; as, for example, a promise to go from New York to London in an hour (1955), or to discover treasure by "magic."

PLAINTIFF. The person or persons making the charge against another in court. He who complains. He who, complains. He who, in personal action, seeks a remedy for an injury to his rights.

PLEA. In Equity, a special answer showing or relying upon one or more things as a cause why the suit should be either dismissed, or delayed, or barred.

At Law. The defendant's answer by matter of fact to the plaintiff's declaration, as distinguished from a demurrer, which is an answer by matter of law. It includes as well the denial of the truth of the allegations

on which the plaintiff relies, as the statement of facts
on which the defendant relies.

PLEA OF <u>NOLO CONTENDERE</u>. The so-called plea of
<u>nolo contendere</u> (I will not contest it) raises no issue
of law or fact under the indictment, is not one of the
pleas, general or special, open to the accused in all
criminal prosecutions, and is allowable under leave
and acceptance by the court. It is in reality a formal
declaration that the accused will not contend with the
prosecuting authority under the charge.

POSSESSION. The detention or enjoyment of a thing which
a man holds or exercises by himself, or by another
who keeps or exercises it in his name.

POST MORTEM. From the Latin meaning "after death,"
the term in legal circles is synonymously used with the
word autopsy.

POWER OF ATTORNEY. An instrument authorizing a person to act as the agent or attorney of the person granting it. It is often called letter of attorney. A general
power authorizes the agent to act generally in behalf of
the principal. A special power is one limited to particular acts.

PRECEDENTS. Legal acts of instruments which are
deemed worthy to serve as rules or models for subsequent cases.

PRELIMINARY EXAMINATION. The hearing given to a person of crime, by a magistrate or judge, exercising the
functions of a committing magistrate or judge, exercising the functions of a committing magistrate, to ascertain whether there is evidence to warrant and require the commitment and holding to bail or the person
accused. Coroners generally have the powers of a
committing magistrate as also have the mayors of
cities in many of the states.

PREMEDITATION. An act is not premeditated unless the
thought of completing it was consciously conceived and
the action was taken with the completion of the act intended. It is the formation of a specific intent and the
consideration of the intended act. It is not necessary
that the intent shall have been entertained for any particular length of time. For example, a person legally
hunting rabbits may suddenly decide to attempt to kill
the next quail (which is not in season) that flies up. On
the other hand, a person hunting rabbits that has no

intention of killing quail, fires at one on the spur of the moment, is not guilty of a premeditated act, although it is an illegal one. Most officers and judges prefer to deal more harshly with a premeditated crime than with a spontaneous one, even though the acts involved may be identical.

PRESUME. To presume is derived from the Latin word praesumere, and signifies to take or assume a matter beforehand, without proof--to take for granted.

PRESUMPTION. An inference affirmative or disaffirmative of the truth or falsehood of any proposition or fact drawn by a process of probable reasoning in the absence of actual certainty of its truth or falsehood, or until such certainty can be ascertained.

PRIMA FACIE. Literally meaning "at first sight." It means that there is sufficient evidence to justify or strongly infer the facts stated. For example, when buildings are fired by sparks from a locomotive, the fire has been held to be prima facie evidence of neglect on the part of those in charge of the locomotive. The proof of the mailing of a letter, duly stamped, is prima facie evidence of its receipt by the person to whom it is addressed. That is prima facie just, reasonable, or correct which is presumed to be just, reasonable, or correct until the presumption has been overcome by evidence which clearly rebuts it. Evidence which if unexplained or uncontradicted would of itself establish the fact alleged.

At first view, on first appearance. For example, the holder of a bill of exchange, indorsed in blank, is prima facie its owner.

PRIVATE POND. To fall within the meaning of the term, the pond must be essentially private. It must be a sheet of water covering exclusively the land of its owner, and must be such as no one could forbid him its use, any more than the cultivation of the soil under- neath, if it was free from water.

PROCEDURE. The methods of conducting litigation and judicial proceedings.

PROOF. The conviction or persuasion of the mind of a judge or jury, by the exhibition of evidence, of the re- ality of a fact alleged. Thus, to prove is to determine or persuade that a thing does or does not exist.

PROSECUTING ATTORNEY. The attorney who conducts proceedings in a court. A public prosecutor. Public officers elected or appointed, as provided by the constitution or statutes of the various states, to conduct suits, generally criminal, on behalf of the state in their respective districts. They are sworn ministers of justice.

PROSECUTION. In Criminal Law. The means adopted to bring a supposed offender to justice and punishment by due course of law. The well-understood, legal signification of the word is, a criminal proceeding at the suit of the government.

PUNISHMENT. In Criminal Law. Some pain or penalty warranted by law, inflicted on a person for the commission of a crime or misdemeanor, or for the omission of the performance of an act required by law, by the judgment and command of some lawful court. The penalty for the transgression of the law.

PUNITIVE. That which inflicts or awards punishment. Whatever is concerned with punishment or penalties such as punitive laws or punitive justice. Also, whatever is involved in or aimed at punishment; such as, a punitive expedition or a punitive section of a code book.

QUALIFIED. Possession fitness or capacity; a person is said to have qualified, or to be qualified, for an office to which he has been elected or appointed, when he has complied with the requirements of the law; as by taking the oath of office and giving an official bond.

RATIONAL. Capable of reasoning; sane.

REASONABLE DOUBT. Such a doubt as will leave the juror's mind, after a careful examination of all the evidence, in such a condition that he cannot say that he has an abiding conviction, to a moral certainty, of the defendant's guilt. A doubt that, arising from a candid and impartial investigation of all the evidence, would cause a reasonable and prudent man to hesitate and pause.

REASONABLE OR PROBABLE CAUSE. As the expression is used in malicious prosecution, it is defined as a reasonable amount of suspicion, supported by circumstances sufficiently strong to warrant a cautious man in believing that the accused is guilty; but mere suspicion alone is not sufficient.

REBUT. To deny; to contradict; to avoid.

REBUTTAL. Testimony addressed to evidence produced by the opposite party; rebutting evidence.

REBUTTING EVIDENCE. Rebuttal evidence is that produced for the purpose of contradicting something previously testified.

That evidence which is given by a party in the cause to explain, repel, counteract, or disprove facts given in evidence on the other side. The term rebutting evidence is more particularly applied to that evidence given by the plaintiff to explain or repel the evidence given by the defendant. It is a general rule that anything may be given as rebutting evidence which is a direct reply to that produced on the other side.

RECLAIMED ANIMALS. Animals wild by nature which have been domesticated.

RECOGNIZE. To try a question of fact; to ratify; to adopt; to become bound by a recognizance.

RE-EXAMINATION. A second examination of a thing. A witness may be re-examined, in a trial at law, in the discretion of the court; and this is seldom refused. In equity, it is a general rule that there can be no re-examination of a witness after he has once signed his name to the deposition and turned his back upon the commissioner or examiner. The reason for this is that he may be tampered with or induced to retract or qualify what he has sworn to.

REHEARING. A second consideration which the court gives to a cause on a second argument. A rehearing cannot be granted by the Supreme Court after the record has been remitted to the court below.

REMIT. To pardon; to remand for a new trial or for further proceedings; to transmit.

REPEAL. The abrogation or destruction of a law by a legislative act. A repeal is express, as, when it is literally declared by a subsequent law, or implied, when the new law contains provisions contrary to or irreconcilable with those of the former law. The power to revoke or annul a statute or ordinance is equivalent to the power to repeal it; and in either case the power is legislative and not judicial in its character.

RES GESTAE. The circumstances, facts, and declarations which grow out of the main fact and are contemporaneous with it, and serve to illustrate its character. The facts of the transaction.

RESIDENCE. Personal presence in a fixed and permanent abode. A residence is different from a domicile, although it is a matter of great importance in determining the place of domicile. The essential distinction between residence and domicile is that the first involves the intent to leave when the purpose for which one has taken up his abode ceases. The other has no such intent.

RESIST. To resist is to oppose by direct, active, and quasi forcible means; to stand against, to withstand. Refusal to obey an officer is not resistance to the officer.

ROTENONE. A certain substance that poisons fish by suffocating them.

RUSTLING. Stealing cattle, or in some cases other domestic livestock. In some states it is a felony.

SANCTUARY. A sacred place where a person who has committed a crime is immune from arrest. A place where wildlife may not be hunted or molested.

SATISFACTORY EVIDENCE. That which is sufficient to induce a belief that the thing is true; in other words, it is credible evidence.

SEARCH WARRANT. A legal writ, executed by competent authority, authorizing the search of the premises named therein and for the express purpose of determining if such unlawful article or articles as are named within the warrant are being secluded or held within the described premises. The goods may be either stolen or illegally possessed.

A warrant requiring the officer to whom it is addressed to search a house, or other place, therein specified, for property therein alleged to have been stolen, and, if the same shall be found upon such search, to bring the goods so found, together with the person occupying the same, who is named, before the justice or other officer granting the warrant, or some other justice of the peace, or other lawfully authorized officer. It should be given under the hand and seal of the justice, and dated.

SELF-DEFENSE. In Criminal Law. The protection of one's person and property from injury. A man may defend himself, and even commit a homicide, for the prevention of any forcible and atrocious crime which, if completed, would amount to a felony.

SENTENCE. A judgment, or judicial declaration made by a judge in a cause. The term judgment is more usually applied to civil, and sentence to criminal, proceedings. Sentences are final, when they put an end to the case; or interlocutory, when they settle only some incidental matter which has arisen in the course of its progress.

SEVERAL FISHERY. An exclusive right to fish in a given place, either with or without the property in the soil at such place. No person other than the owner of the fishery can lawfully take fish at such place.

SHERIFF. The office of sheriff is one of the oldest known to the common law. It is inseparably associated with the county. The name itself signifies keeper of the shire or county. The office is said to have been created by Alfred when he divided England into shires, but Coke believed it to have been of Roman origin.

SOUND MIND. That state of a man's mind which is adequate to reason and comes to a judgment upon ordinary subjects like other rational men. The law presumes that every person who has acquired his full age is of sound mind, and, consequently, competent to make contracts and perform all his civil duties; and he who asserts to the contrary must prove the affirmation of his position by explicit evidence, and not by conjectural proof.

SPECIAL AGENT. An agent who is only authorized to do specific acts in pursuance of particular instructions, or with restrictions necessarily implied from the acts to be done.

SPECIAL JUDGE. A judge appointed to act in a particular case because of the disqualification of the regular judge. The authority of such a judge is not limited to the term during which he is appointed, but extends to subsequent terms until the disability of the regular judge is removed.

STATE. A body politic, or society of men, united together for the purpose of promoting their mutual safety and advantage, by the joint efforts of their combined strength.

STATEMENT. The act of stating, reciting, or presenting verbally or on paper.

STATE POLICE POWER. That power under which the states or their municipalities may enact statutes and ordinances to protect the public health, the public morals, the public safety, and the public convenience.

STATE'S EVIDENCE. The evidence of an accomplice who testifies for the prosecution in the hope of being released or punished more lightly.

STATUS QUO. The existing state of things at any given date.

STATUTE. A law properly enacted by the authorized lawmaking body of a state or nation. A law established by the act of the legislative power. An act of the legislature. The written will of the legislature, solemnly expressed according to the forms necessary to constitute it the law of the state. This word is used to designate the written law in contradistinction to the unwritten law.

STATUTE OF HUE AND CRY. According to Webster, a loud outcry with which felons were anciently pursued, and which all who heard it were obligated to take up and join in pursuit. Later a written proclamation for the capture of a felon or stolen goods.

A statute or act by which the inhabitants of an area were liable for the loss of the goods taken unless they produced the robber.

STATUTE OF LIMITATIONS. The time within which an action may be brought against a person for a crime. The time varies with the crime and the laws of the state where the crime is committed.

SUBPOENA. A legal instrument issued by competent authority, requiring the presence of a person to testify of his own knowledge concerning certain acts or information.

A process to cause a witness to appear and give testimony, commanding him to lay aside all pretenses and excuses, and appear before a court or magistrate therein named, at a time therein mentioned, to testify for the party named, under a penalty therein mentioned. This is called distinctively a subpoena ad testificandum. On proof of service of a subpoena upon the witness and that he is material, an attachment may be issued against him for a contempt if he neglects to attend, as commanded.

SUMMONS. The name of a writ commanding the sheriff, or other authorized officer, to notify a party to appear in court to answer a complaint made against him and in the said writ specified, on a day therein mentioned.

SUPREME COURT. A court of superior jurisdiction in many of the states of the United States. The name is properly applied to the court of last resort, and is so used in most of the states.

SWEAR. To take an oath administered by some officer duly empowered. One may swear who is not duly sworn; and in such case the oath is not administered, but self-imposed, and the swearer incurs no legal liability thereabout.

TESTIMONY. The statement made by a witness under oath of affirmation.

Oral evidence spoken by a human witness, as contrasted with evidence presented in documentary form by innate objects.

TRIAL. In Practice. The examination before a competent tribunal, according to the laws of the land, of the facts put in issue in a cause, for the purpose of determining such issue.

VENUE. The county in which the facts are alleged to have occurred, and from which the jury are to come to try the issue. Some certain place must be alleged as the place of occurrence for each traversable fact.

VERDICT. The decision of the proper authority hearing the action. The decision made by a jury and reported to the court on the matters lawfully submitted to them in the course of a trial of a cause.

VESTED INTEREST. An interest when vested, whether it entitles the owner to the possession now or at a future period, is fixed and present; so that the right of ownership, to the extent of the estate, may be aliened.

VIOLATION. The result of an act done unlawfully and often with force. This word has also been construed under this statute to mean carnal knowledge.

VOLUNTARY STATEMENT. In criminal proceedings, a defendant's statement, to have been voluntarily made, must have proceeded from the spontaneous suggestion of his own mind, free from the influence of any extraneous disturbing cause.

WANTONLY. Done in a licentious spirit, perversely, recklessly, without regard to propriety or the right of others; careless of consequences, and yet without settled malice.

WARRANT. A legal instrument, properly executed by competent authority, requiring the arrest and apprehension of the person named therein. A writ issued by a justice of the peace or other authorized officer, directed to a constable or other proper person, requiring him to arrest a person therein named, charged with committing some offense, and to bring him before that or some other justice of the peace. An order authorizing a payment of money by another person to a third person.

WEIGHT OF EVIDENCE. This phrase is used to signify that the proof on one side of a cause or issue is greater than on the other. When a verdict has been rendered against the weight of the evidence, the court may, on this ground, grant a new trial; but the court will exercise this power not merely with a cautious but a strict and sure judgment, before they send the case to a second jury.

WILD ANIMALS. Animals wild by nature, such as deer in the forest, pigeons in the air, and fish if in public waters or the ocean.

WILDLIFE. Any wild animal. Either fish or game, or both.

WILFULLY. Intentionally as distinguished from accidentally or involuntarily.

WITNESS. A person testifying concerning matters of law and sworn to speak the truth, the whole truth, and nothing but the truth.

One who testifies to what he knows. One who testifies under oath to something which he knows of first hand.

WRIT. A mandatory precept, issued by the authority and in the name of the sovereign or the state, for the purpose of compelling the defendant to do something therein mentioned.

WRITTEN INSTRUMENT. A Missouri statute defines the term as including every instrument, partly printed and partly written, or wholly printed with a written signature thereto, and every writing purporting to be a signature.

X-RAY PHOTOGRAPH. A photograph made by the aid of a particular electrical ray whereby there may be secured reliable representations of the bones of a flesh and bones body, although they are hidden from direct view by the surrounding flesh, and also of metallic or other solid substances which may be imbedded in the flesh.

Appendix B
Forms, Charges, and Specifications

Copy to Judge

STATE OF IDAHO

DEPARTMENT OF FISH AND GAME

CITATION TO APPEAR IN COURT

Name___Jack Poacher_____

Address_Arbon, Idaho_____

Age___38___Height__6'__1"___Weight_194___Sex__Male___

Occupation_Shipping Clerk___Employer___Idaho Central___

Vehicle____Dodge_____Lic. No._____191_____

Game Lic. No.___183456_____Purchased at____Arbon_____

Place of Violation___Knox Canyon_____

County__Power___Date_Oct. 16, 1950_Time__10:00__A.M.__P.M.

Violation___Hunting deer with the aid of a dog_____

_____

_____

You are hereby notified to appear before___I. M. Tuff____
                                      Justice of the Peace
                                           Probate Judge

at____American Falls_____,Idaho

on the___17___day of_October__, 19_50_at__10__A.M.__P.M.
then and there to answer to the above charge.
Receipt of Citation Acknowledged

_____   JOHN LAW_____
      Defendant   Conservation Officer

241

ACKNOWLEDGEMENT OF NO LICENSE

This is to certify that I, _____ Joe Careless _____

of _____ Homedale _____, State of _____ Idaho _____, was

(hunting) (~~fishing~~) (~~trapping~~) in _____ Power _____County

on the __15__ day of _October___, 19_50_, at ____9:00_____o'clock

and that I was approached by Conservation Officer____ John Law _____

_____, and that I did not have a license

as required by law in my possession at the time, I further claim

that I purchased a license from ___Joe's Garage_____
                                        (Vendor)
of _____ Homedale _____ on__October 14, 1950_____
                                             (Date)

Witness____ Jack Law _____ Signature____ Joe Careless _____
                                    Date_____October_____

Information checked at ____American Falls____ Date ___Oct. 17, 1950___

License was (~~was not~~) purchased as shown.
License No.___187547_____

242

IN THE JUSTICE COURT OF   AMERICAN FALLS   PRECINCT
COUNTY OF   POWER   STATE OF IDAHO

STATE OF IDAHO, Plaintiff,   }

          vs.   }   COMPLAINT--CRIMINAL

   Jack Poacher   }
          Defendant)

     Personally appeared before me this 17 day of October ,19 50
       John Law, Conservation Officer of American Falls

in the county of   Power , who, first being duly sworn,

complains of Jack Poacher of Arbon, Idaho and charges him with the

public offense of   Hunting deer with the aid of a dog

committed as follows, to-wit: That the said   Jack Poacher

at   Knox Canyon , in the County of   Power   and State of Idaho

on the   16   day of October   , 19 50   , did then and there

willfully and unlawfully violate Section 36-1407 of the State of Idaho

    Fish and Game Code by hunting deer with the aid of a dog.

     all of which is contrary to the form of the statute in said State
made and provided and against the peace and dignity of the State
of Idaho.

     Said complainant therefore prays that a warrant may be issued
for the arrest of said   Jack Poacher

and that he may be dealt with according to law

                  (Signed)_____John Law_____

Subscribed and sworn to before me this 17 day of October   , 19 50

                       I. M. Tuff
               Justice of the Peace of Said Precinct

IN THE JUSTICE COURT

of __American Falls__ Precinct County of ___Power___

State of Idaho

THE STATE OF IDAHO:

To any Sheriff, Constable, Marshal or Policeman of the County

of _____Power_____

INFORMATION, on oath, having this day been laid before me by

John Law, Conservation Officer   that the crime of

Hunting deer with the aid of a dog (as contrary to Section 36-1407

of the State of Idaho Fish and Game Code)

has been committed, and accusing   Jack Poacher of Arbon, Idaho

thereof, you are commanded forthwith to arrest the above named

          Jack Poacher of Arbon, Idaho

                    and bring him before me, forthwith,

at my office at American Falls in said Precinct, County of Power

  Dated at · American Falls   In said Precinct, County of Power

at the hour of 10:00 A.M. , this 17 day of October , 19 50.

                              _____
                                   I. M. Tuff
                              Justice of the Peace

THE ABOVE NAMED   Jack Poacher of Arbon, Idaho

having been brought before me under this warrant

committed for examination to the Sheriff of the County of Power

  Dated this   17   day of Oct. , 1950

                              _____
                                   I. M. Tuff
                              Justice of the Peace

IN THE PROBATE COURT

OF THE COUNTY OF ___POWER___, STATE OF IDAHO

State of Idaho,
                         Plaintiff,
        vs.

_____)
_____)   COMPLAINT--CRIMINAL
_____)
        Jack Poacher   )
                    Defendant

PERSONALLY APPEARED Before me this __17__ day of _October_, 19_50_

John Law, Conservation Officer, of ___American Falls___

in the County of____Power____, who, being duly sworn, complains
and says:
        That___Jack Poacher_____

of ___Arbon, Idaho___, on the ___16___ day of___October___, 19_50_

at ___Knox Canyon___, in the County of____Power____, and State

of Idaho, ___did then and there willfully, knowingly, and unlawfully___

___violate Section 36-1407 of the State of Idaho Fish and Game Code___

___by hunting deer with the aid of a dog.___

All of which is contrary to the form of the statute in such
case made and provided and against the peace and dignity of the
State of Idaho.

Said complainant therefore prays that a warrant may be issued
for the arrest of said ___Jack Poacher___

and that __X_he_X__ may be dealt with according to law.

                              ___JOHN LAW___

Subscribed and sworn to before me this __17__ day of_October_, 19_50_

                              ___I. M. TUFF___
                              Probate Judge

No._____Filed_____, 19____ _____, Clerk.
                         Recorded in Book_____, Page____

245

POWER OF ATTORNEY

Dated at __American Falls__, this _17_ day of _October_, 19 _51_
I, _____Jack Poacher_____, of the city of _____Arbon_____,
State of ___Idaho___, hereby acknowledge that I am guilty of the
crime of ___Hunting deer with the aid of a dog___
on which charge I have been arrested by ___John Law___
and I hereby authorize and empower ___Rex Bleep___
as my attorney in the State of Idaho, to enter a plea of guilty
for me to a complaint filed on the above charge in the
~~Probate~~ Justice Court of ___American Falls___ ___Power___, County, Idaho.
                              City

Witness to my signature: Jack Poacher
                                Signed

___Joe Loosends___   Arbon, Idaho
                                Address

246

STATE OF IDAHO

DEPARTMENT OF FISH AND GAME
Boise

STATE GAME DIRECTOR,
   Boise, Idaho.

Dear Sir:

I herewith make report of the arrest of __Jack Poacher__
                                          (Name)
of____Arbon, Idaho_____
                        (Address)
at____Knox Canyon_____on___October 16_____, 195_0_

Nature of offense charged__Hunting deer with the aid of a dog____

Defendant arraigned before__I. M. Tuff_____
Justice of the Peace⎫ at_American Falls___on___October 17___, 195_0_
~~Probate Judge~~   ⎭

Plea entered_____Guilty_____

If plea of not guilty is entered give date and result of trial_____

_____

_____

Fine imposed, $__100____Suspended, $_____Net Find, $_100_

Jail Sentence____30 days_____Suspended___30 days_____

Prosecuting Attorney_____

Defendant's Attorney_____

Equipment Seized_____

Disposition of Equipment Seized_____

   If game, birds, fish, hunting or fishing paraphernalia are seized
in connection with this case, a full report must be made to the
State Game Director regarding same.

REMARKS:_____

_____

_____

Report No._____   (Signed)___JOHN LAW_____
   (For office use only)   Conservation Officer

247

IN THE PROBATE COURT

COUNTY OF ___Power___, STATE OF IDAHO

The State of Idaho   Plaintiff)

          vs.   )   SUBPOENA--CRIMINAL

Jack Poacher   Defendant)

THE STATE OF IDAHO SENDS GREETING TO

Mr. Bashful Observer

WE COMMEND YOU, That all and singular business and excuses being set aside, you appear and attend before the said Probate Court, in and for the County of   Power   State of Idaho, at a term of said Court to be held at the Court room of said Court, in the said County of Power   , on the 20th day of October , 19 50 at 10 o'clock a.m., then and there to testify in the above entitled cause on behalf of the State of Idaho, Plaintiff

ATTEST My hand and seal of said Court this 17th day of October , 1950

_____
S. Hand
Clerk

No._____Filed_____, 19____._____,Clerk

Recorded in Book_____, Page_____

State of Idaho   Department of Fish and Game

                        HUNTER'S STATEMENT

Hunting License No.___183456___ Car License No.___I 191___

    I, the undersigned, after having been advised of my constitu-
tional rights and that any statement I may make may be used
against me, freely and voluntarily and without any promise of
immunity wish to state that on___October 16_____, 19_50_

in _Power_____County, State of Idaho, I was__Hunting deer___

_____with the aid of a dog_____

and at said time approached by_____John Law_____

an Idaho State Conservation Officer.

                              _____Jack Poacher_____
                                         (Signed)

Date__October 16_____, 19_50_.   Address___Arbon, Idaho___

Appendix C
Sample Examination Questions

1. There are a number of legal devices used to promote wildlife conservation. Name five.
2. What is a technical defect in a fish-and-game law? Cite an example.
3. What is the main action that a fish and game commission can take against a violator to prevent continued violations?
4. What are some basic differences between wildlife law enforcement and that of other law enforcement work?
5. What are the five "w's" in crime detection?
6. Give the five basic steps in an arrest procedure.
7. All game law violations are said to fall under one or more of five subdivisions. What are these five major units?
8. List three basic reasons why people violate game laws.
9. List at least five basic reasons why people do not violate game laws.
10. When does an individual, during a deer hunt, actually have legal title to the deer?
11. When is it possible for a person to be twice held in jeopardy as regards fish and game violations?
12. Criminal evidence is said to involve what three things?
13. An enforcement officer who encourages a person to break the law, and then arrests him, is guilty of what?
14. Assuming there are basically two types of law violations, list and very briefly discuss them.
15. Define the term "reduce to possession."
16. The duties of a law enforcement officer fall into what main categories?
17. The basic principles applying to an arrest situation are said to vary but little from that of a successful military operation. They are referred to as the four "s's." List them.
18. Is it true that the question of when an arrest shall or shall not be made is a very simple one for a highly-trained law enforcement officer?
19. It is often stated that when a law enforcement officer approaches a suspect it is necessary for the officer to

first identify himself. Under certain conditions this is not necessary. Name them.

20. When is a person actually under arrest?
21. When, in handling a wildlife law violation, is it permissible for an officer to use side arms?
22. When, in dealing with an arrest suspect, is it permissible to use profanity?
23. When strong physical resistance is encountered during the course of an arrest and the prisoner is forceably subdued, what should the arresting officer do as soon as it is practical in order to protect himself from some future complaint?
24. When does an arrest warrant expire?
25. A warrant arrest may be made at night, for a misdemeanor, under what circumstances?
26. Some wildlife law enforcement officers carry side arms. When this is the case, what is the common reason for this?
27. The director of the fish and game department calls you, the chief law enforcement officer of the department, in and instructs you to proceed in a matter which you feel is absolutely wrong in both policy and technique. However, it is neither legally nor morally wrong. After a brief discussion in which you fail to convince the director that you are right, he dismisses the subject. How should you proceed?
28. You are a conservation officer patrolling a sage grouse hunt in County Y of State X. County Y has a small population of sharptails located within the sage grouse habitat. Prior to the season the fish and game department and local newspapers have conducted an intensive campaign to inform hunters about the differences in appearance of the two species. However, you check three hunters in one party that have a "legal limit" of sharptail which they claim are sage grouse. It is obvious that these hunters unknowingly shot sharptails for sage grouse. What are you going to do?
29. Discuss the advantages and disadvantages of state court systems that permit suspensions of part (or all) of a penalty, and those that make a penalty mandatory for conviction of a misdemeanor. Under which system is more responsibility placed upon the officer?
30. Discuss the differences between misdemeanors and felonies.

31. Discuss the differences between criminal and civil courts. Who are the plaintiffs and defendants in each?

32. What are the fallacies in these statements:

    a. Poor people should not be arrested for killing deer out of season since they never waste the meat.

    b. The law should be amended to include one hen pheasant in the bag and possession limit so that if one is shot accidentally it will not be wasted.

    c. "Party hunting" should be made legal.

33. What are the advantages and disadvantages of all states adopting identical fish and game codes?

34. X tells you, a conservation officer, that he saw Y shoot an elk out of season. X refuses to sign a complaint against Y, but says that he will testify against Y. In addition, X takes you to the spot of the killing where you find blood and elk hair on the ground. You get a search warrant and search Y's premises but fail to find the carcass. What do you do now?

35. You are a conservation officer patrolling a deer hunting area in State X. You check a hunter in the field; the hunter claims that he has a hunting license but that it was left in his car which is about one-half mile away. The fish and game code of State X states that hunters must be able to produce hunting licenses upon demand of a conservation officer. What are you going to do? Make an arrest? Why?

36. Discuss conditions under which you are going to issue a citation to appear in court rather than placing the violator under immediate arrest.

37. You are a conservation officer patrolling Duck Lake during waterfowl season. You see a hunter leave a blind from the south end of the lake, enter a boat, start the motor, and travel to the north end of the lake by a direct route. During the trip the hunter frightens a large flock of waterfowl from the middle of the lake. The hunter talks for several minutes to the occupant in the north blind, then enters the boat, and returns by the same route to his blind on the south edge of the lake. Federal regulations state that it is unlawful to molest waterfowl. Are you going to make an arrest? Why?

38. You are a conservation officer patrolling a marsh during waterfowl hunting season. You notice two hunters

remaining in a duck blind three-fourths of an hour after legal shooting time. The hunters still have a dozen duck decoys scattered in front of the blind. You conceal yourself to determine whether the hunters will shoot any waterfowl. Several flocks of ducks fly within 75 yards of the hunters; they conceal themselves but fail to fire at the ducks. Finally it becomes dark so you approach the hunters, identify yourself, and request permission to examine both shotguns. Each gun is loaded with three shells. Federal regulations state that it is unlawful to kill, shoot, or hunt waterfowl after legal hours. Do you have a case? If so, what evidence will you present in court?

39. You are patrolling a deer hunting area in State X during the first day of the season. While in the field you check a party of hunters at a camp located one mile from the nearest highway. The only deer in the camp is untagged; the laws of State X declare that the deer must be tagged immediately after being shot and before being transported. The hunter who killed the deer states that he did not tag the carcass for fear of losing the tag when the deer was carried through heavy brush. You note that the deer is a fawn. Are you going to arrest the hunter for failing to tag the carcass? Why?

40. You arrest a hunter for violation of the fish and game code and take him to the nearest Justice of the Peace. While preparing a complaint you note that the violator and Justice are conducting a very friendly conversation. The gist of the conversation suggests that the two are related. What are you going to do?

41. Discuss the disadvantages of the following penalties sometimes imposed by courts:

   a. Monetary fine
   b. Jail sentence
   c. Confiscation of hunting and fishing equipment
   d. Revocation of hunting and fishing license
   e. Publication of names and offense in local papers

42. In State X a violator was acquitted because of a technical defect in the wording of the complaint signed by the conservation officer. The complaint charged that Y was unlawfully fishing through the ice. Why was Y acquitted? How would you reword the charge?

43. In County X you find a reported fur poacher with a sack of cold, unskinned muskrats near a woodshed; the animals appear to have been dead three or four days. Muskrat trapping in County X does not open for two weeks and has not been open the past several months. The trapper states that he caught the animals in distant County Z which has had a muskrat season open for a week. What should an officer do?

44. You are a conservation officer operating a checking station in State X during the regular pheasant season. You stop a car and the driver informs you that he has four limits of pheasants. He states that one limit is his while the remaining three belong to three friends that are in another car. The driver gives you the names, addresses, and car description of the friends. The driver states that the three friends completed hunting but wanted to visit other friends before returning from the hunt; the three gave their birds to the driver of the first car so that he could get them home and quickly place them in cold storage. The driver states that he cannot wait for the three friends to arrive. Laws of State X state that it is unlawful to have more than one possession limit of pheasants. What are you going to do?

*45. When are prisoners handcuffed to solid objects?

    a. never   d. for a short time only
    b. always   e. when they are extremely
    c. rarely   dangerous

46. Effective wildlife law enforcement officers depend heavily on:

    a. strong-arm   d. good public relations.
       tactics.   e. preventing violations by
    b. a bold front.   making pals with everyone.
    c. side arms.

47. Considerable pressure is sometimes exerted on newspaper editors to suppress game violation stories because:

    a. most people want favorable public approval.
    b. people dislike publicity.

---

*In multiple choice questions mark the one answer that is correct, or most nearly so.

c. it is not the job of a newspaper to publicize game law violations.

d. it is unethical to publicize law violations.

e. drawing public attention to such violations causes an increase in the type of violation committed.

48. In most states game violations are handled by:

a. probate court.
b. district court.
c. justice of peace.
d. supreme court.
e. none of these.

49. Game laws, in the final analyses, are enforced by:

a. judges or juries.
b. justices of the peace.
c. attorney general.
d. game wardens.
e. county prosecutor.

50. When arresting a dangerous subject, there is one time that is all important to the officer. When is it?

a. if and when the subject tries to escape
b. the first moment of initial contact
c. if the subject tries to draw a gun
d. when the officer identifies himself
e. when the subject is moved

51. When is a subject actually under arrest?

a. when the subject apparently agrees to the arrest
b. when the subject puts up his hands
c. when the resistance of the subject has been overcome
d. when the subject has been informed he is under arrest
e. when the subject is approached by the arresting officer

52. Probably the most fool-proof method of searching a subject for a dangerous weapon is known as:

a. the wall search.
b. the face-to-face search.
c. the back-to-face search.
d. the prone position search.
e. the partial strip search.

53. As a federal game management agent, you stop an automobile on a federal highway. The people in the auto are not dressed to hunt. You have no particular evidence of their having committed a wildlife violation.

There are no guns in sight. You ask to look in the locked trunk. They refuse. How should you proceed?

a. shoot the lock off .
b. arrest the driver .
c. search for guns .
d. hold the auto .
e. let them go .

54. A federal migratory bird hunting stamp is required:

a. to possess migratory birds .
b. to hunt certain migratory birds .
c. to hunt ducks, geese, and coots .
d. to hunt ducks and geese .
e. to hunt migratory game .

55. An important document of English history applied to game the same as the Magna Charta applied to the people. What is it?

a. the Migratory Bird Act
b. the Lacey Act
c. the Charger of the Forest
d. the Magna Charter of <u>Ferae Naturae</u>
e. none of these

56. In State X a man sets traps at noon for muskrats, 24 hours before the season opens. Eight hours after the traps are set a muskrat is caught in one of them. The man does not come to his trapline until after the season opens the following noon. He then claims the animal was taken legally. How can you prove the complaint?

a. You are a game warden so your word is better than that of the defendant.
b. Make the man confess by threatening him.
c. Figure the man will later confess so let it go.
d. Tag muskrat with time, date, place, and temperature of animal. Point out to the court that muskrats are largely nocturnal.
e. None of these.

57. A man draws an antelope permit. He injures himself before the hunt so gives the permit to a friend. Do you have a case, and if so, why?

a. No, because the permit allows one animal to be shot, and who shoots it makes no difference.
b. Yes, because the man with the permit stayed home.

    c. No, because the man that killed the animal was just doing the injured man a favor.

    d. Yes, because licenses and permits are non-transferable.

    e. None of these.

58. When big game populations exceed the carrying capacities of ranges on national forest lands, the Forest Service normally:

    a. Sets seasons and regulates the kill without regard to state's rights.

    b. Prohibits public hunting in accord with their policy of maintaining all resources in a natural state.

    c. Seeks the cooperation of the state in arriving at satisfactory hunting regulations.

    d. Improves the range to meet the demand.

    e. Does nothing about the game situation because their primary interest is with timber.

59. For what animal was there an act passed that now specifically protects that animal only?

    a. trumpeter swan   d. black bass
    b. sandhill crane   e. bald eagle
    c. labrador duck

Paragraph A

    a. You, as a conservation officer, are patrolling the Portneuf River, State X, on August 19, 1951. As you are checking a fisherman, you notice that he has just purchased his fishing license that morning. Fishing season ends September 10.

    b. In order to avoid arousing the fisherman's suspicions, you make a mental note of his name (M. J. Funny) and address, along with where he purchased the license.

    c. The next day you locate Funny's house at 1322 South 4th Street in Pocatello, but he is not at home. You go next door and try to find out how long Funny has lived at his present address. As you expected, you are told that Funny has lived at the address about seven weeks and that he moved there from City Y, which is in another state. Since it is necessary to live in State X six months before being considered a resident, Funny has apparently violated the law by purchasing a resident fishing license when he should have purchased a non-resident fishing license. You go back and wait in front of the neighbor's house until Funny returns home from work. In half an hour Funny drives up in a Buick with State Y' license plates. You approach him and recall the previous meeting yesterday. You ask Funny if you may check his license again. Funny, sensing that something is wrong, pulls the license out of his pocket and tears it up before you can grasp it. Funny says, "There's not much that you can do now."

    d. You look next door and happen to see, in the garage, the car that Funny drove to his fishing spot yesterday. This seems to be a clear-cut case of a deliberate violation, as Funny borrowed the neighbor's car so as not to arouse suspicion about his not being a resident of State X.

60. Paragraph A, Item b. The next day you, as a conservation officer, should:

    a. follow the man.
    b. check with Funny's employer as to his honesty.
    c. go to the license vendor and talk to him.
    d. go to the license vendor and get a copy of the license sold to Funny.
    e. drop the matter.

61. Paragraph A, Item c. Following your encounter with Funny, you:

    a. charge him with illegal destruction of his fishing license.
    b. inform him that you have a copy of his fishing license and that, based on previous information, you are putting him under arrest, and tell him why.
    c. you grab Funny and shove him into your car and start for the nearest court.
    d. you tell Funny that he is correct, there is nothing you can do now that he has destroyed his license.
    e. you issue Funny a warning since it is a borderline case.

62. Paragraph A, Item d. The logical disposition of the case is:

    a. case dismissed because of insufficient evidence.

    b. Funny convicted and given minimum penalty for being an out-of-stater.

    c. Funny convicted and given penalty because of intent to defraud.

    d. case dismissed because of illegal tactics of the conservation officer.

    e. Funny is convicted of a felony because of his acts in connection with the case, and fined and given a jail sentence.

63. Paragraph A, Item e. The charge against Funny is:

    a. purchase of a wrong class fishing license.

    b. resisting an officer.

    c. poor sportsmanship.

    d. driving an automobile with an out-of-state license tag.

    e. accidental purchase of a wrong class fishing license.

Paragraph B

    a. You are patrolling Fritz Creek in State X with John Doe, state conservation officer at City Y, on August 15, 1951. As you walk past a sheep camp on the way to a beaver colony upstream, you see bits of hair on the ground. You pick up some of it, examine it, and are certain that it is either deer or antelope hair. Both animals are present in the area. You walk closer to the sheep camp, find more hair and even an empty wool sack with blood stains. The camp tender is nearby so you tell him that you have reason to believe that there has been a violation of the fish and game laws and ask his permission to search the camp. He states the herder is away but gives permission to search. Underneath his mattress you find a sack with four freshly-skinned grouse (no open season) and a leg of unidentified meat. Enough feathers are on the birds to establish their identity as grouse, but you are not certain what species they are. The sheep camp tender denies knowing anything about the bag.

    b. In the meantime you compare the bones from the legs of antelope and deer. You also compare hairs and are finally convinced beyond a reasonable doubt that the leg is from a deer.

64. Paragraph B, Item a. Your action, as a conservation officer, should be:

   a. go to the nearest court and swear out a warrant for the camp tender.
   b. charge the camp owner with illegal possession of grouse meat, but do not put him under arrest.
   c. charge the camp owner with illegal possession of grouse meat and place him under arrest.
   d. charge the camp tender with illegal possession of grouse meat and place him under arrest.
   e. issue a warning.

65. Paragraph B, Item a. Now assume you have placed the camp tender under arrest. If he resists, you should:

   a. force him to accompany you, using the necessary amount of force or persuasion.
   b. let him go.
   c. get more help and come back for him.
   d. draw your gun and threaten to shoot him in the leg.
   e. forget the whole thing and warn the camp tender that he will be smart to do likewise.

66. Paragraph B, Item b. Your action is:

   a. file a charge for illegal possession of deer meat against the camp tender.
   b. do nothing, because you did not originally file a charge.
   c. do nothing, because one charge covers both violations.
   d. do nothing, because it appears the camp tender cannot be convicted.
   e. try to get a confession from the camp tender before you proceed further.

67. Paragraph B, Items a and b. During this case what section or sections of the code was/were most actively involved?

   a. right of seizure
   b. unlawful possession of game
   c. right to search
   d. resisting an officer
   e. right of search and unlawful possession of game

Paragraph C

It is 3:00 p. m. on November 1, 1951, and you are patrolling the streams of State X. Trapping season opened at 12:00 noon on November 1. While driving along you see a car parked by a slough and a man skinning muskrats. Since the season is only three hours old, you wonder how this is possible. You park the truck and walk toward the trapper. You see that he has a pile of about 40 muskrats. You begin a casual conversation in order to find out how he got them. He tells you that he set the traps a day ago. You then inform him that it was unlawful to set rat traps until 12:00 noon on November 1. You then ask to check his license and you find that his name is Thomas Block of Hoboken. Block then changes his story and says that he put out his traps without actually setting the springs. Later he set them and then made another trip, picking up 40 muskrats.

68. Paragraph C. As a conservation officer, your action is:

    a. do nothing because of lack of evidence.
    b. tell Block he is lucky that you did not catch him with the muskrats before noon, November 1.
    c. charge Block with illegal possession of muskrats.
    d. charge Block with trapping out of season.
    e. seize the muskrats and warn Block.

69. Paragraph C. The most damaging evidence against Block is:

    a. his original statement that he set the traps before the season opened.
    b. the fact that it was almost, if not entirely, impossible to set out his trap line, run it, and take 40 muskrats and return to the automobile and skin part of them all in three hours, since rats are chiefly nocturnal.
    c. that Block was skinning freshly-caught muskrats.
    d. changing his story in regard to his activity for the day.
    e. the fact that some of the muskrats were starting to freeze.

70. You are a conservation officer patrolling a trout stream three weeks prior to the opening of fishing season; you find two 12-year-old boys fishing in the creek. What are you going to do?

a. arrest them.

b. seize their fishing poles and tell them to go home.

c. take the boys home and let their parents render punishment.

d. explain the purpose for a closed fishing season and tell the boys to come back in three weeks.

e. take the boys to the probate judge and have him censure them.

71. Before a hunter can claim legal ownership of game he must:

a. legally reduce the animal to his possession.

b. wound an animal and be pursuing it.

c. have a legal tag attached to the animal (if so required).

d. be close on the trail of the animal.

e. none of the above.

References

Benedict, Nelson, and George Laycock. 1954. Murder in the woods. Field and Stream 51.1:19-21, 88-89.

Connery, Robert H. 1935. Governmental problems in wildlife conservation. Columbia University Press. 250 pp.

Day, Albert M. 1949. North American waterfowl. New York: Stackpole and Heck, Inc. 329 pp.

DuPont Company, The. 1930. Wild game--its legal status. The DuPont Co. 50 pp.

Furst, S. Dale, Jr. 1946. Outlook in wildlife law enforcement. Delivered before the International Assn. of the Game, Fish, and Forestry Commissioners, Denver, Colorado. 1 p.

Gabrielson, Ira N. 1951. Wildlife management. New York: The Macmillan Co. 274 pp.

Hardy, J. I., and Thora M. Plitt. 1940. An improved method for revealing the surface structure of fur fibers. U. S. Fish and Wildlife Service Wildlife Circular 7. 1-10 pp.

Kelly, Claude. 1953. What our courts must learn: game laws are no joke! Utah ·Fish and Game Bulletin. 10.5:1,3,6. 10.6:6-8.

Nelson, William. 1762 (XVII). The laws concerning game. Of hunting, hawking, fishing and fowling, etc. And of forest, chases, parks, warrens, deer, doves, dove-cotes, conies. 6th edition. London: Printed by E. Richardsen and C. Lintot for T. Waller. 255 pp.

Schultz, William F., Jr. 1953. Conservation law and administration. New York: Ronald Press. 607 pp.

Sigler, William F. 1954. What is wildlife management? Utah Fish and Game Bulletin 10.12:1-2.

Sutherland, Edwin H. 1947. Principles of criminology. 4th edition. Chicago, Philadelphia, New York: J. B. Lippincott Co. 643 pp.

United States Army. 1951. Criminal investigation. Washington, D. C.: U. S. Government Printing Office, Dept. of the Army Field Manual FM 19-20. 258 pp.

United States Government. 1951. Manual for courts-
    martial. Washington, D. C.: U. S. Government
    Printing Office. 665 pp.
Wertham, Frederick. 1954. Let's look at the comics.
    Scouting 42.7:2-3, 19-20.

Suggested Reading*

Bibliographies

Culver, Dorothy Campbell (compiler). 1934. Bibliography of crime and criminal justice, 1927-1931. New York: H. W. Wilson Co. 413 pp.

Culver, Dorothy Campbell (compiler). 1939. Bibliography of crime and criminal justice, 1932-1937. New York: H. W. Wilson Co. 391 pp.

Cumming, Sir John. 1935. A contribution towards a bibliography dealing with crime and cognate subjects. 3rd ed. London: Receiver for the Metropolitan Police District, New Scotland Yard, S. W. 1.

Federal Bureau of Investigation. 1950. Bibliography--juvenile delinquency and crime control. Washington, D. C.: Federal Bureau of Investigation, U. S. Dept. of Justice. 21 pp. (mimeo.)

Greer, Sarah. 1935. A bibliography of civil service and personnel administration. New York: McGraw-Hill Book Co., Inc. 143 pp.

Greer, Sarah. 1936. A bibliography of police administration and police science. New York: Institute of Public Admin., Columbia University. 152 pp.

Kuhlman, Augustus Frederick. 1929. A guide to material on crime and criminal justice. New York: H. W. Wilson Co. 633 pp.

Lunden, Walter A. 1935. A systematic outline of criminology with selected bibliography. Pittsburgh, Penn.: Univ. of Pittsburgh. 115 pp.

Menefee, Louise Arnold, and M. M. Chambers. 1938. American youth--an annotated bibliography. Washington, D. C.: The American Council on Education. 492 pp.

Sellin, Thorsten, and J. P. Shalloo. 1935. A bibliographical manual for the student of criminology. Philadelphia, Penn.: Univ. of Penn. Press. 41 pp.

---

*Taken, in part, from a bibliography of crime and kindred subjects released by the Federal Bureau of Investigation, October 1, 1950.

Spector, Herman K. 1944. Bibliography on criminology--
penology and allied subjects. New York: Dept. of
Correction. 190 pp. (mimeo.)

Tompkins, Dorothy C. (compiler). 1947. The crime
problem in California--a selected bibliography.
Berkeley, Calif.: Univ. of Calif. Press., Bureau of
Public Admin. 16 pp.

Birds

Bump, Gardiner, Robert W. Darrow, Frank C. Edminster,
and Walter F. Crissey. 1947. The ruffed grouse.
New York State Conservation Dept. 915 pp.

Grange, Wallace B. 1948. Wisconsin grouse problems.
Madison 2, Wis.: Wisconsin Conservation Dept. 49
plates, 17 fig., 35 tables, 318 pp.

Kortright, Francis H. 1943. The ducks, geese, and swans
of North America. Washington, D. C.: The American
Wildlife Institute. 36 plates, 476 pp.

Low, Jessop B. 1945. Ecology and management of the Red-
head (Nyroca americana) in Iowa. Ecological Mono-
graphs, Vol. 15. 35-69 pp.

Patterson, Robert L. 1952. The sage grouse in Wyoming.
Denver: Wyoming Game and Fish Commission, Sage
Books, Inc. 54 tables, 18 fig., 87 ill., 341 pp.

Stokes, Allen W. 1954. Population studies of the Ring-
necked Pheasants on Pelee Island, Ontario. Technical
Bull., Wildlife Series No. 4. Toronto: Ontario Dept.
of Lands and Forests. 154 pp.

Cost of Crime

Dorr, Goldthwaite H., and Sidney P. Simpson. 1931.
Report on the cost of crime and criminal justice in the
United States. Washington, D. C.: U. S. Government
Printing Office. 657 pp.

Ettinger, Clayton J. 1932. The problem of crime. New
York: Ray Long and Richard R. Smith, Inc. 538 pp.

Gillin, John Lewis. 1945. Criminology and penology.
3rd ed. New York: D. Appleton-Century-Crofts, Inc.
600 pp.

Crime Surveys

Harrison, Leonard V. 1934. Police administration in
Boston. Cambridge, Mass.: Harvard University
Press. 203 pp.

Michael, Jerome, and Mortimer J. Adler. 1932. An institute of criminology and of criminal justice. New York: Columbia University Press. 531 pp.

Smith, Bruce, Raymond Moley, and others. 1926. Missouri crime survey. New York: The Macmillan Co. 587 pp.

Wigmore, John H. 1929. The Illinois crime survey. Published by Illinois Assn. for Criminal Justice, in cooperation with the Chicago Crime Commission. 1108 pp.

Criminal Law and Procedure

Alexander, Clarence. 1949. The law of arrest. Buffalo, New York: Dennis and Co., Inc. Vol. 1, 1133 pp. Vol. 2, 2260 pp.

Council of State Governments. 1949. The handbook of interstate crime control. Chicago, Illinois: The Council of State Governments. 91 pp.

Cummings, Homer, and Carl McFarland. 1937. Federal justice. New York: The Macmillan Co. 576 pp.

Frank, Jerome. 1949. Courts on trial. Princeton, New Jersey: Princeton University Press. 441 pp.

Goebel, Julius, Jr., and T. Raymond Naughton. 1944. Law enforcement in colonial New York. New York: The Commonwealth Fund. 867 pp.

Holtzoff, Honorable Alexander (ed.). 1946. Federal rules of criminal procedure--with notes prepared under the direction of the Advisory Committee appointed by the United States Supreme Court. New York: New York University School of Law. 335 pp.

President's Research Committee on Social Trends. Recent social trends (in the United States). New York: McGraw-Hill Book Co., Inc. 1933 (2 vol.), 1568 pp. Last printing December 1948, 1568 pp.

Radzinowicz, Leon. 1948. A history of English criminal law and its administration from 1750. New York: The Macmillan Co. 853 pp.

Radzinowicz, Leon, and J. W. C. Turner, 1948. The journal of criminal science. New York: The Macmillan Co. Vol. 1. 207 pp.

Vanderbilt, Arthur T. (ed.). 1949. Minimum standards of judicial administration. Newark, New Jersey: The Law Center of New York University for the National Conference of Judicial Councils. 752 pp.

Criminology

Branham, Vernon C., and Samuel B. Kutash (ed.). 1949. Encyclopedia of criminology. New York: Philosophical Library. 527 pp.

Cantor, Nathaniel F. 1939. Crime and society. New York: Henry Holt and Co. 459 pp.

Fink, Arthur E. 1938. Causes of crime. Philadelphia, Penn.: University of Penn. Press. 309 pp.

Haynes, Frederick E. 1935. Criminology. New York: McGraw-Hill Book Co., Inc. 497 pp.

Inbau, Fred E. 1948. Lie detection and criminal interrogation. Baltimore, Maryland: The Williams and Wilkins Co. 193 pp.

MacDonald, John C. R. 1939. Crime is a business. Stanford University, Calif.: Stanford University Press. 263 pp.

Morris, Albert. 1935. Criminology. New York: Longmans, Green and Co. 590 pp.

O'Hara, Charles E., and James W. Osterburg. 1949. An introduction to criminalistics. New York: The Macmillan Co. 705 pp.

Perkins, Rollin M. 1942. Elements of police science. Brooklyn, New York: The Foundation Press, Inc. 651 pp.

Sannié, Charles. 1954. The scientific detection of crime. Publ. 4190, Smithsonian Institution. (Reprint from Impact of Science on Society, Vol. 4, No. 3, 1953. Publ. by UNESCO.) 337-369 pp.

Snyder, LeMoyne. 1947. Homicide investigation. Springfield, Illinois: Charles C. Thomas. 287 pp.

Taft, Donald R. 1942. Criminology. New York: The Macmillan Co. 708 pp.

Vollmer, August. 1949. The criminal. Brooklyn, New York: The Foundation Press, Inc. 462 pp.

Von Hentig, Hans. Crime, causes and conditions. New York: McGraw-Hill Book Co., Inc. 1947, 379 pp. Last printing January 1949, 532 pp.

Documents

Brewster, F. 1932. Contested documents and forgeries. Calcutta, India: The Book Co., Ltd.

Carvalho, David N. 1904. Forty centuries of ink. New York: Banks Pub. Co.

Lee, C. D., and R. A. Abbey. 1922. Classification and identification of handwriting. New York: D. Appleton-Century-Crofts, Inc. 113 pp.

Mitchell, C. Ainsworth. 1922. Documents and their scientific examination. London: Charles Griffin and Co., Ltd.

Mitchell, C. Ainsworth, and T. C. Hepworth. Inks, their composition and manufacture. London: Charles Griffin and Co., Ltd.

Osborn, Albert S. 1926. The problem of proof (especially as exemplified in disputed document trials). Newark, New Jersey: The Essex Press. 539 pp.

Osborn, Albert S. 1944. Questioned documents. Albany, New York: Boyd Printing Co. 737 pp.

Quirke, Captain Arthur J. 1930. Forged, anonymous, and suspect documents. London: George Rutledge and Sons, Ltd. 282 pp.

Saudek, Robert. 1928. Experiments with handwriting. London: George Allen and Unwin, Ltd. 394 pp.

Saudek, Robert. 1933. Anonymous letters. Strand, London: Methuen and Co., Ltd.

Ecology

Allee, W. C., Alfred E. Emerson, Orlando Park, Thomas Park, and Karl P. Schmidt. 1950. Principles of animal ecology. Philadelphia, Penn.: W. B. Saunders Co. 837 pp.

Chapman, Royal N. 1931. Animal ecology. New York: McGraw-Hill Book Co., Inc. 464 pp.

Clarke, George L. 1954. Elements of ecology. New York: John Wiley and Sons. London: Chapman and Hall, Ltd. 534 pp.

Hesse, Richard, W. C. Allee, and Karl P. Schmidt. 1947. Ecological animal geography. New York: John Wiley and Sons, Inc. 597 pp.

Woodbury, A. M. 1954. Principles of general ecology. New York: Blakiston Co. 504 pp.

Fingerprints

Battley, Harry. 1930. Single fingerprints. London: His Majesty's Stationery Office, Director of Publications. 98 pp.

Bridges, B. C. 1942. Practical fingerprinting. New York: Funk and Wagnalls Co. 374 pp.

Chapel, Charles Edward. 1941. Fingerprinting (a manual of identification). New York: Coward-McCann, Inc. 299 pp.

Cummins, Harold, and Charles Midlo. 1943. Finger prints, palms and soles. Philadelphia, Penn.: The Blakiston Co. 309 pp.

Federal Bureau of Investigation. 1945. Classification of fingerprints. Washington, D. C.: United States Government Printing Office. 137 pp.

Galton, Francis. 1892. Finger prints. New York: The Macmillan Co. 216 pp.

Henry, Sir E. R. 1937. Classification and uses of fingerprints. London. His Majesty's Stationery Office, Director of Publications. 142 pp.

Kuhne, Frederick. 1942. The fingerprint instructor. New York: Scientific American. 182 pp.

Pearson, Karl. 1930. The life, letters, and labours of Francis Galton. Cambridge, England: The University Press.

Wentworth, Bert, and Harris Hawthorne Wilder. 1932. Personal identification. Chicago, Illinois: T. G. Cooke. 383 pp.

Fire and Fire Prevention

Bond, Horatio. 1942. Fire defense. Boston, Mass.: National Fire Protection Assn. 222 pp.

Curtis, Arthur F. 1936. A treatise on the law of arson. Buffalo, New York: Dennis and Co., Inc. 688 pp.

International City Managers' Assn., The. 1942. Municipal fire administration. Chicago, Illinois: The International City Managers' Assn. 666 pp. 5th edition, fall 1950 575 pp.

Rethoret, H. 1945. Fire investigations. Toronto and Montreal, Canada: Recording and Statistical Corp., Limited. 467 pp.

Firearms: ammunition and ballistics

Johnson, Melvin M., Jr., and Charles T. Haven. 1943. Ammunition (its history, development and use, 1600-1943). New York: William Morrow and Co. 374 pp.

Sharpe, Philip B. 1937. Complete guide to handloading. New York: Funk and Wagnalls Co. 2nd edition, December 1941. Reprinted 1944. 465 pp.

Simmons, Richard F. 1947. Wildcat cartridges. New
York: William Morrow and Co. 333 pp.
Whelen, Colonel Townsend. Small arms design and ballis-
tics. Plantersville, South Carolina: Small-arms
Technical Pub. Co. Vol. I, Design, 1945, 352 pp.
Vol. II, Ballistics, 1946, 315 pp.

Firearms: General

Brown, Earle B. 1949. Basic optics for the sportsman.
New York: Stoeger Arms Corp. 259 pp.
Camp, Raymond R. 1948. The hunter's encyclopedia.
Harrisburg, Penn.: Stackpole and Heck, Inc. 1152 pp.
Chapel, Charles Edward. 1943. Gun collecting. New
York: Coward-McCann, Inc. 256 pp.
Hatcher, Julian S. 1947. Hatcher's notebook. Harrisburg,
Penn.: The Military Service Pub. Co. 488 pp.

Firearms: Gunsmithing

Chapel, Charles Edward. 1943. Gun care and repair.
New York: Coward-McCann, Inc. 454 pp.
Howe, James Virgil. 1941. Reprinted 1944. The modern
gunsmith. New York: Funk and Wagnalls Co. Vol. I,
424 pp. Vol. II, 424 pp.
Howe, Walter J. 1946. Professional gunsmithing. Plantersville, South Carolina: Small Arms Technical Pub.
Co. 526 pp.
Vickery, W. F. 1945. Advanced gunsmithing. Plantersville, South Carolina: Small Arms Technical Pub. Co.
429 pp.

Firearms: Identification of Domestic and Foreign Arms

Hatcher, Julian S. 1935. Textbook of firearms investigation, identification and evidence; together with the textbook of pistols and revolvers. Plantersville, South
Carolina: Small-Arms Technical Pub. Co. 5th printing 1946. 533 pp.
Sharpe, Philip B. 1938. 2nd ed., 1947. The rifle in
America. New York: Funk and Wagnalls Co. 782 pp.
Smith, Walter H. B. 1948. Pistols and revolvers.
Harrisburg, Penn.: National Rifle Assn. of America;
and the Military Service Pub. Co. Vol. I, Pistols
and revolvers, 638 pp. Vol. II, Rifles, 546 pp.

Smith, W. H. B. 1955. Small arms of the world. Harrisburg, Penn.: The Military Service Pub. Co. 768 pp.

Wilson, R. K. 1944. Textbook of automatic pistols. Plantersville, South Carolina: Small-Arms Technical Pub. Co. 350 pp.

Fishes

Beckman, William C. 1952. Guide to the fishes of Colorado. Leaflet No. 11. Boulder, Colorado: University of Colorado Museum. 110 pp.

Berg, Leo S. 1947. Classification of fishes both recent and fossil. Ann Arbor, Michigan: J. W. Edwards. 517 pp.

Bigelow, Henry B., and William C. Schroeder. 1953. Fishes of the Gulf of Maine. Fishery Bulletin 74. Washington, D. C.: United States Dept of the Interior, Fish and Wildlife Service, United States Government Printing Office. 577 pp.

Carl, G. Clifford, and W. A. Clemens. 1948. The freshwater fishes of British Columbia. Handbook No. 5. British Columbia Provincial Museum, Department of Education. 132 pp.

Carlander, Kenneth D. 1950. Handbook of fresh-water fishery biology. Dubuque, Iowa: Wm. C. Brown Co. 276 pp.

Carlander, Kenneth D. 1953. First supplement to handbook of fresh-water fishery biology. Dubuque, Iowa: Wm. C. Brown Co. 277-429 pp.

Clemens, W. A., and G. V. Wilby. 1946. Fishes of the Pacific coast of Canada. Bulletin No. LXVIII. Fisheries Research Board of Canada, Ottawa. 368 pp.

Dymond, J. R. 1932. The trout and other game fishes of British Columbia. Ottawa: The Department of Fisheries. 51 pp.

Eddy, Samuel, and Thaddeus Surber. 1947. Northern fishes with special reference to the upper Mississippi Valley. Revised edition. Minneapolis: University of Minnesota Press. 276 pp.

Harlan, James R., and Everett B. Speaker. 1951. Iowa fish and fishing. State Conservation Commission. 237 pp.

Hinks, David. 1943. The fishes of Manitoba. Province of Manitoba. The Department of Mines and Natural Resources. 102 pp.

Hubbs, Carl L., and Karl F. Lagler. 1947. Fishes of the Great Lakes region. Cranbrook Institute of Science, Bulletin No. 26. Bloomfield Hills, Michigan: The Cranbrook Press. 186 pp.

Lagler, Karl F. 1952. Freshwater fishery biology. Dubuque, Iowa: Wm. C. Brown Co. 360 pp.

Roedel, Phil M. 1948. Common marine fishes of California. Fish Bulletin No. 68. State of California: Department of Natural Resources, Division of Fish and Game. 158 pp.

Rounsefell, George A., and W. Harry Everhart. 1953. Fishery science: its methods and applications. New York: John Wiley and Sons, Inc. 444 pp.

Schultz, Leonard P. 1948. Keys to the fishes of Washington, Oregon, and closely adjoining regions. Vol. 2, No. 4. Seattle: University of Washington. 103-228 pp.

Schultz, Leonard P., with Edith M. Stern. 1948. The ways of fishes. New York: D. Van Nostrand Co., Inc. 264 pp.

Schultz, Leonard P., Earl S. Herald, Ernest A. Lachner, Arthur D. Welander, and Loren P. Woods. 1953. Fishes of the Marshall and Marianas Islands. United States National Museum Bulletin 202, Smithsonian Institution. Washington, D. C.: United States Government Printing Office. 685 pp.

Sigler, William F. 1953. The collection and interpretation of fish life history data. Logan: Utah State Agricultural College. 46 pp.

Smith, J. L. B. 1949. Marine fishes of South Africa. Capetown Pub. Co., Ltd. 1132 pp.

Umali, Agustin F. 1950. Guide to the classification of fishing gear in the Philippines. Research Report 17, Fish and Wildlife Service, United States Department of the Interior. Washington, D. C.: United States Government Printing Office. 165 pp.

Walford, L. A. 1937. Marine game fishes of the Pacific coast from Alaska to the Equator. University of California press. 205 pp.

History of Wildlife Law

Kirby, Chester. 1933. The English game law system. American Historical Review XXXVIII(2):240-262.

Oke's game laws. 1897. 4th ed. E. C. London: Butterworth and Co., 7 Fleet Street. First edition published in 1861.

Palmer, T. S. 1912. Chronology and index of the more important events in American game protection, 1776-1911. U. S. Dept. of Agri. Biol. Survey Bulletin 41.

Palmer, T. S., and H. W. Olds. 1900. Laws regulating the transportation and sale of game. U. S. Dept. of Agri. Biol. Survey Bulletin 14.

Radcliffe, William. 1926. Fishing from the earliest times. 2nd ed. New York: E. P. Dutton and Co. 494 pp.

U. S. Department of Commerce. 1938. A summary of game fish laws for 1937-1938, with special reference to black bass. Fish Cir. 27. 50 pp.

Williams, R. W., Jr. 1907. Game commissions and wardens: their appointment, powers, and duties. U. S. Dept. of Agri. Biol. Survey Bulletin 28.

Identification--Legal Medicine

Bamford, Frank. 1947. Poisons--their isolation and identification. Philadelphia, Penn.: The Blakiston Co. 304 pp.

Best, Charles Herbert, and Norman Burke Taylor. 1950. The physiological basis of medical practice. Baltimore, Maryland: The Williams and Wilkins Co. 1341 pp.

Cook, E. Fullerton, and Eric W. Martin. 1948. Remington's practice of pharmacy. Easton, Penn.: The Mack Pub. Co. 1511 pp.

Gonzales, Thomas A. 1940. Legal medicine and toxicology. New York: D. Appleton-Century-Crofts, Inc. 754 pp.

Hamilton, Alice, and Harriet L. Hardy. 1949. Industrial toxicology. New York. Paul B. Hoeber, Inc. 574 pp.

Henry, Thomas Anderson. 1949. The plant alkaloids. Philadelphia, Penn.: The Blakiston Co. 804 pp.

King, Earl Judson. 1947. Micro-analysis in medical biochemistry. New York: Grune and Stratton, Inc. 168 pp.

Patty, Frank A. Industrial hygiene and toxicology. New York: Interscience Publishers, Inc. Vol. I, 1948, 531 pp. Vol. II, 1949, 1138 pp.

Radley, Jack A., and Julius Grant. 1948. Fluorescence analysis in ultra violet light. London: Chapman and Hall, Ltd.

Rehfuss, Martin Emil, F. Kenneth Albrecht, and Alison Howe Price. 1948. A course in practical therapeutics. Baltimore, Maryland: The Williams and Wilkins Co. 824 pp.

Schiff, Fritz, and William C. Boyd. 1942. Blood grouping technic. New York: Interscience Publishers, Inc. 248 pp.

Simpson, Keith. 1947. Forensic medicine. Baltimore, Maryland: The Williams and Wilkins Co. 335 pp.

Smith, Sydney (ed.). 1948. Taylor's principles and practice of medical jurisprudence. London: J. & A. Churchill, Ltd. Vol. I, 723 pp. Vol. II, 841 pp.

Sollmann, Torald. 1948. A manual of pharmacology and its applications to therapeutics and toxicology. Philadelphia, Penn.: W. B. Saunders Co. 1132 pp.

Wiener, Alexander S. 1945. Blood groups and blood transfusion. Springfield, Illinois: Charles C. Thomas. 438 pp.

Williams, Richard Tecwyn. 1949. Detoxication mechanism. (The metabolism of drugs and allied organic compounds.) New York: John Wiley and Sons, Inc. 288 pp.

Invertebrates

Brown, Frank A., Jr. 1950. Selected invertebrate types. New York: John Wiley and Sons, Inc. 597 pp.

Hegner, Robert W. 1933. Invertebrate zoology. New York: The Macmillan Co. 570 pp.

Hyman, Libbie H. 1940-1951. The invertebrates. Vols. I, II, and III. New York: McGraw-Hill Book Co., Inc. 1848 pp.

Kudo, Richard R. 1950. Protozoology. 3rd ed., 3rd printing. Springfield, Illinois: Charles C. Thomas. 778 pp.

Pennak, Robert W. 1953. Fresh-water invertebrates of the United States. New York: The Ronald Press Company. 769 pp.

Limnology

American Public Health Association. 1946. Standard methods for the examination of water and sewage. New York: 1790 Broadway. 286 pp.

Morgan, Ann Haven. 1930. Field book of ponds and streams. New York: G. P. Putnam's Sons. 448 pp.

Ruttner, Franz. 1953. Fundamentals of limnology. Univ. of Toronto Press. 242 pp.

Sverdrup, Harold U., Martin W. Johnson, and Richard H. Fleming. 1946. The oceans. New York: Prentice-Hall. 1087 pp.

Welch, P. S. 1935. Limnology. New York: McGraw-Hill Book Co., Inc. 471 pp.

Welch, P. S. 1948. Limnological methods. New York: Blakiston Co. 381 pp.

Mammals

Allen, D. L. 1943. Michigan fox squirrel management. Lansing, Michigan: Conservation Department. 404 pp.

Anthony, H. E. 1928. Field book of North American mammals. New York: G. P. Putnam's Sons. 48 ill., 674 pp.

Cahalane, Victor H. 1947. Mammals of North America. New York: The Macmillan Co. 682 pp.

Durrant, Stephen D. 1952. Mammals of Utah. University of Kansas Publications, Museum of Natural History, Vol. 6. 549 pp.

Goldman, Edward A. 1950. Raccoons of North and Middle America. Washington, D. C.: United States Government Printing Office. 22 plates, 2 fig., 153 pp.

Grinnell, Joseph, Joseph S. Dixon, and Jean M. Linsdale. 1937. Fur-bearing mammals of California. Berkeley: University of California Press. Vol. I, 7 plates, 138 fig., 375 pp. Vol. II, 6 plates, 206 fig., 777 pp.

Murie, Olaus J. 1951. The elk of North America. Harrisburg, Penn.: The Stackpole Co.; and Washington, D. C.: Wildlife Management Institute. 29 ill., 32 fig.; 376 pp.

Murie, Olaus. 1954. A field guide to animal tracks. Boston: Houghton Mifflin Co. 374 pp.

Penology and Reformation

American Prison Assn. Published annually. Proceedings of the annual Congress of Correction of the American Prison Association. New York: The American Prison Assn.

Barnes, Harry Elmer, and Negley K. Teeters. New horizons in criminology. New York: Prentice-Hall, Inc. 1943, 1069 pp. 1947, 1070 pp.

East, W. Norwood. 1936. Medical aspects of crime. Philadelphia, Penn.: The Blakiston Co. 437 pp.

Johnston, James A. 1949. Alcatraz Island Prison (and the men who live there). New York: Charles Scribner's Sons. 276 pp.

Reckless, Walter C. 1940. Criminal behavior. New York: McGraw-Hill Book Co., Inc. 532 pp.

Robinson, Louis N. 1931. Should prisoners work? Philadelphia, Penn.: John C. Winston Co. 353 pp.

Photography

Eastman Kodak Company. 1948. Photography in law enforcement. New York: Eastman Kodak Co. 112 pp.

Radley, J. A. 1948. Photography in crime detection. London: Chapman and Hall, Ltd. 186 pp.

Scott, Charles C. 1942. Photographic evidence. Kansas City, Miss.: Vernon Law Book Co. 922 pp.

Police Administration

Cooper, R. Weldon. 1938. Municipal police administration in Texas. Austin, Texas: The University of Texas. 320 pp.

Floherty, John J. 1943. Inside the FBI. Philadelphia, Penn.: J. B. Lippincott Co. 192 pp.

Glover, E. H. 1934. The English police. London: The Police Chronicle.

Harrison, Richard. 1949. Scotland Yard. New York: Ziff-Davis Pub. Co. 269 pp.

Look, Editors of. 1947. The story of the FBI. New York: E. P. Dutton and Co., Inc. 286 pp.

Monroe, David Geeting. 1941. State and provincial police. Evanston, Ill.: The State and Provincial Section, International Assn. of Chiefs of Police, and the Northwestern University Traffic Institute. 251 pp.

Pettee, George S. 1946. The future of American secret intelligence. Washington, D. C.: Infantry Journal Press. 120 pp.

Smith, Bruce. 1949. Police systems in the United States. New York: Harper and Brothers. 351 pp.

Vollmer, August, and Alfred E. Parker. 1935. Crime and the state police. Berkeley: University of California Press. 226 pp.

Psychology and Sociology

Abrahamsen, David. 1944. Crime and the human mind. New York: Columbia University Press. 244 pp.

Children's Bureau, U. S. Dept. of Health, Education, and Welfare. 1954. Specialized courts dealing with children. Washington, D. C.: United States Government Printing Office.

Ellingston, John R. 1948. Protecting our children from criminal careers. New York: Prentice-Hall, Inc. 374 pp.

Federal Civil Defense Administration. 1952. Police services. Washington, D. C.: United States Government Printing Office. 50 pp.

Gleuck, Shelton and Eleanor. 1936. Preventing crime. New York and London: McGraw-Hill Book Co. 496 pp.

Gross, Hans. 1918. Criminal psychology. Boston, Mass.: Little, Brown, and Co. 514 pp.

Hooton, Earnest Albert. 1939. Crime and the man. Cambridge, Mass.: Harvard University Press. 403 pp.

Introductory essays by a number of writers. 1944. Mental abnormality and crime. New York: The Macmillan Co. 316 pp.

Kelker, George H. 1943. The state-sportsman-landowner triangle. Journal of Wildlife Management 1:7-10.

Mannheim, Hermann. 1946. Criminal justice and social reconstruction. New York: Oxford University Press. 290 pp.

Rhodes, Henry T. F. 1937. The criminals we deserve. New York: Oxford University Press. 257 pp.

Reptiles and Amphibians

Bishop, Sherman C. 1943. Handbook of salamanders. Ithaca, New York: Comstock Pub. Co., Inc. 555 pp.

Blanchard, Frank N. 1939. A key to the snakes of the United States, Canada, and lower California. Ann Arbor, Mich.: University of Michigan Press. 65 pp.

Breckenridge, W. J. 1944. Reptiles and amphibians of Minnesota. Minneapolis, Minn.: The University of Minnesota Press. 202 pp.

Dickinson, W. E. 1949. Field guide to the lizards and snakes of Wisconsin. Milwaukee Public Museum, Popular Science Handbook Series No. 2. Milwaukee, Wisc. 70 pp.

Schmidt, Karl P., and D. Dwight Davis. 1941. Field book of snakes. New York: G. P. Putnam's Sons. 365 pp.

Smith, Hobart M. 1946. Handbook of lizards. Ithaca, New York: Comstock Pub. Co. 557 pp.

Stebbins, Robert C. 1954. Amphibians and reptiles of western North America. McGraw-Hill Book Co. 528 pp.

Wright, Albert Hazen, and Anna Allen Wright. 1949. Handbook of frogs and toads. Ithaca, New York: Comstock Pub. Co. 639 pp.

Sex and Crime

American Social Hygiene Assn., Inc. 1948. Problems of sexual behavior. New York: American Social Hygiene Assn., Inc. 138 pp.

Blackwelder, Helen McLarin. 1947. Tell girls why. Atlanta, Georgia: Turner E. Smith and Co. 98 pp.

DeRiver, J. Paul. First printing 1949. Second printing 1950. The sexual criminal. Springfield, Illinois: Charles C. Thomas. 281 pp.

Doshay, Lewis J. 1943. The boy sex offender and his later career. New York: Grune and Stratton, Inc. 206 pp.

Gould, George, and Roy E. Dickerson (compiled under the direction of Bascom Johnson). 1942. Digest of state and federal laws dealing with prostitution and other sex offenses. New York: The American Social Hygiene Assn., Inc. 453 pp.

Henry, George W. Sex variants. New York: Harper and Brothers. 1941 (2 vol.), 1179 pp. 1949 (1 vol.),

Hirschfeld, Magnus. 1941. The sexual history of the World War. New York: Cadillac Pub. Co. 346 pp.

London, Louis S., and Frank S. Caprio. 1950. Sexual deviations. Washington, D. C.: The Linacre Press, Inc. 702 pp.

Pollens, Bertram. 1938. The sex criminal. New York: The Macaulay Co. 211 pp.

Rickles, N. K. 1950. Exhibitionism. Philadelphia, Penn.: J. B. Lippincott Co. 198 pp.

Sherwin, Robert Veit. 1949. Sex and the statutory law. New York: Oceana Publications. 74 pp.

Shoenfield, Allen. 1950. The sex criminal. Detroit, Michigan: The Detroit News. 63 pp.

Thoinot, L. 1930. Medicolegal aspects of moral offenses. Philadelphia, Penn.: F. A. Davis Co. 487 pp.

Statistics

Annual report of the National Automobile Theft Bureau. Dallas, Texas: National Automobile Theft Bureau.

Annual report of the Judicial Council, State of New York. New York: The Judicial Council.

Bureau of the Census, Washington, D. C. 1927. Instructions for compiling criminal statistics. Washington, D. C.: Supt. of Documents, Government Printing Office. 64 pp.

Committee on Uniform Crime Records. 1929. Revised 1935. A guide for preparing annual police reports. Washington, D. C.: International Assn. of Chiefs of Police. Issued by Federal Bureau of Investigation. 37 pp.

Committee on Uniform Crime Records. 1930. Uniform crime reporting--a complete manual for police. Washington, D. C.: International Assn. of Chiefs of Police. Issued by Federal Bureau of Investigation. 464 pp.

Criminal statistics, England and Wales. London: His Majesty's Stationery Office, Director of Publications. Published annually.

Federal Bureau of Investigation. Ten years of uniform crime reporting. (A ten year history of Uniform Crime Reporting in U. S., 1930-1939.) 163 pp. (mimeo.)

Federal Bureau of Investigation. 1943. Uniform crime reporting handbook; suggestions for the preparation of uniform crime reports. 33 pp.

Federal Bureau of Investigation. Uniform crime reports (for the United States and its possessions). Issued semi-annually as a bulletin.

Hotchkiss, Willis Livingstone. 1931. Uniform classifications for judicial criminal statistics. Baltimore, Maryland: The Johns Hopkins Press. 133 pp.

National Safety Council. 1949. Accident facts. Chicago, Illinois: National Safety Council. 96 pp.

Ridley, Clarence E., and Orin F. Nolting. 1950. The municipal year book. Chicago, Illinois: The International City Managers' Assn. 598 pp.

Robinson, Louis N. 1911. History and organization of criminal statistics in the United States. New York: Houghton Mifflin Co.

Warner, Sam Bass. 1934. Crime and criminal statistics in Boston. Cambridge, Mass.: Harvard University Press. 150 pp.

Wildlife Law Enforcement

Brohn, Allen, and LeRoy J. Korschgen. 1950. Precipitin test--a useful tool in game law enforcement. Trans. 15th No. Am. Wildlife Conf. 467-476 pp.

Bumgarner, Willis Clifton. 1952. Guidebook for wildlife protectors institute of government. Chapel Hill, N. Carolina: University of North Carolina. 221 pp.

California Fish and Game Commission. 1948. Fish and game warden's manual. Compiled by H. C. Jackson. 47 pp.

Callaghan, F. P.____Instructions for the guidance of U. S. game management agents (restricted). Washington, D. C.: U. S. Fish and Wildlife Service. 68 pp.

Gascoine, D. R. 1949. Law enforcement problems in waterfowl management. Trans. 14th No. Am. Wildlife Conf. 95-99 pp.

Idaho Fish and Game Department. 1954. Conservation officers' manual. Idaho Fish and Game Department. 39 pp.

Leedy, Daniel L. 1948. Aerial photographs--their interpretation and suggested use in wildlife management. Jour. Wildlife Mgt. 12.2:206-207.

Sigler, William F. (ed.) 1950. Wildlife law enforcement. Utah State Agricultural College. 219 pp.

Swanson, C. D. 1949. Manual of instruction for the guidance of Alaska enforcement agents, patrol agents, and deputy Alaska game wardens. U. S. Fish and Wildlife. 70 pp. and appendix.

Turner, R. G. 1941. Law enforcement. Trans. 6th No. Am. Wildlife Conf. 66-67 pp.

Washington State Department of Game. Protectors' manual. State of Washington. Dept. Game. 87 pp. (mimeo.)

Wildlife Management

American Fisheries Soc. Published annually.

Carhart, A. W. 1946. Hunting North American deer. New York: The Macmillan Co. 232 pp.

Davis, H. S. 1953. Culture and diseases of game fishes. Berkeley: University of California Press. 332 pp.

Edminster, Frank C. 1947. Fish ponds for the farm. New York: Charles Scribner's Sons. 114 pp.

Gabrielson, Ira N. 1943. Wildlife refuges. New York: The Macmillan Co. 32 ill., 17 fig., 257 pp.

Gabrielson, Ira N. 1947. Wildlife conservation. New York: The Macmillan Co. 32 plates, 24 fig., 250 pp.

Graham, E. H. 1944. Natural principles of land use. New York: Oxford University Press. 274 pp.

Grange, W. B. 1949. The way to game abundance. New York: Charles Scribner's Sons. 365 pp.

Journal Wildlife Mgt. Published quarterly.

Leopold, Aldo. 1939. Game management. New York: Charles Scribner's Sons. 35 fig., 53 tables, 481 pp.

North American Wildlife Conference Trans. Published annually.

Rounsefell, George A., and W. Harry Everhart. 1953. Fishery science: its methods and applications. New York: John Wiley and Sons, Inc. 444 pp.

Stoddart, Lawrence A., and Arthur D. Smith. 1953. Range management. 2nd edition. New York: McGraw-Hill Book Co., Inc. 433 pp.

Trippensee, Reuben Edwin. 1948. Wildlife management. New York: McGraw-Hill Book Co., Inc. 479 pp.

Trippensee, Reuben Edwin. 1953. Wildlife management. Vol. II. New York: McGraw-Hill Book Co., Inc. 572 pp.

Wing, Leonard W. 1951. Practice of wildlife conservation. New York: John Wiley and Sons, Inc. 412 pp.

General Index

Abet, defined, 185
Abide, defined, 185
Abrogate, defined, 185
Abrogation, defined, 185
Accessory, defined, 185
Accessory after the fact, defined, 185
Accessory before the fact, defined, 186
Accessory to the fact, defined, 59
Accident, defined 186
Accomplice, defined, 186
Accusation, defined, 186
Acknowledgment, defined, 186
Acknowledgment of no license, model form, 241
Acquittal, defined, 186
Act, defined, 187
Action, defined, 187
Act of Gòd, defined, 187
Acts cited
  Act of August 11, 1916 (39 Stat. 446, 476; 16 U.S.C.
    683). Authorized president to protect and control wild-
    life, 33
  Act of July 3, 1890 (26 Stat. 215). Organic Act of Idaho.
    Recognizes Nez Perce Tribe treaty rights, 64
  Bald Eagle Act, 29
  Black Bass Act, 28, 29
  Lacey Act. Regulates interstate commerce of game, 24
  Legislative Act of 1915 (North Carolina Code Ann., 1939,
    Sec. 2099). Consents to let Federal Government con-
    trol game animals, 33
  Migratory Bird Hunting Stamp Act. Provides funds to
    implement Migratory Bird Treaty Act, 27, 28
  Migratory Bird Treaty Act. Protects migratory birds
    and game mammals, 25, 27
  National Forest Administration Act. Extends federal
    control to all phases of wildlife regulation, 30, 32
  Weeks Law, 33
Administrators, problems facing, 178
Admissible, defined, 187

283

Index of Cases Cited